Walter Johnson

Walter Johnson
A Life

by Jack Kavanagh

Diamond Communications, Inc.
South Bend, Indiana

1996

Walter Johnson
A Life

Copyright © 1995 by Jack Kavanagh

10 9 8 7 6 5 4 3 2 1

Manufactured in the United States of America

Diamond Communications, Inc.
Post Office Box 88
South Bend, Indiana 46624-0088
(219) 299-9278
FAX (219) 299-9296

Library of Congress Cataloging-in-Publication Data

Kavanagh, Jack.
    Walter Johnson : a life / by Jack Kavanagh.
       p. cm.
    Includes index.
    ISBN 0-912083-81-6 : $24.95
    1. Johnson, Walter Perry, 1887-1946. 2. Baseball players--United
States--Biography. I. Title
GV865.J6K386 1995
796.357'092--dc20
[B]   94-42221
                                             CIP

Contents

In loving memory of my wife, Sally,
who was to me as Hazel was to Walter Johnson

Acknowledgments

The Society for American Baseball Research (SABR) deserves the largest share of appreciation for the detailed content and authenticity of information in this long-overdue biography of Walter Johnson. SABR's microfilm library, available to all members, provided *The Sporting News* which covered Walter Johnson's entire career, and *The Sporting Life* which reported Johnson's career through 1917. SABR colleagues had already researched many statistical aspects of Johnson's career. Details of his shutouts, those pitched or endured; home runs, hit and given up; opening day contests; matchups with Babe Ruth and with Ty Cobb and events involving Johnson were identified; in short, the time-consuming detail of many particulars of a long career had already been printed in annual editions of SABR's *Baseball Research Journal* or *The National Pastime*. Other special Johnson information came from SABR's file of presentations made at its national conventions. In addition, SABR colleagues were unfailingly responsive in checking information in their local or regional newspapers.

Frank Williams, whose monumental analysis of Johnson's complete major league pitching record was taken from carefully reviewed original score sheets, not only provided certified authenticity, but saved hundreds of research hours. Those games in which Johnson participated as a pitcher were already identified, making it unnecessary to examine all of the intervening games.

This book benefits substantially from the generous response from many libraries and their research staffs. Dave Kelly, from the Library of Congress, expedited microfilm of the *Washington Post* and the *Washington Star* which was obtained through interlibrary loan requests by my own library, the North Kingstown (RI) Public Library. Its outstanding reference staff, led by Susan Berman, Linda Caisse, and Ann Salisbury, were supportive and tolerant of having their microfilm viewers and printers utilized extensively. The library at Dartmouth College also provided microfilm of the *Washington Post*. The University of Rhode Island library's microfilm of the *New York Times* and the use of its facilities aided. The New York Public Library and the Providence (RI) Library were sources of copies of magazines with Johnson material. Of special value was the Coffeyville (KS) Library and its most helpful reference director, Karyl L. Buffington. A request for local coverage of several events in Johnson's life during the years he made Coffeyville his home, revealed that a trove of material was stored in the library's files.

Other libraries which provided copies of local newspaper accounts of events in Johnson's career, were those of Schenectady, New York, Joplin, Missouri, and Tulsa, Oklahoma.

Of substantial help was the Baseball Hall of Fame Library, directed by Tom Heitz. Direct assistance by Bill Deane was generous and promptly given. This book can claim to be the first researched, in part at least, at the library's expanded facilities, during a December, 1993, visit.

It is always risky to single out one or several among the dozens who volunteered to help with the research for this book. Or those whose published material was utilized. However, the contribution of Fred Schuld deserves special recognition. Not only did he let me know of Woodrow Wilson's meeting with Larry, Cleveland's pet and mascot, he sent extensive coverage of Johnson's unhappy managerial career with the Indians and helped locate photos from that era.

Lt. Col. Al Kermisch, Ret., a painstaking researcher of the career of Walter Johnson, generously reviewed portions of this manuscript to ensure their validity. The "discovery" of Johnson and his California activities had been warped out of shape by earlier writers. Along with research by A. D. Suehsdorf of Johnson's pre–major league experiences, coverage is possible with assurance of its accuracy.

Frank Fortunato, who is writing a biography of Walter Johnson, shared research into aspects of Johnson's career. Johnson deserves additional biographical coverage.

Others who aided in preparing this book are: Charles Alexander, Mark Alvarez, Bob Boynton, Norton Chellgren, L. Robert Davids, Jim Feeney, Larry Gerlach, Raymond Gonzalez, Dr. Stanley Grosshandler, Steven H. Heath, Fred Ivor-Campbell, Frank Keetz, Jim Kreuz, Jim Langford, Len Levin, Ron Liebman, Tim McNamara, Norman Macht, Jeffrey and Kerry and Kevin Martin, Jim Milton, Neil Munro, Don O'Hanley, Emil Rothe, Joel D. Treese, John Schwartz, John Spalding, Lyle Spatz, Paul Warburton, Joe Wayman. Although coming under the heading of "Membership Services," the responses from SABR's executive director, Morris Eckhouse, and office manager, John Zajc, were fast and accurate. SABR can be joined by those with an interest in baseball's history: P.O. Box 93183, Cleveland, OH 44101.

Foreword

Heck, Jack Kavanagh had to be a seven-come-11 natural to write about Walter Johnson, the best pitcher *ever*, because he'd also written charmingly well about the best pitcher who *never* pitched—Joe Matson.

I fell in love with Kavanagh as a baseball researcher with a sense of humor when he did an essay on the best-that-never-was for the Society of American Baseball Research, a group of doctors, bakers, and electric-bulb makers with whom we're both proud to hold membership.

For SABR, Kavanagh crafted a honey of reminiscence for many readers of the *Baseball Joe* series about the boy Matson, who went from teenager to a pitching star so great—hope you can stand this friends!—that he once struck out 27 big leaguers in a game. Uh-huh, and because a big bloke named Babe Ruth proved a great pitcher might also be a great hitter, Matson became the top home run hitter, too. How about five in one game!

Matson, "born in 1894 and dead of overachievement in 1928," as Kavanagh put it, a "one-dimensional demigod," inspired many of us—if we couldn't pitch or hit like him—to write baseball and perhaps with fewer cliches than "Henry Chadwick," obviously the *nom de knickers* of one or more authors.

Actually, "Matson" was a contraction of Christy Mathewson, the early-day giant of the Giants. The Greek god with a cowlick was so good that he finished just ahead of Walter Johnson in the famous First Five elected to the National Baseball Hall of Fame in 1936. To this day, although unable to demand a recount, I suspect that a predominance of New York reporters with baseball writing membership were responsible for the Big Six having the voting edge over the Big Train.

Playing with poorer teams, Johnson won more games than Mathewson or any other great except Cy Young, who played in a different century, in a different game. I shy from writing too much about Johnson, not only because I once tried to encapsulate his colorful career in *SuperStars of Baseball*, a Diamond Communications publication, but because I don't want to tread on Kavanagh's writing pleasure or your reading enjoyment.

I do know that Sir Walter was a Galahad in life—didn't smoke, drink, or swear—and even there he had an edge on Matty, who knew the difference between rye whiskey and Rye, New York, and, though poison gas had filled his lungs in World War I, he couldn't resist a good cigar.

Like Matty—dead in 1925 on an October day as his rival toed the World Series pitching rubber for Washington at Pittsburgh—Walter Perry Johnson didn't live long enough. He was only 59 when he died of brain cancer late in 1946, but even by then they had named a high school for him in Bethesda, Maryland.

I've been a sucker for years for good stories about "Barney," as friends called the heavy-footed driver. Waite Hoyt, himself a Hall of Famer, imitated Johnson's sidearmed fling for me and it makes the mind wince over potential physical handicap. Another Hall of Famer, catcher and manager Al Lopez, remembers the thrill of catching Johnson as a kid of 17 at Tampa, Florida, in 1925—and then watching in awe as the pitching legend pulled on a woolen sweater and trotted five times around a mile racetrack.

Shirley Povich—best known as Maury Povich's pop but one of the greatest sportswriters ever (even when listed as a Woman-of-the-Year candidate)—had a close relationship with the quiet, humble hero. Povich even convinced Sir Walter to sit with him and watch a young Cleveland fireballer named Bob Feller. Discreetly, the writer queried if Feller threw as hard as Johnson…"No," Johnson said softly, "and not as fast as Lefty Grove, either."

Whenever I hear any Johnny-Come-Smartly argue that Johnson couldn't throw as hard as the top pitchers now—aware that when he piled up his strikeouts, hitters jabbed for contact rather than swing for power—I like to think of the time fearless, peerless Ty Cobb was asked about his most trying moments: "Facing Walter Johnson on any dark day in Washington," said the Georgia Peach.

I'm glad Jack Kavanagh took typewriter or computer in hand and wrote about the best pitcher *ever*. After all, when the man who wrote about the best pitcher *never*, Joe Matson, got around to giving the Big Train the championship honors he'd earned (1924), the 37-year-old gaffer not only had won 23 games, but, shades of *Baseball Joe*, he'd also hit .433!

—*Bob Broeg*
St. Louis, Missouri
October 1994

1

A Star Rises in the West

RUMORS OF A YOUNG GIANT striking out astonishing numbers of batters on mining town teams in Idaho reached several major league clubs in 1906. They grew more persistent in 1907. Fuzzy legend says that insistent letters from volunteer scouts, local boosters, and traveling men passing through Idaho, tipped off big league teams to an amazing pitching prodigy. One of these bird dogs with informal links to the major leagues was an itinerant umpire we know only as McGuire. He told George Moreland, a respected baseball writer and one of the game's first historians, about a pitching phenom whose games he had worked. Moreland passed the word to Fred Clarke, the Pittsburgh manager, who wrote the prospect's name in his notebook. After Walter Johnson's name appeared in the sports headlines, Clarke remembered too late why it was familiar. It was still in his notebook. Even though the Pirates trained in Hot Springs, Arkansas, 500 miles closer to Weiser, Idaho, than Pittsburgh is, Clarke had missed his chance to look at Johnson in the spring of 1907. A train ticket would have cost $9.

The Detroit Tigers, like Pittsburgh a contender for pennants, also missed an opportunity to snare Johnson. They were bombarded with letters from the proverbial talent-spotting traveling salesman who had visited Weiser, Idaho, while drumming up trade for a line of cigars. William Yawkey, who owned the Tigers, brought one of the letters to general manager Frank Navin, who is said to have scoffed, "If this salesman knows so much about baseball, what's he doing peddling cigars in bush towns out in Idaho?"

Actually, it was networking among veteran baseball people that got Walter Johnson to the big leagues with the last-place Washington Nationals. Even before he emerged as a super semipro prospect in the Rocky Mountains, the teenage Johnson had been spotted on the sandlots of southern California. He was an untested but not unvalued prospect, and one local professional player, Jack Burnett, suggested the teenager make baseball his career.

There was an opening with Tacoma, with whom outfielder Burnett played. The city had dropped out of the Pacific Coast League and joined the newly formed Northwestern Association. While Walter Johnson's 1906 bid for a place in professional baseball was not an earthshaking event, one of major seismic significance had occurred. One effect of the San Francisco earthquake was to make a great many experienced West Coast baseball players available. As the Bay Area teams dug out of the rubble, Tacoma decided they did not need a pitching prospect when they could sign seasoned players.

Walter Johnson had pitched only once for Tacoma, in a Red Cross Relief Fund game, and lost, 4-3. His fastball was too much for an inexperienced local catcher named Mathews to handle. Shortly after Tacoma's season began, Walter Johnson was out of a job. His parents had given their 18-year-old son permission to try his hand at pitching professionally, and he could have wired home for train fare. However, Jack Burnett lined up a semipro job in Weiser, Idaho, for his young friend. Almost 20 years later, in a nationally syndicated biographical series, Walter Johnson still appreciated the help given by his friend, although he recalled him as Barnett. He also remembered the shock of being cut loose 1,000 miles from home, paid off with only one week's salary of $40. The next year when Tacoma, hearing of his success at Weiser, tried to tempt him back, he turned them down. The man who would smile away a teammate's error was singularly bitter about the way he had been treated in Tacoma.

"One day," he recalled years later, "I received a half dozen telegrams from the club asking me to return to the Coast. In the last message they offered me $350 a month, which was a record price for that league. However, I said from the start that I would never again play for Tacoma for people who, when I was with them, had not given me a fair shake to make good.

"If I had gone back to Tacoma perhaps my whole baseball future would have been in a different setting. I might have been sold to some club other than Washington."

A return to Tacoma would have been a step in the wrong direction for young Walter Johnson. His evident ability made it unnecessary. His pitching at Weiser in 1906, his work in winter ball around Los Angeles, and a spectacular start when he returned to Weiser in 1907, made Johnson a well-known prospect.

In 1913 an article appeared in the *San Francisco Chronicle*, written by Joe Burke, a popular West Coast baseball figure. He, among many others, claimed to have "discovered" Johnson. Burke wrote: "I discovered Walter Johnson as a pitcher when he was about 14 years old, a big, overgrown, awkward, lazy boy. One day Jack Burnett and I stood up to bat a few of the kid's pitches. He threw us a dozen or so balls apiece and we couldn't touch him."

Burke went on to describe how Walter Johnson, with other teenagers, put together a makeshift team using discarded gloves and taped baseballs and repaired bats to play pickup games. These led to more formal play that brought Johnson up against players from professional leagues. Burke said, "We had Walt discovered long before he went to Weiser. Olinda, the place where Walt got his start, is in an oil district, close to a valley of oranges and walnuts. Olinda is a place of rugged attractions, where derricks on brown hillsides are lifted skyward and where men sweat and toil and have their men's fun and frolics. Where the derricks dotted the landscape, there were bunkhouses, rough office buildings, company eating-houses, a store or two and a livery stable. I was a bookkeeper for the Santa Fe Railroad, which has wells at Olinda. Old Frank Johnson, Walt's dad, was a teamster for the Santa Fe wells, and Walt drove a team when he was not going to school."

Burke concluded his reminiscences by describing how Johnson had pitched. "He had his own fast, under-handed style. That was his natural sling. Many a time when Walt was growing into his baseball manhood older players told him he was pitching all wrong. He instinctively knew better." Actually, no one had to "discover" Walter Johnson. Like the Pacific Ocean or the Rocky Mountains, you could not miss such an obvious natural wonder once you came upon it.

In Washington, D.C., the new manager of the American League club, Pongo Joe Cantillon, was plugged into the West Coast circuit of baseball's "old-boy network." He had played for Oakland in the California League in the early 1890s. Between seasons Cantillon had also run a saloon on San Francisco's notorious Barbary Coast. He was a genial Irishman, whose propensity for writing letters to old friends kept him in contact with them. One of these was Joe Shea, who had played in the California League with him. It was Shea's tip about young Johnson that first alerted Cantillon.

Pongo Joe's odd nickname stemmed from his permanent simian grin. Someone with erudition enough to know that "pongo" refers to anthropoids, usually to orangutans, linked the name to Cantillon. It is unlikely he knew the origin of his nickname and anyone who explained it to him would have had a terrific fight on his hands. What Pongo Joe did know was that he was saddled with the worst team in the young American League. He also knew that he had to recruit talent for his tailenders on a shoestring budget. He did not even have a scout to send to confirm that the Johnson boy was a real prospect. Then his reserve catcher, Cliff Blankenship, split a finger and was available to go on a western scouting trip.

Cantillon was also aware of a fleet-footed young outfielder with Wichita, Kansas, in the Western Association. Clyde Milan (Mill-in) was available to the first team to make a firm offer. Cantillon talked owner Thomas C. Noyes into bankrolling Blankenship's trip, which paid great dividends. Not only was Milan, who went on to 16 outstanding seasons with Washington and displaced Ty Cobb as the base-stealing champ in 1912 and 1913, bought from Wichita, but Blankenship snared Walter Johnson as well.

Milan, who became Walter Johnson's closest friend on the Washington team and roomed with him for the 16 years they were teammates, was bought by Washington for $900 on June 24. He was to report after Wichita ended its season. Milan commented later on Blankenship's lack of enthusiasm for riding a train farther west to track down a reported phenom, a teenager named Walter Johnson. "Probably he's just some wild, hard-throwing kid who'll walk the ball park," griped the big league catcher. Cliff Blankenship's pessimism turned to exuberant enthusiasm when he got to Weiser. Although he did not actually see Johnson pitch in a game, he watched him warm up. He saw a blistering-fast ball that made his decision easy.

Blankenship had reached Weiser, Idaho, on June 26. As Johnson did not report to Washington until July 26, there is a month's span which has been inaccurately reported in published material about Walter Johnson. Much of the confusion stems from Johnson's own indifference to details when telling reporters throughout the years about how he was discovered. He glossed over the particulars in a 1914 first-person account given to Billy Evans, a major league umpire and prolific writer of magazine and newspaper baseball articles. Evans had umpired Johnson's debut game in 1907. Addressing the elusive truth about his movement from Weiser to Washington to young readers of the upscale *St. Nicholas Magazine*, Johnson observed: "Every year I read a dozen new stories about how I got my start in baseball. If all of them were true, I would be the protégé of at least 100 different baseball enthusiasts. To tell the truth, I don't know who is most directly responsible for my getting a chance in the Big League."

Johnson blurs the particulars of the trip eastward by saying: "That trip from Weiser to Washington is a sufficiently long one. Never having made such a journey before, I was not at all clever in picking out my trains, and, as a result, I was delayed in arriving."

Even more distortion was introduced over the years of Johnson's celebrity. The trip's itinerary and details of its ending were embellished by journalists whose editors accepted their copy without confirming it. Everyone who wrote a comprehensive piece about Johnson felt obliged to account for his discovery in Weiser, and many added their own spin to the story. Forget such fanciful tales as Blankenship neglecting to bring a contract form and improvising one on wrapping paper from a Weiser butcher shop. Almost everything which has been grafted onto the discovery and delivery of Walter Johnson is warped or invented.

Walter Johnson agreed to sign with Washington but only after he had visited the city. The nation's capital was a long way from his home in California. He was not sure he wanted to make his career in baseball in a city so far from his family and friends. One of the recurring tales of his signing makes a point either about Johnson's insecurity or his prudence. He insisted on a guarantee that he would be able to get home again. He wanted to be protected against a repetition of the Tacoma fiasco.

Blankenship wired the "good news–bad news" information about Johnson's tentative acceptance to Joe Cantillon, who was in New York City for a series with the Highlanders. Cantillon immediately staked his claim to the young phenom in a special bulletin to the *Washington Post* datelined June 29, 1907. Cantillon announced that Walter Johnson belonged to Washington. The report informed the fans that the young phenom had pitched 75 innings without allowing a run. He had struck out 166 batters in 11 games. The Washington manager said the recruit would join the team after the Idaho State season closed on July 14.

The ebullient Cantillon hyped the acquisition of the boy wonder of the Rockies by saying, "If this fellow is what they say he is we won't have to use but only two men in a game, a catcher and Johnson. He strikes out most of the men, so why have an infield and an outfield? I shall give all the boys but the catchers days off when Johnson pitches." This was Pongo Joe's way of creating expectations to be lived up to by the young pitcher.

Lt. Col. Al Kermisch, Ret., a Washington-based historian, has specialized in Walter Johnson's career. He has done more to put the record straight than anyone, although invented accounts recur whenever something about Walter Johnson is written. Baseball writers of the past spun fanciful "facts" and others continue to weave them into later works.

Al Kermisch dug into the accounts in Rocky Mountain newspapers to establish a "paper trail" that determines Walter Johnson's whereabouts during the month between Blankenship's arrival in Weiser and Johnson reaching Washington. The following account appeared in the *Idaho Daily Statesman* on July 23: "...Johnson, the pitcher, left this morning for Washington, D.C. The American League sent Johnson a draft for $250 to pay his expenses to Washington. Upon his arrival there and as soon as he signs the contract with the club he will receive a bonus of $500 and a ticket to his home in California and be placed on the payroll at $400 a month." The newspaper account explained that Johnson did not expect to actually play for Washington that season but only to train with them. The paper also admired Johnson for never using intoxicating liquors nor tobacco.

Although Cantillon had agreed that Johnson would finish his season in Idaho and not leave until the 14th, there was no hurry for Walter Johnson to report to Washington. There would be no one there to check him in. After they left New York, the team played in Philadelphia and Boston before heading west. Not until they had also visited Cleveland, Detroit, Chicago, and St. Louis would the team return to Washington. It was the expectation of the Washington newspapers that Johnson would join the team on its road trip. Writers did not accompany the ball club. The sports editors depended on whatever team notes came with the play-by-play game accounts telegraphed from the ballparks. When Cliff Blankenship appeared in the lineup in Chicago on July 12, the papers assumed Walter Johnson had arrived with him. They were so convinced that Pongo Joe Cantillon was holding out his ace prospect they complained when he was not given at least some experience in several lopsided games. Actually, of course, Johnson was still in Weiser.

Before Walter Johnson headed for the big leagues, a big game with the rival mining community of Caldwell was played on June 30 and a crowd of 2,000 jammed the stands. Large sums of money were bet on the game and town pride demanded victory. Caldwell had imported Irv Higginbotham to pitch. He had been kept by Tacoma when Johnson was cut, and later in 1906 he pitched for the St. Louis Cardinals.

Thousands of fans poured in from all over the Idaho hills and special trains brought well-heeled sports from Boise and Billings, Montana. The betting on these games was heavy. The partisan crowd saw Higginbotham and Walter Johnson hook up in a memorable pitching duel. The first 10 innings were scoreless, extending Johnson's string of shutout innings to 85. He had allowed only two hits and struck out 15 men when the game reached the bottom of the 11th inning. After two men were out, an error put a runner on first. He stole second and reached third when Johnson's next pitch got through the catcher's hands for a passed ball. The next batter's seeing-eye ground ball bounded through the infield and Johnson's shutout string at Weiser was ended.

Walter Johnson looked back on his stay in Weiser with fondness in a 1924 interview with Will Wedge, sports editor of the *New York Sun*. He remembered Weiser as a mining town with a lively sprinkling of cattle- and sheepmen. Weiser formed one of the jumps in a little semi-pro league. Games were played about once a week and a brass band was at each game, as were the sheriff and his deputies to squelch expected riots. Johnson described a typical encounter with their rivals at Caldwell:

"Our manager was the sheriff of the county and he sat on the bench armed as if he were out after the James boys. Our first baseman was a deputy sheriff and the game was hardly an inning old before he was in a fight. Soon a merry riot was raging all over the unfenced field. I stood on the mound wondering if this was the way all professional games were conducted. Just as I was about to get embroiled in the fuss myself, our sheriff and the chief of police of Weiser came out with impressive-looking hardware.

"They said, 'Don't budge kid, we ain't going to let you hurt your arm swinging at some worthless coyote. You get paid for pitching for us, but we can get everybody in town to fight for us for nothing.' "

Johnson also told about the June 30 game with Caldwell: "The rival mayors bet everything but the jails and courthouses on the game. The Weiser wager was that they could go to Caldwell and beat anything that represented that town on the diamond. We found that covered too wide a range, for when the Weiser special and six bands and about 1,600 folks pulled into Caldwell, we found our wily opponents had five ringers in the lineup—fellows from the Coast and Northwestern Leagues. We went into the 10th inning tied 0 to 0. Weiser got a man around to third. The town doctor was on our bench and he offered the batter $750 if he'd bring the run in. That was half what the Doc figured to win on the game.

"The batter tried the squeeze play. The pitcher fielded the ball, but threw past the catcher. But our silly runner on third got flustered and he turned around and slid back to the hot corner. Then he saw the ball going by the catcher and started for home only to be thrown out. The next inning our infield made enough errors to let Caldwell romp off with the game. It cleaned out Weiser like the Dempsey-Gibbons fight cleaned out Shelby, Montana, some years later."

Johnson described Weiser as having 15 saloons for 2,500 people. "It was a big-hearted, hard-fisted town, but it kept itself surprisingly in order. They never teased me to drink. When they found out I had never tasted hard liquor, they said, 'Good boy, keep away from it always' and that's what I have done."

Walter took his time saying goodbye to Weiser. There was talk that the baseball season would be extended. He was 19 years old and a local favorite. Folks wanted him to stay and go on pitching for Weiser. They even offered to set him up in business. Local boosters said they would provide him with a tobacco shop. Even before Honus Wagner ground the cigarette industry under his spiked heel by forcing his baseball card to be removed from their offerings, the young Johnson was making his teenage decisions about smoking, drinking, and gambling. There was plenty of each in the wide-open mining town of Weiser available for him to sample.

Later he would admit to having gingerly tried some of the vices which tempted him. He declared that while he had nothing against those who gave in to them, he recognized that players with drinking problems had shorter careers and gave the fans less than their best effort at all times. He never touched anything more alcoholic than beer and said he just did not care for the taste of it. He would sit around a table in a saloon with his friends and unabashedly sip lemonade. And, if young Walter ever puffed on a cigarette, like our current United States president, he probably didn't inhale. As for gambling, Walter Johnson had been raised in a thrifty, hardworking family. The thought of wagering on a roll of the dice, a spin of a wheel, or a card game never tempted him, although he eventually became a pretty good card player. He enjoyed a low-stake game of cassino to wile away time on road trips.

One explanation why Walter Johnson dallied around town even though he had the fare to board an eastbound train is that the manager of the Weiser team wanted to keep his ace pitcher available until the season ended on July 14. The manager refused to pay him his salary any sooner. Johnson, who was to take a strong interest in his earnings all his life, stayed to collect what he had earned. After the big game with Caldwell, Johnson defeated Boise, 3-2. The game at the state capital drew 5,000 fans. Johnson pitched again on July 7 and was in games on three successive days, July 13, 14, and 15. He bowed out of Idaho's semipro circles with a farewell shutout, winning a makeup game with the Mountain Home team, 4-0. Another version has it that Johnson could have left earlier because the local sports and boosters were willing to make up any salary he would have to leave behind. They wanted him to show the baseball world what kind of a ballplayer Weiser could produce.

Even so, Johnson remained in Weiser for another week, either vacillating or vacationing. He was a youthful blend of modesty and self-confidence. Then on July 23, 1907, the young phenom strapped his suitcase shut with the belt from his Weiser baseball uniform and climbed aboard the train that would carry him to his destiny.

2
Here Comes Walter...

WALTER JOHNSON had his train fare, the $250 he had received in advance to pay his way to Washington. Whether he went by Pullman, traveling in a sleeping car, or saved money by sitting up in a coach, we do not know. He never said much about his first trip east. The important thing for baseball is that he got there.

Appropriately it was the form of transportation that provided his most enduring nickname, "the Big Train." Grantland Rice, a nationally syndicated sports columnist, gave Johnson his nickname, comparing the fireballer with the era's symbol of juggernaut power. Rice, whose metaphorical leads include describing the Notre Dame backfield as "the Four Horsemen," told his readers, "The Big Train is coming to town." This nickname implied both power and dependability. Trains once arrived precisely on time. It was said about a train's dependability, "You could set your watch by it." Local people would snap open their watches and compare them with the train's schedule. "The Big Train" served as a perfect metaphor for Walter Johnson. He was powerful, fast, and dependable.

Johnson enjoyed reading, and magazines of the time had stories by Jack London, Owen Wister, Zane Grey, and others who wrote outdoor tales. They might have been handed to him by friends who came to the Weiser train station to see him off. If Johnson bought the baseball weeklies, *The Sporting Life* and *The Sporting News,* at depot newsstands along the way, he would have read confused accounts of his joining Washington. Paul W. Eaton was the correspondent for *The Sporting Life*. Much of what we know about Johnson, apart from his ball field exploits, comes from Eaton's weekly notes. Eaton was not a full-time journalist and never traveled with the team; in fact, he was a diplomatic correspondent for the State Department. He was an avid baseball follower, who had been a Marietta College fraternity brother of Ban Johnson, the founder of the American League. When the team was on the road, Eaton got his information from the Washington newspapers. If they were wrong, he was wrong. Johnson might have read, as his train approached Washington, that a misinformed Eaton had already reported he had joined the team in Chicago.

Finally, on Saturday, July 27, the *Washington Post* reported:

Phenom Johnson Is Here

There was a full length, one-column picture of Johnson in his Weiser baseball uniform, and the story which ran underneath it read:

> Walter Johnson, the Idaho State League phenom, who has a record of pitching 85 innings without allowing a run and has struck out 166 men in twelve games, arrived in the local camp yesterday.
>
> Johnson left his home in Idaho on Monday at noon and has been on the road ever since. With eyes, ears, and hair filled with cinders, the young fellow reported to Manager Cantillon last night tired and worn, but full of confidence that he will be able to pitch winning ball in the American League.
>
> Because of his great showing in Idaho, Johnson was the center of attraction at the Regent Hotel last night. He complained of being stiff and sore as a result of his long trip, and is anxious to get into a uniform and limber up with the rest of the players.

There is a dissonant note in the account of Johnson's departure from Weiser. The *Idaho Daily Statesman* had said on a Tuesday that Johnson had left that morning. Johnson told the Washington reporters it was the noon train on Monday. The only morning train out of Weiser was at 2:25 A.M. It was the Oregon-Washington Limited. The other Chicago and North Western Line cross-country train was the China Japan Mail. That train left Weiser at 4:00 P.M. They were the mainstays of the Union Pacific Overland Route. We'd bet that Johnson, having sipped lemonade with his buddies in a Weiser saloon until the early morning hours, still considered it Monday when he climbed aboard the Oregon-Washington Limited. The newspaper would, with journalistic accuracy, have reported the train as departing

11

"in the morning." Despite the noontime reference, we'll rest a case hardly worth making except to illustrate the flimsiness as evidence of after-the-fact recall and hurriedly written newspaper copy. Few of us can remember what we had for dinner last Sunday, yet we take as gospel details recounted by former players of events long blurred by time.

Forty-four years after Johnson's arrival in Washington, a writer for the temporarily revived *The Police Gazette*, once a principal sporting paper of the late 19th and early 20th century, vividly recalled the details of July 26, 1907. Edward J. Bruen remembered the young man's appearance:

> Walter wore on that eventful afternoon a suit of snuff-colored goods made up after the snappy styles of five years previous or thereabouts. That was in the age of see-more, tight-fitting coats and skimpy-cut trousers. An uncomfortable high collar garroted Walter's neck, while a brilliantly hued necktie of the narrow string variety was rakishly draped over a pink shirt. The socks were near-purple and the low-cut shoes were yellow—a howling yellow.

Before Joe Cantillon tucked his travel-weary recruit into bed for the night, he got his signature on a contract. He would be paid $1,300 for the rest of the season and, yes, his return-trip ticket was assured. Johnson gave out various accounts of his arrival in Washington in interviews throughout the years. They varied somewhat, but all were characteristically modest and poked fun at himself. In 1924, at the zenith of his career, having dramatically won the seventh game of the World Series against the New York Giants, Johnson told an interviewer about his arrival in the major leagues.

"I can see now," mused Johnson, "how funny I must have appeared in those days, but I can assure you it wasn't funny at the time." Johnson laughingly told of the plight that he found himself in the first day that he joined the Washington team:

"When the game was over the players left the field in a hurry. I did not know the reason for this and took my time. When I got outside of the ballpark there was no one around, so I started to walk downtown.

"You must remember that was in the days when we had no club-houses and the players dressed in the hotel. I walked down Pennsylvania Avenue in my uniform while a curious crowd of kids followed me. I do not know how long I walked when a fellow stopped me and offered me a ride. He asked me why I did not take the bus that the players chartered after the game and I told him that I did not know anything about it."

Johnson continued to work out the kinks of train travel during several days of practice. The Detroit Tigers were in town and, despite Frank Navin's out-of-hand dismissal of the cigar salesman's tip, word was out about the raw-boned young giant. They sized him up themselves, and Ty Cobb, only a year older but already established as a superstar, watched for any weakness he could exploit. When Joe Cantillon named Walter Johnson as the starting pitcher for the second game of a doubleheader on August 2, 1907, the Tigers had an advance idea of the youngster's potential.

The game has been extensively written about, particularly in the recollections by Davy Jones and Sam Crawford of the Detroit Tigers, who told historian Lawrence Ritter about Walter Johnson's debut for his collection, *The Glory of Their Times*. Jones, the Detroit leadoff man who was the first to face Johnson in the major leagues, and Crawford, who homered, recalled with awe the first encounter with Johnson. Davy Jones said, "Boy, could that guy ever fire that ball! He had those long arms, absolutely the longest arms I ever saw. They were like whips, that's what they were. He'd just *whip* the ball in there."

Sam Crawford also remembered Johnson's speed: "…You'd hardly see the ball at all, but you'd hear it. *Swoosh* and it smacks into the catcher's mitt. He had such an easy motion it looked like he was just playing catch. That's what threw you off. He threw so nice and easy— and then *swoosh*, and it was by you."

J. Ed Grillo was the veteran baseball writer for the *Washington Post*. He had covered baseball in Cincinnati in the 1890s. When the American Association was formed in 1902, he became one of its early presidents. As a close friend of Ban Johnson, founder of the American League, he knew talent when he saw it. Grillo's game account says:

> Walter Johnson, the Idaho phenom, who made his debut in fast company yesterday, showed conclusively that he is perhaps the most promising young pitcher who has broken into a major league in recent years. He pitched eight of the nine innings and was only taken out [for a pinch hitter] in the eighth.
>
> In those eight innings Johnson allowed but six hits, three of which were scratches, while he issued but a single

pass to first. He had terrific speed and the hard-hitting Detroit batsman found him about as troublesome as any pitcher they have gone against. If the youngster showed any weakness, it was in fielding his position and it was this failing which gave the visitors their first run.

For the first six innings Johnson had allowed but three hits and two of these were bunts which a more experienced man would have handled. In the second inning Cobb and Rossman laid down bunts which were allowed to roll safe and *Cobb went from first to third on one of them* and then scored on a fly ball. With one out in the fourth...*Cobb stole second and third* [but] Johnson kept him there by fanning Downs.

In the first meeting between Johnson and Cobb, the fireballer held Cobb to a bunt single in four times at bat. However, he had a pyrotechnic afternoon in his other specialties. In addition to his spectacular base running, he had three assists, cutting down two runners at the plate and doubling another off first base. In a sacrifice bunt situation of his own, Johnson hurt his cause by letting the ball hit him for an out. In the end, it had been a gallant first effort by an inexperienced youngster, who lost, 3-2.

In his fine biography of baseball's greatest hitter, Charles C. Alexander quotes Cobb as saying after facing Johnson for the first time, "I encountered the most threatening sight I ever saw on a ball field. The ball just hissed with danger."

The rivalry between Johnson and Cobb lasted through careers that almost completely overlapped. Cobb was in his third season and was a year older when Johnson broke in, and his big league career outlasted Johnson's by part of a season. There was never enmity between the two, although the patience of the Washington pitcher was constantly tested by the fiery Detroit outfielder. This worked to Cobb's advantage in many instances, but against him, too. Sam Crawford, Cobb's teammate whose home run in the debut game was the only one Johnson would give up until two seasons later, had a friendly relationship with the pitcher. Perhaps it helped that he was from Nebraska, a neighboring state of Kansas. He was called "Wahoo Sam" for his hometown. Crawford was as well-liked by Detroit's opponents as Cobb was widely loathed.

Crawford later told Lawrence Ritter about his relationship with Walter Johnson and about how Cobb's style affected the fireballing pitcher. "Walter Johnson and I were very good friends, and once in awhile Walter would sort of 'give' me a hit or two, just for old time's sake. But when Ty came up there, Walter always bore down all the harder. There was nothing he enjoyed more than fanning Ty Cobb. Cobb never could figure out why I did so well against Walter, while he couldn't hit him with a 10-foot pole."

Alexander says Cobb batted .335 in 67 games against Johnson. Cobb's performances against various pitching greats were among materials Alexander found at the library of the Baseball Hall of Fame in Cooperstown. It was probably the work of Ernest J. Lanigan, the veteran historian and statistician who was the library's first director. Crawford's recollection of how Cobb fared against Johnson also might have been correct. His career ended considerably sooner than Cobb's and perhaps the Georgia Peach solved Johnson better in the later years of their careers. Or, maybe, Crawford just remembered it the way he told it because it made a better story.

Grillo's newspaper account traced Johnson's debut game, play by play, as the youngster who had never pitched a single inning in professional baseball battled the American League's leading team. Detroit could not afford to take it easy on the rookie. They were in a neck-and-neck battle for the pennant, the first of three they would win in succession. Detroit matched Johnson with Ed Siever, who was on his way to an 18-win season. Hughie Jennings, the aggressive manager of the Tigers, was known for his "eeeyah" scream and distracting antics in the third base coaches' box. For Johnson's debut game, he was suffering from a bad case of laryngitis. In New York, where the Tigers played before coming to Washington, the hoarse-throated Detroit manager had brought a cornet to the coaching lines. The Highlanders had protested to the league president, Ban Johnson, so Jennings substituted a whistle to try and shake up the rookie pitcher. His ear-piercing blasts had no effect on Walter Johnson. Perhaps he had learned to block out such distractions back in Idaho; the untamed western fans were known to fire off their revolvers during games played in frontier towns. Jennings was the first to discover that nothing disturbed Johnson's equilibrium during a ball game.

The *Washington Post* estimated 5,000 fans had attended the Friday afternoon doubleheader. Washington, firmly mired in last place, lost both games. Hughie Jennings put away his whistle and observed about the young pitcher, "In two years he'll be greater than Mathewson." The fans had seen the debut of that rare phenom, one who would live up to his advance notices.

On the 20th anniversary of Walter Johnson's initial appearance, the team invited everyone who had been at the inaugural game to come to the ballpark as the club's guests. Johnson had pitched the second game of a Friday doubleheader, and his debut had been well advertised. Many fans had come late and crowded into the cheaper seats in right field. When they spilled over onto the playing field a ground rule holding balls hit into the crowd to doubles was imposed. For the 10th anniversary, the ball club offered free tickets to the original spectators. Of the *Post*'s "estimated 5,000," some 15,000 wrote to claim that they had been in the ballpark when Walter Johnson took the mound for Washington for the first time.

3

The Phenom
Pays Off

WALTER JOHNSON was an immediate sensation with the
Washington fans. Long accustomed to last-place teams,
they had never had a star prospect of such promise to cheer.
Johnson rewarded them in his next start by easily defeating the
Cleveland Naps, 7-2, on August 7. It was the first of the 417 regular-
season victories he would pitch for Washington and a forerunner of
Johnson's style of coasting to easy victories. Cleveland's first run was
unearned and the other scored when he eased up in the ninth. Had
Walter Johnson pitched in modern times with incentive bonuses, the
impressive records he left behind would have been even more astonishing. It was his style to win without humiliating an opponent. His
already unbreakable lifetime total of 110 shutouts would have been
much higher had his team's defense been steadier and he less generous to batters when a game was safely won.

Larry Lajoie, popularly called Napoleon, was the playing manager
for Cleveland, who were called the Naps in his honor. His leadoff batter, Elmer Flick, a future Hall of Famer, singled to start the game, and
Lajoie also welcomed the rookie with a base hit. That was it for those
two. Flick, a hard-to-strike-out slap hitter, was fanned twice. Lajoie,
too, was handcuffed for the rest of the game.

The overjoyed fans reacted as though their tailenders had won a
championship. They rushed onto the field, intent on carrying young
Johnson off on their shoulders. The players jumped into a chartered
touring car, which carried them to their hotel. Their clubhouse had
burned down and had not yet been rebuilt. The fans followed Johnson
and his teammates into town, cheering the young pitcher's first victory.

A week later, when Johnson made his first road trip, he lost another type of game that was to characterize his career. He was defeated
1-0 as three Washington runners were thrown out at the plate. Not

only would Johnson set a career record by pitching 110 shutouts, 38 of them came in the pressure of a 1-0 game. He also lost 1-0 squeakers 26 times. Johnson, who later would go through six errorless seasons, allowed the only St. Louis run when he threw to second base for a force-out but no one covered the bag.

Washington was again shut out in his next start, a 3-0 loss at Cleveland, although Johnson fanned Lajoie this time, and Flick, too. At Detroit he was charged with losses as he relieved on successive days to drop his record to 1-5. He returned to the victory column with a 2-1 defeat of Boston on August 29. J. Ed Grillo, the *Washington Post* sports editor, commented, "...The visiting players on the bench never take their eyes off the youngster and they marvel at his ability. His terrific speed, quick curve and absolute control are so rare in a young pitcher that Johnson is in a class by himself."

In Philadelphia, Johnson, still learning to field bunts, threw away a sacrifice by Lave Cross in the ninth and beat himself, 3-2. However, he followed with his first career shutout, blanking Boston, 1-0, and followed that in New York with a 2-0 win over the Highlanders on September 12. Then, in the opening game of a doubleheader with Chicago, Johnson lost, 2-1, when his third baseman, Pete O'Brien, booted in the two White Sox runs.

Walter Johnson characteristically never blamed his fielders for an error. He must have set a record for forbearance in his next start against the Browns. He had pitched six shutout innings when the cumulative effect of five Washington errors upset him to the extent that he gave up two tainted runs in the seventh inning and yielded four more runs in both the eighth and ninth innings. In all, Johnson was racked for 14 hits, although walking none.

Walter Johnson had an effect on the American League pennant race as the season reached October. He lost to the Tigers on October 1, 5-3, on a bitterly disputed call of a ball hit down the foul line. Detroit, in a blazing finish of their pennant drive, won the four-game series from Washington. Ty Cobb drove himself to exhaustion while racking up 13 hits in 18 times at bat. He rampaged on the bases, stealing four bases in one game. In the last game, October 3, caught in a rundown, he collapsed short of home plate and was tagged out where he lay by Jim Delahanty.

It was a demonstration of Cobb's fiery will to win. While the 19-year-old Johnson surely was impressed, his own style was more methodical with far less visible emotion. The day after Detroit left town, Johnson helped them wrap up their first American League pennant. Johnson knocked the Philadelphia Athletics out of the pennant race when he out-pitched Eddie Plank, who was trying for his 25th victory, winning 2-1 in 10 innings. In St. Louis, Detroit won its pennant clincher.

Johnson's record over the last nine weeks of the 1907 season was 5-9. His earned run average was 1.88. He started 12 games and completed 11 of them. His opponents scored 35 runs and batted a composite .245. In the revealing comparative statistic, strikeouts against bases on balls, the rookie had walked only 20 batters in $110\frac{1}{3}$ innings while fanning 71.

> NOTE: Johnson's 1907 statistics are the work of SABR member John Schwartz. Frank Williams, a super statistical sleuth also from the Society for American Baseball Research, completed the Schwartz analysis of Johnson's career records which appear in this book. Williams spent his vacations for five years at the Baseball Hall of Fame Library where they are stored, closely examining the actual score sheets of all Johnson's games. Original errors in information from these sources will be noted and a revised, true record of Johnson's statistics is included in this book.

In reporting the end of the season dispersal of the players of the Washington Nationals, it was noted, "Walter Johnson and Cliff Blankenship have returned to California."

The Johnson family welcomed their son safely back from the world of big league professional baseball. As soon as he unpacked, Johnson looked for somewhere to play baseball. Unlike the years when he was learning how to pitch, this time the teams came to him.

Johnson spent a week in San Diego showing his southern California admirers the fastball that had dazzled the major league batters. He joined the Pickwicks, the Southern State League Champions and defeated the Pacific Coast League Champions, the Los Angeles Angels, 1-0. He held the PCL champs to three hits and struck out 16, beating Sleepy Bill Burns, the Angels ace who would be Johnson's teammate the next season in Washington. Burns was later a peripheral figure in the 1919 Black Sox scandal.

Then Johnson hooked up with Santa Ana of the California Winter League, for whom he would pitch between major league seasons for three years until he and his family moved back to Kansas. The winter league was fast company featuring a number of major leaguers and others from the PCL and other minor leaguers who wintered in southern California. The weather, so unlike wintry Kansas, made it possible for Johnson to play baseball year-round. That he was getting paid for it, was Walter Johnson's idea of the good life.

The *Washington Star* told local fans that their pitching hero was turning into a slugger. Calling him "Home Run Johnson," the paper reported a letter he had written to a friend, an attaché in the Senate, saying, "I have played ball nearly every Sunday since I came home, and my arm is in fine shape. I never let it out too much, but just toss the ball over." Then, with boyish immodesty, he continued, "You ought to see me bat. I bat better than any man in the league, and there are some good hitters and pitchers out here. I don't pull away like I used to back there. I hit two over the fence for two home runs thus far."

Walter Johnson enclosed a newspaper clipping which told that in the seven games he had pitched for Santa Ana he had struck out 98 batters. He had made 13 hits in 25 times at bat for an average of .520.

However, as winter went on, the dispatches back to Washington became ominous. Johnson was increasingly ineffective, and finally gave up pitching. An abscess had formed behind his right ear and a case of mastoiditis developed. Thomas Alva Edison's mastoid problems, which resulted in deafness in one ear, had recently been in the news. Then in a story datelined March 1 from Washington D.C., reporting a special dispatch from Los Angeles, came word that Johnson had been operated on for mastoiditis. In what sounds like kitchen-table surgery, the account reported that the operation was done at the Johnson home in Olinda, California, a small city now part of Fullerton. It said, "An abscess back of the right ear was opened and *a piece of bone cut from the skull.*"

Reports from the West Coast varied between optimistic assurances that Walter Johnson would be as fit as ever and ready to open the season to statements further extending his promised arrival in the East. The 1908 season was well underway, with the Nationals snug in their customary cellar berth, before an underweight Walter Johnson joined them on the road in St. Louis. He had pressed to hurry his return and, of course, had missed spring training altogether. He would have to pitch himself into shape. On June 11 he started against the Browns at Sportsman's Park in St. Louis. He lasted less than four innings, giving up five hits, walking one, and allowing four runs. He struck out no one. The 6-3 victory went to Rube Waddell in relief. The eccentric lefthander, whom Johnson said many years later was the greatest pitcher he ever saw, had worn out the patience of Connie Mack in Philadelphia. He was to win 19 games in St. Louis that season before his brilliant pitching ability was dimmed by a lifestyle that Johnson later recalled: "He had the stuff and should have lasted for years, but he did not take proper care of himself. Sometimes he would pitch a great game, then at other times, showing the effects of poor condition, he would pitch a mighty poor game."

Johnson was held out of action for 12 days and seemed to have regained his ability in a match with Boston's Ed Cicotte. But Johnson weakened late in the game, and Boston got single runs in the eighth and ninth innings to tie the game. After Johnson left for a pinch hitter in the ninth, the game went to the 11th inning before Boston won, 3-2. Johnson lost his next time out when his team was shut out by the Philadelphia Athletics on June 29. He gave up three runs in seven innings. Walter Johnson's first win in 1908 was not recorded until July 4. It was a comfortable 6-2 nightcap win in a doubleheader at home with New York. However, the games that followed went into the loss column for two reasons. One reason was the usual inability of his team to score runs. The Washington Nationals were, of course, impartial in this shortcoming. They rarely scored many runs for any of their suffering pitchers.

The other reason Johnson lost some of his games was the caliber of pitchers other teams sent against him. It was as though the youngster was the newest challenger riding down the dusty streets of a western frontier town. The seasoned "fast guns" of the league took him on in start after start. After a debilitating illness, he still held his own against an array of pitchers who were their team's top starter, many of whom reached the Baseball Hall of Fame.

After his first victory, Johnson lost a three-hitter and a four-hitter. Errors again beat him in the first of these and then Ed Cicotte, whose Hall of Fame destiny self-destructed with the 1919 Black Sox scandal, edged him out, 3-2. Next, Addie Joss, whose own career was tragically cut short when he died just before the 1911 season began, knocked off the new challenger.

Johnson dueled Bill Dinneen for 16 innings before winning, 2-1. Big Bill, who had won three games in the first World Series played in 1903, was still going strong and won 19 games in 1908.

21

Next time out Johnson beat the White Sox spitball wonder, Ed Walsh, 5-3. In 1908 Walsh absolutely dominated everyone except Walter Johnson. He won an incredible 40 games, overextending his arm to the detriment of his later career, by pitching 464 innings. He led the American League with a .727 average, pitched 11 shutouts, and doubled in relief with six saves. Big Ed Walsh also led in strike-outs with 269.

Almost every time Johnson took the mound in 1908 he was tested by the other team's best pitcher. The venerable Cy Young, still capable of winning 21 games that season, got into the fray, as did Jack Chesbro of the New York Highlanders, an earlier 40-game winner (41 in 1904). Johnson won shutouts against Happy Jack, 3-0 on September 4 and 4-0 on the seventh. They were part of one of Walter Johnson's most celebrated accomplishments. *He pitched three successive shutouts against the Highlanders in four days.* New York City still observed God's prescribed day of rest and professional baseball was not allowed on Sunday. Otherwise, Joe Cantillon might have sweet-talked his young pitcher into throwing four successive shutouts in four days. There is an embroidery to this feat that Johnson, whose third shutout came in the opener of a twin bill, ducked the chance to make it four-for-four. He is supposed to have hidden from the manager until the second game had started. It's a good story, but Johnson was lucky to finish the first game after an exasperated Chesbro had drilled him with a pitch late in the game. The ball hit Johnson on the bicep of his pitching arm. An anxious Cantillon massaged the arm for five minutes according to Billy Evans, who was once again the umpire for a historic Johnson occasion. He let his meal ticket finish, but between games the arm became so sore that Cantillon decided against further risk.

After his famous three shutouts in four days in New York, Johnson beat Eddie Plank, another Hall of Famer from Connie Mack's Philadelphia A's, 2-1. Johnson now had allowed only one run in 36 innings. When he pitched another nine-inning game the day after defeating Plank, he had won five games in eight days. The testing went on during September. Ed Walsh won, 1-0, and Rube Waddell beat Johnson, 2-1, in 10 innings. Johnson was charged with a loss in relief in a game which Addie Joss started on September 26. He came in with one out in the fourth inning and held Cleveland scoreless until the seventh when the Naps tied the score on hits by Bill Bradley and Larry Lajoie. The box score commentary concludes with a mystifying comment: "After the game the crowd of 16,836 paraded with three bands for half an hour."

A fabled event took place while Johnson dueled with the league's best pitchers. His catcher, Gabby Street, earned legendary fame by catching a baseball dropped from the top of the Washington Monument on August 17. Although the files of the *Washington Post* for Sunday, August 26, 1894, carried a fully documented, witnessed account of the same catch being made by Pop Schriver of Cap Anson's Chicago White Stockings, Street's feat was hailed as a unique first-time accomplishment. Shirley Povich, in his history of Washington baseball published by Putnam & Sons in 1950, heatedly defended Street's catch against rumors of the earlier catch.

Johnson's own activities were more routine that day. Mike Kahoe, not Street, whose hands were possibly still stinging from the catch, was behind the plate as the Nationals and the White Sox played to a 4-4 tie. The game was called because of darkness with the tireless Ed Walsh pitching in relief of Doc White.

A game in New York on October 1 drew this news note: "The visitors' bats went astray somewhere between the station and the ball park and Washington had to use bats borrowed from New York." Maybe it was the strange bats, but Jack Chesbro gained some vengeance. He had lost two of the three shutout games Walter Johnson pitched earlier in the four-day span. This time he won a 2-1 game. Two days later Johnson's record fell below .500 with a 3-2 loss to the Highlanders. However, when New York came to Washington for a season-ending series, Johnson evened his final record at 14-14. It took an 11-inning shutout against Jack Warhop to reach that plateau. Warhop is best remembered in trivia contests as the pitcher who gave up Babe Ruth's first home run.

Walter Johnson had pitched .500 ball for a team that played at a seventh-place .441 percentage. He had missed April, May, and half of June and had to pitch himself into shape after he finally arrived from his California home. Although earned run averages were not officially compiled for the American League until 1913, Johnson's 1.65 ERA can be worked out from his 47 earned runs in $256\frac{1}{3}$ innings pitched. His strikeout-to-walks ratio was three to one as he fanned 160 batters and walked only 53. Not yet 21, Walter Johnson had established himself, mostly in head-to-head encounters, as the peer of the best pitchers in his league.

4

Coming of Age in the Big Leagues

AFTER THE 1908 SEASON, Walter Johnson was invited to stop off in Chicago on his way home to California. Backed by a team of major leaguers, he would pitch against the popular Logan Squares, a top-notch independent team. He always found it hard to decline offers to pitch off-season games for extra income. This turned out to be an offer he should have resisted. Organized baseball was directed by a three-man national commission which consisted of the presidents of the American and National Leagues, with the well-regarded Garry Herrmann, owner of the Cincinnati Reds, striving to be the impartial tiebreaker in disputes. This time the three members were unanimous in enforcing a rule against such exhibitions until the World Series was profitably out of the way. Particularly as half of the Series games in 1908 would be played at the Chicago Cubs park, they did not want any diversions across town. The players who were to have played the game were declared ineligible to be signed to 1909 contracts and were fined $200 each. Two of Johnson's teammates, Jim Delahanty and George McBride, were slapped down, too.

Chastened, Walter Johnson continued back to California. He no longer thought of sitting up in a coach to save fare. He dressed the way young men did in the nation's capital. He had been to New York City, to Philadelphia, to Boston. Johnson was interested in the cities he visited, sending picture postcards of their landmarks home to his family and friends.

The World Series ended on October 16 with the Cubs making quick work of the Tigers in five games. It was safe for Walter Johnson to listen to another offer to pitch in a post-season game. On October 22 he put on a uniform of the Olives, a semipro outfit in Los Angeles, to pitch against the Los Angeles Colored Giants.

The divisiveness of politically correct language was far, far in the future. What divided white from black players was that only the white ones could make a living in organized baseball. Colored teams, the term in use then, were forced into the insecurity of barnstorming. There is nothing in Johnson's entire life to show any bias against blacks, nor was he ever particularly moved to take up their cause. He came from hardworking people who took it for granted that they had been born with white and others with dark skins. It was not impossible for blacks to succeed, only harder.

The Los Angeles Colored Giants were a powerful team which had won 35 of 36 games before facing Walter Johnson. They beat him, too, although it took 11 innings before the final score of 6-5 was reached. Johnson fanned 20 batters, but his inexperienced catcher could not handle him very well. Nonetheless, the Giants racked up nine hits off Johnson and demonstrated the folly of segregated baseball. Johnson probably would have agreed to a mixed team that day as he surely could have used their catcher.

Walter Johnson had been paid $3,000 for his first full season in the big leagues, even though he had not pitched all of it. Washington offered him an increase to $3,500 for 1909. Johnson, who was to respond in all salary negotiations with the self-interest of the professional ballplayer, asked for $4,000. The matter of his suspension was still a cloud, although no sensible person would think that organized baseball would ban Johnson, already a powerful gate attraction, over such a minor offense. Eventually the matter was settled. Johnson paid the $200 fine, which later events indicate may have been reduced to $50. Even so, Walter Johnson resented it. He accepted the team's $3,500 offer without further argument and got ready for what he hoped would be a truly complete season without the delays of illness. He continued to pitch Sunday baseball with Santa Ana and wrote to the team that he had gained 14 pounds, all of it muscle. Hard off-season outdoor work would keep him fit all his life. He was now a six-footer who weighed 200 pounds, an appropriate size for the coming strikeout king.

Washington trained in Galveston, Texas, and, shortly after beating Houston of the Texas League in a nine-inning exhibition, Walter Johnson caught a cold. It was the forerunner of a persistent pattern of respiratory problems which plagued Johnson throughout his career. A robust man, he was careless in avoiding situations which were popularly held to cause colds. He would sit in his shirtsleeves playing cards by an open train window or sit out on deck on a chilly crossing of

Lake Erie going from Cleveland to Detroit. Even as a manager, he would pitch batting practice, hit ground balls, and then, neglecting to put on a warm-up jacket, sit on cold cement steps. Granted, while present-day medical wisdom says these circumstances do not cause colds, had antibiotics been available during Johnson's career, he might well have broken Cy Young's record of 511 career wins.

During his career, Walter Johnson was sidelined and hospitalized several times by pneumonia, and grippe and influenza constantly recurred. He even caught malaria. He rarely missed a contest because of injury but was often felled by ailments he might have avoided or cured quickly with modern medical techniques and better self-care. In 1908 he had been delayed by mastoiditis and an operation. Now, in 1909, he was in bed with a massive cold when the season opened in Washington and was hardly fit to appear at all when he made his first start in New York in late April.

The season, already off to a ruinous start for Washington and a disappointing one for its young star pitcher, worsened on April 24. The Nationals were humbled by the Highlanders, 17-0, and Johnson was knocked out of the box after giving up five runs on six hits and six walks. Nine days later he tried again in Boston. He went six innings but lost, 7-1. Four days later he seemed to be on track. He was not winning, but the games he lost were the low-scoring kind. In Philadelphia, Jack Coombs beat him, 1-0, when a ninth-inning run scored on a throwing error. On May 10, as Washington went down to a third successive shutout, Johnson held the fort for 10 scoreless innings before giving way. He had given up only three hits before he weakened and a lone run beat him in the 11th.

Washington continued to reel through a season-destroying road trip. Johnson did not get to pitch before a home crowd in 1909 until his 10th appearance. By then his record was 2-6. He had won his first game in Cleveland, beating Addie Joss, 3-2, singling in the winning run himself in the 10th inning. His second win came cheaply under the scoring rules of the time. He was taken out of a game, too sick to continue, leading 2-1 after three innings. Long Tom Hughes rescued Johnson in great style, striking out 11 batters in six relief innings. Johnson was credited with the victory, however.

Despite friendly fans in the stands, Johnson's first appearance at home dropped his record to 2-7. It took 11 innings on June 5 to lose, 6-3, after two Washington runners were thrown out at the plate trying to score the winning run in regulation innings.

Despite the admiration of such stars as Kid Elberfeld and Wild Bill Donovan, Johnson was rarely at the top of his form all season. Elberfield told the sporting press, "I think the greatest pitcher baseball has ever known is Walter Johnson. I have batted against all the present day cracks except Mathewson. Why, Johnson can tell you what's coming up and still you can't hit it."

Donovan, who had mastered the wildness that got him his nickname, said of the pitcher he called the greatest youngster to ever break into the game, "Here is a mere boy, not yet of age, who did not have a single day's minor league experience, pitching as good ball as any pitcher in the American League and he does it all without any apparent effort. But there is much room for improvement in Johnson's work, which experience alone can bring him. When he learns the fine points of the pitching game his work will be easier and more effective. If ever there was a youngster who stands a chance of duplicating the great record of Cy Young, it is Walter Johnson."

Donovan was right on target. Johnson was still relying almost entirely on his fastball, and with the debilitating effects of a lingering illness, he tired late in ball games. Again, had the present custom of lifting a starting pitcher after six of seven so-called "quality innings" been in effect, and if Washington had a relief specialist, a "stopper" in today's terms, Donovan's prediction that Johnson would equal Cy Young's record would have been greatly enhanced.

There were flashes of form by Johnson. On August 17 he went 12 innings for a shutout win, 1-0, over Chief Bender of the A's. He had started the game the day before but lasted only six innings. That game was memorable for his first home run. The ball cleared the left-field fence, a feat done less than half a dozen times before, according to the press.

It was a long, long season for Washington. Joe Cantillon's days were numbered as his team lost repeatedly. In late August the Nationals lost 12 of 13 games on a road trip. Only Johnson's struggling 6-5 win in 10 innings on August 25 at Cleveland broke the string. At that, Johnson gave up 15 hits. In his next start he left the game after five innings, trailing Ed Walsh, who pitched a two-hitter, 1-0. After the game Walter Johnson reported he had a sore arm. The general opinion was that he had simply caught a cold in his arm. Johnson was sent back to Washington and remained idle for three and a half weeks. Even with this loss of time, and his delayed start, he pitched almost 300 innings before the season ended. Johnson pitched the team's 100th loss, losing 6-5 at Philadelphia.

It was not a pleasant season for Walter Johnson to contemplate. Luckily, he was not a brooding type of player. He had lost 25 games, which in a way is a sign of a superior pitcher. You have to be well regarded to have that many opportunities for defeat.

Walter Johnson was hailed as the pitcher of the future and offered an opportunity to do what he liked doing best. Instead of going back to California to play Sunday ball, he was invited to join a squad of National Leaguers and play a barnstorming trip with the Philadelphia Athletics.

Frank Bancroft, who had been the off-field manager of the Providence Grays in 1884 when Ol' Hoss Radbourn had won 60 games and a National League pennant, was a veteran entrepreneur. He had led the first American team to visit Cuba in the 19th century. He was now the business manager of the Cincinnati Reds and would still hold that post when they won a tainted World's Championship from the Chicago White Sox in the 1919 Black Sox scandal series.

Connie Mack was on the verge of winning four pennants in five seasons and the idea of post-season tour for his developing youngsters seemed a good one. Eddie Collins and Frank Baker were just breaking into the major leagues. With Jack Barry also in the lineup, they needed only the arrival of Stuffy McInnis the next season to form "the $100,000 Infield." It is a discount metaphor at today's rates, but at the time it described an almost priceless value. Philadelphia had finished a close second to Detroit in 1909. Their pitching staff was headed by two future Hall of Famers, Eddie Plank and Chief Bender.

The team with which Walter Johnson would travel featured a trio of New York Giants. Larry Doyle, in only his third season but already captain of John McGraw's team, expressed the exuberance of youth when he exclaimed, "It's great to be young and be a Giant." Twenty-year-old Rube Marquard was on the verge of shedding the label "the $11,000 Lemon." McGraw had paid a then-exorbitant sum to buy a minor league prospect who had stumbled at the start. Marquard, like Walter Johnson, was a pitcher still reaching toward his potential. Chief Meyers, a Cahuilla Indian from California who had been Johnson's catcher when he pitched for the Pickwicks in San Diego, was a first-year backstop for the Giants. Meyers had been educated at Dartmouth. The A's Eddie Collins was a graduate of Columbia, Jack Barry had captained Holy Cross, Eddie Plank was from Gettysburg, and Jack Coombs was an alumnus of Colby College.

Joe Jackson, who had joined the Athletics before the end of 1909, was not on the squad that made the tour. He had bolted for home in the piney hills of South Carolina as soon as the season ended. Shoeless Joe had been ridiculed for his illiteracy when he joined the Athletics late in the season. He wanted no part of a tour with players who had made fun of his rural ways. He was so adamant about not playing with them that Connie Mack virtually gave him away to Cleveland after the next year.

The teams, the A's and Bancroft's Nationals, would play most of their games in California. Johnson had been added because of his local popularity as well his national acclaim. It was a cooperative arrangement with all participants putting up $200 to cover such expenses as would not be met out of gate receipts. They would share the profits the tour expected to make. Bancroft made the arrangements. The tour began with games in Chicago, and the teams worked their way west. The California part of the trip started in the San Francisco Bay area with a week-long series of games, either between the traveling teams or individually against local teams. Then the teams would play their way down to Los Angeles for another week-long set of games. Walter Johnson was billed as "the local hero." From there the tour would cross the Southwest and end a week before Thanksgiving Day in New Orleans. Then the players, after splitting the profits, would head for their homes.

In most respects, the trip was a success. It put the A's in shape to win pennants in four of the next five seasons. Doyle, Meyers, and Marquard of the Giants would see their Philadelphia friends in the World Series in 1911 and 1913 and play Boston in 1912, the year the A's missed making it five in a row. Walter Johnson, however, would have to wait until 1924 before he would reach a World Series. Still, he gained a great deal of experience from the tour. He was the sort of young man who would benefit from the travel and the companionship of other young players, stars on the rise like himself.

The downside of the experience was that after leaving Los Angeles, the tour, which had been profitable to that point, encountered a string of rained-out contests which could not be rescheduled. The itinerary called for the teams to hit a town, play a game, get back on their chartered train, reach the next town and play again, and keep going. When it rained at every stop, there were no gate receipts. New Orleans had already had a week of torrential downpours when the soggy athletes reached there. There was no hope to play a game, and the young athletes were homesick with thoughts of Thanksgiving. At the end, there were no profits to share. However, each player had his $200 deposit returned and was given a ticket home. Johnson and some of the California players returned to Los Angeles for additional games. As such ventures go, Walter Johnson had enjoyed a wonderful experience.

5

An Opening Day Tradition Is Born

THE NEXT TIME Walter Johnson saw the Athletics, the team he had barnstormed with between seasons, was on Opening Day, 1910. It was a "first time" occasion: the first of 14 opening day games Walter Johnson would pitch in his 21-year career. When he could, from 1910 on, he was on the mound when the American League baseball season began. Sometimes he appeared even when medical advice warned otherwise. He was in top shape in the 1910 opener and almost set a record when he beat Eddie Plank, 3-0. Not until Bob Feller, something of a latter-day Walter Johnson, did it while pitching for Cleveland in 1940, would anyone pitch an opening day no-hitter. Johnson barely missed being the first.

Frank "Home Run" Baker took a lusty cut at a pitch and lifted a high pop fly down the right-field foul line. Three fielders converged, but just as Doc Gessler reached for the ball, some clod whose foot stuck out from under the rope that held back an overflow crowd tripped the outfielder. The ball fell safely for a very scratchy hit.

However, Walter Johnson's near-miss no-hitter that Opening Day was overshadowed by a man who cast a considerable one. The nearly 300-pound William Howard Taft, the president of the United States, attended the game. Taft, a knowledgeable baseball fan, had as president been to big league games before in Washington and other cities. When he received a handsome, leather-bound season pass to all 1910 Washington games, he put it to use at the earliest opportunity by agreeing to throw out the first ball of the season.

Club owner Thomas C. Noyes, delighted that his invitation was accepted, hunted up a chair to hold the president's broad proportions and set it up in a field box. The practice of having someone of celebrity throw out the first ball of an important contest had been in vogue since the 19th century. Customarily, the pitch was made from the mound. Taft made his from his box. He handed his top hat to his wife and peeled off his kid gloves. Then with great effort he threw the ball toward Walter Johnson, who saved the president a throwing error by short-hopping the ball out of the dirt. Johnson, with a fine sense of historical significance, rolled the ball to the bench with an instruction that it be saved for him.

The teams took the field and the pear-shaped president squeezed into his chair. He stayed there for the full nine innings, tugging free only as the home team came to bat in the seventh inning, then sitting down again. One of the more charming deceits passed down from one fanciful baseball writer to the next, connects Taft with initiating the seventh-inning stretch, and some versions even pinpoint it to Opening Day in 1910. Not true. Folks in Boston were doing it when Ol' Hoss Radbourn was a colt.

Walter Johnson was at the top of his form, striking out nine batters and bouncing a double off the distant left-field wall to drive in the only run he would need. The fans cheered as the president and his party made their way from the ballpark. They stayed to applaud the players as they trooped into the rebuilt clubhouse. 1910 was a great year for baseball. Before the season was over, fans were singing Jack Norworth's new song, "Take Me Out to the Ball Game."

The next day, young Walter Johnson sent the "opening day ball" President Taft had thrown to him to the White House. His note asked the president to autograph it for him. Taft did even better; he inscribed it, "To Walter Johnson with the hope that he may continue to be as formidable as in yesterday's game. William H. Taft. April 15, 1910.

Among other changes in Walter Johnson's circumstances in 1910 was the departure of Joe Cantillon as Washington's manager and the arrival of Jimmy McAleer. A celebrated fly chaser with Cleveland teams in the 1890s, McAleer had helped Ban Johnson start the American League. He led Cleveland in 1901 and the St. Louis Browns from 1902 through 1909. After a second-place finish in 1902, McAleer's Browns were almost as perennially doomed to second division as was Washington. However, McAleer had the backing of the powerful Ban Johnson, and the American League's founder wanted a strong franchise in the nation's capital. Vaudeville jokes that Washington was "first in war, first in peace and last in the American League," rankled the dour Ban Johnson. McAleer had a certain jaunty panache to take the place of Pongo Joe Cantillon's perpetual simian grin. McAleer, who next would become a part-owner of the Boston

Red Sox, could present himself in the best social circles. Cantillon, who was more at home in saloons than salons, went back to his minor league domain and successfully ruled for years in Minneapolis as owner and manager.

Cantillon had brought four star players to Washington, led by Walter Johnson. Clyde "Deerfoot" Milan, called Zeb by his mates, in center field, George McBride at shortstop, and Gabby Street behind the plate were standout players. Except for Street, who departed when McAleer did, the others were the nucleus of Washington's teams for a decade. Eventually, all three would also manage the team.

Walter Johnson bounced back in 1910 from a hardly deserved 13-25 record the season before to almost reverse the figures. He won 25 and lost 17 games. He did this for a team that would have been deep in last place without him. Even so, Washington could only barely manage a seventh-place finish.

Along the way, Walter Johnson pitched heroically, winning or losing by one-run margins 17 times. He pitched eight shutouts and lost 1-0 twice and 3-0 once. Johnson narrowly missed a no-hitter again at St. Louis on September 25. Frank Truesdale, a 5-foot-6, 145-pound second baseman, was the Browns' leadoff batter. His dinky fly ball dropped in safely to mar Johnson's near-perfect game. He walked none and only 28 men came to bat. Truesdale was the pesky type of batter who often hit Johnson best. Whether they played on his sympathy or just took contact pokes at the ball, such players fared better against Johnson than free swingers. He rated the diminutive shortstop Donie Bush as the Detroit Tiger batter who gave him the most trouble, not Ty Cobb.

Cobb, whose later published recollections were warped to serve his unquenchable ego, self-effacingly confessed to having exploited Johnson's fear of seriously harming a batter by crowding the plate. Johnson managed to overcome his qualms about pitching inside 206 times during his career and established an all-time mark for hit batsmen. Unlike today's easily enraged dig-in sluggers, no one ever charged the mound after a close pitch from Johnson. If it hit them, they were glad they survived.

The 1910 season belonged to Connie Mack and his Philadelphia Athletics. Even Johnson could win only two of six starts against them. After his opening day shutout, Johnson twice lost one-run games when he weakened in the ninth inning. He lost 4-3 on May 6 and 3-2 on July 5 as Eddie Plank evened the score for the opening day game. The A's also beat him, 7-5, on July 30. However, the pendulum swung

Walter Johnson's way on September 3. He was leading 3-1, the A's tally being the customary gift run coming on a Washington error. Then in the eighth inning, Connie Mack gave Walter Johnson an opportunity to make the record book. He sent three successive pinch hitters to the plate and Johnson struck them all out. Ten days later, in Philadelphia, Johnson again lost by one run, 2-1.

The final time Walter Johnson pitched against the Philadelphia Athletics was to prepare them for the 1910 World Series. The Chicago Cubs were concluding a National League schedule that took a week longer to complete than that of the American League. To keep the A's sharp for their coming encounter with the Cubs of "Tinker to Evers to Chance" fame, the American League arranged a series with an All-Star team. The Red Sox sent Tris Speaker and Jake Stahl, and the White Sox provided Harry Lord and pitcher Doc White. The rest of the team consisted of players from the Washington Nationals. Even Doc White was a D.C. resident between seasons, a practicing dentist in the nation's capital.

Jimmy McAleer managed the All-Stars, and from his own team had Kid Elberfeld, Germany Schaefer, Clyde Milan, George McBride, and the battery of Gabby Street and Walter Johnson. If the set of games was intended to bolster the confidence of Mack's team, having Johnson pitch was no way to do it. On Monday, October 10, with the A's "Big Three"—Bender, Plank, and Coombs—taking three-inning turns, the All-Stars coasted to an easy 8-3 win. Johnson allowed the AL champs only three hits and struck out eight, three of them in the third inning. He also doubled and singled.

Two days later, after Doc White had pitched a two-hitter against the A's, Walter Johnson was back to beat them again, 4-1. He gave up only five hits, two of them doubles coming in the ninth inning when "he slackened his speed," according to baseball historian Francis C. Richter, who covered the game for *The Sporting Life*. He was the editor of the Philadelphia-based baseball paper.

The A's did defeat Big Ed Walsh, the Chicago White Sox super spitballer, who had led the AL with a 1.27 ERA despite leading in losses with 20 defeats. Walter Johnson may have overwhelmed the Philadelphia Athletics, but he did not ruin their confidence. Having warmed up on Johnson, White, and Walsh, the A's made quick work of the Cubs. They took the first three games, losing the fourth to Three Finger Brown by one run, and wrapping up the 1910 World Series with a final victory the next day.

When the 1910 pitching stats were tallied, Walter Johnson dominated them. He pitched the most games, 45; started the most, 42; and completed the most, 38. He had pitched the most innings, 373, and struck out 313 to lead the league for the first time. With a temporary memory lapse, the press failed to remember that Rube Waddell had struck out 349 batters in 1904. They hailed Johnson for setting a new strikeout record. A purse of $500 was raised by the fans and thrust upon the young pitcher, who modestly accepted it. Actually, the records the reporters had failed to look up gave Waddell only 348 strikeouts in 1904. It was not until Bob Feller in 1946, his first season back from wartime Navy duty, also struck out 348, that Waddell's record was reexamined. An overlooked strikeout was belatedly added to the Rube's record.

Walter Johnson's life was not confined to the ball field during 1910. On his way to spring training he had stopped off in Kansas to visit an uncle who lived in Coffeyville. It had once been a rip-roaring cow town, where the Clanton gang met the finality of frontier justice. Three of the outlaw brothers were gunned down as they overreached themselves and tried to rob both the town's banks at the same time. Since then, Coffeyville had settled down to being a much quieter place to live and raise a family.

California had not been the promised land the Johnsons had expected. Frank, with a prize pair of work horses, had supported his family hauling pipes to the oil fields. But he was too independent to work for someone else, and it wasn't farming. With Walter now playing baseball on the East Coast, they thought it might be better to get closer by returning to Middle America.

The Johnsons moved to Coffeyville, in the southeast corner of Kansas, where they bought a 160-acre farm across the Verdigris River east of town. When the baseball season ended, Johnson joined his parents and younger brothers and sisters and pitched in to fashion a working farm for all the Johnsons. Later, Walter Johnson would buy his own farm and be known during much of his career as "the Coffeyville Express." Relocating the Johnson family made it all the more urgent to make the most money he could from baseball.

During the 1910 season Walter Johnson had been tempted by a promoter, D.A. Fletcher. An unknown, it was his idea to create an All-Star tour to travel the country following the season. He set about recruiting the top players in both leagues, offering them $3,000 apiece to make the trip. The Cincinnati-based promoter had an even grander scheme. He proposed leveraging the tour into a new major league. He would create a six-team league and recruit the best players from the

16 major league teams. Fletcher was an archetypical hustler; he intended to do this with other people's money. He claimed as much as $8 million in available backing and tapped into his sources for enough up-front money to make an impressive start.

Apart from the evident hurdles before him, such as having ballparks to play in, circumstances had placed Fletcher in the home city of Garry Herrmann, chairman of baseball's ruling triumvirate, the National Commission, and of Frank Bancroft, the dean of barnstorming. Herrmann and Bancroft got D.A. Fletcher evicted from his office and apartment in the Havlin Hotel in Cincinnati. They told its manager he would lose the patronage of the National League clubs. When they played the Reds in the future they would stop elsewhere. The Havlin Hotel asked Fletcher for his key.

In Washington, the business-wise Jimmy McAleer, whose star players were succumbing to Fletcher's wiles, pointed out they were only being asked to sign options on contracts. No money would change hands until the promoter had an impressive number of star players willing to jump to a new league. Then he would use these "contracts" to draw the millions in backing he would need. McAleer scoffed that such an approach would never succeed. However, Fletcher's claims that stars such as Ty Cobb and Honus Wagner were signed for the tour and would play in the new league were not denied.

The Sporting Life carried the following information, datelined October 3 and filed from Cincinnati: "According to Chicago dispatches, while the Washington team was in that city, pitcher Walter Johnson frankly stated that he, McBride, Milan and Street had signed with Fletcher's proposed new league. Johnson said that the new league was practically organized and added:

" 'I do not know exactly how many players have been signed up, but I do know that three members of our team beside myself have already signed contracts. They are McBride, Milan and Street. We will each get $10,000 bonuses if everything goes through all right, and we have assurance from Mr. Fletcher that the possibility of a hitch is past.' "

When asked where D.A. Fletcher would get the money to carry out his proposals, Johnson answered, "Fletcher hasn't any money to speak of himself, but I understand he has several millions of backing. Fletcher isn't a capitalist but a promoter—and a good one." The dispatch from Cincinnati concluded by saying that the players had wired the Washington papers to deny they had signed with the new league.

Though D.A. Fletcher moved his headquarters to New York City just after the World Series and continued to issue boastful claims, his scheme faded. However, he had found a potential market, and the expansion of major league franchises was left for someone else to exploit. Four years later, others with more secure backing from men who longed to own big league ball clubs, brought the Federal League into its two-year existence. Just as he was easily drawn into Fletcher's scheme, Walter Johnson's need for money to support his own ventures would make him willing to be exploited.

6
The Express
Stops at Coffeyville

WITH D.A. FLETCHER'S grand tour abandoned, Walter Johnson headed for his family's new home in Kansas. His father now ran a dairy farm and there would be ample work to keep his oldest son busy. He had outgrown playing Sunday baseball just for the fun of it. He was no longer a willing youngster looking for a game. As Kansas winters did not allow for year-round baseball, Johnson left his glove and toe plate in his equipment bag.

A dinner was held in his honor on October 30. Coffeyville had a new "hometown hero" and would regard him as its number-one citizen during the years the Washington pitcher made the city his off-season home. There was a symbiotic pairing of the town and its new celebrity. Each had the same middle-class values that the other appreciated. Coffeyville sought respectability after its founding fathers had stopped shooting up the town on Saturday nights. Johnson, reared in a hardworking, self-sufficient family, welcomed an off-season alternate to the high-life style of Washington.

Walter Johnson could have lived anywhere he wished. He had grown up on a Kansas farm. He had gone through adolescence in southern California. He had begun his professional life as an Easterner in Washington, D.C. In 1911, he chose the prairie lifestyle of Kansas. Baseball players of Walter Johnson's time came mostly from rural America. When the baseball season ended, they headed home, looking forward to the autumn hunting season. Johnson was drawn to the blood sports. His greatest pleasure during his time away from baseball was to follow a pack of hound dogs as they flushed out targets for his shotgun. Rabbits, quail, whatever scurried or flew, were quarry for his game bag. And best of all in Johnson's estimation, were nocturnal ventures into wooded lands on coon hunts with his friends.

Even though plans for a new league had fallen through, D.A.

Fletcher had raised Walter Johnson's salary expectations. He had been paid $4,500 for 1910 but had envisioned twice that much according to Fletcher's proposed wage scale. Johnson decided he was worth $9,000, "The same as Ty Cobb gets."

In March, the unsigned Walter Johnson went to Hot Springs, Arkansas, a popular spa where out-of-shape athletes readied themselves for the coming season. Johnson did not need to soak out a winter's excesses, but he did enjoy the informal ball games that were played against local teams. With him were his roommate, Clyde "Zeb" Milan, and Germany Schaefer, whose off seasons included vaudeville tours and relaxing in saloons with his friends. Germany's exercise between seasons consisted largely of blowing the foam off steins of lager. He had long been a pre-season denizen of Hot Springs, turning up there on a regular basis when with Detroit.

Johnson's batting drew comment, the press reporting: "His two home runs astounded the natives, one of them the longest home run ever hit here. This gives Johnson two parks where he has hit the longest home run. The other is Detroit."

Johnson's salary appetite, whetted by Fletcher's rosy promises, now required more appeasement than the Washington management claimed it could afford. They offered an increase to $6,000, a raise of $1,500. Johnson went to Atlanta where the team was training and began working out while he negotiated a new contract. The offer was increased to $6,500, and there management dug in its heels. Walter Johnson met Christy Mathewson when the Giants came through Georgia. Maybe Matty had advice for the young pitcher. He was the highest-paid pitcher in baseball but had a greater claim on early 20th-century megabucks than the relative newcomer. Johnson had also read Ty Cobb's revelation that he was being paid $9,000 a season for three years. The young pitcher wanted the same amount; if not in equal yearly payments, then a three-year total of $27,000.

It was pointed out that Cobb played 140 or more games a season and Johnson only pitched about 40. However, Cobb's box-office value could not be identified as specifically as Johnson's. When he pitched, the gate receipts nearly doubled. Walter Johnson was 23 years old and immature in many ways. However, he was not inexperienced in dealing with the management of professional baseball teams. He would never forget being cut loose in Tacoma. Although his friends on the team, Gabby Street, Dolly Gray, Bob Groom, and Kid Elberfeld, tried to talk him into signing, Johnson told them, "They won't give me what I want and I don't intend to sign up for what they offer."

To show the team had reached its limit, Manager McAleer bought Johnson a ticket back to Coffeyville. The two men shook hands and Johnson walked out of the team's hotel and left Atlanta on the 4:10 P.M. train. He was back in Coffeyville late the next night. And by the following Wednesday, he was in Washington ready to sign a compromise contract. Management had the advantage of the reserve clause, which bound a player exclusively to one club. Johnson's alternatives were limited. He could barnstorm, play outlaw ball, or raise chickens with his father. Still, he had held out to some advantage. Agreement was reached to pay the pitcher $7,000 a year for three years. It was below Johnson's demands but higher than he had originally been offered. Considering what he would achieve over the coming three seasons, he had sold himself too cheaply. However, knowing he had a good-paying job for three years meant a lot to Walter Johnson. Although only 23, he had no youthful delusions about immortality. He already knew that when a pitcher lost his fastball, he also lost his job. The harangue over salary had taken some of the edge off Walter Johnson's spring training preparation, and he would not be ready for the season's opener.

Even while Johnson's contract was being negotiated, owner Tom Noyes faced a far more expensive problem. A fire had razed his ballpark only 25 days before the 1911 season was to begin. Only the right- field bleachers remained. However, there was land available beside the old ballpark, and a new one was built to be "bigger and better than ever" in time to open the season. A roof over the grandstand would have to wait. To shade the patrons from Washington's hot summer sun, large canvas screens were erected. However, when it came to playing baseball, the ballpark was ready before Johnson was. Pitching the opening day game had not yet become a Johnson tradition. He had done it only once, the year before when President Taft had glorified Opening Day by throwing out the first ball. A top-hatted President Taft was on hand again for 1911's opening day ceremonies, but Johnson watched from the bench. The hurriedly rebuilt ballpark had seats for 12,000 and nearly another 3,000 found places to stand. This time the president made a better ceremonial toss, but not to Walter Johnson. Dolly Gray beat the young Red Sox ace, Smokey Joe Wood, 8-5.

Three days later, Johnson was almost ready. Although he lost, 6-2, in the fifth inning he fanned four batters for another unusual record. After pitcher Ray Collins struck out, so did Larry Gardner. But the third strike got away from Eddie Ainsmith, and the batter reached first on a passed ball. Gardner then stole second and, with two strikes, Tris Speaker doubled and drove in the game's first run. Johnson then struck out the next two batters, Duffy Lewis and Clyde Engle. Washington made three errors in the next inning and the Red Sox scored three runs. The game, played on a cold, damp day, had mixed results for Johnson. He struck out eight, but he also walked eight and gave up 11 hits.

More than a week went by before Johnson started again, and this time he lost to New York, 5-3. In Philadelphia, Johnson won for the first time of the season, 2-1, outdueling his frequent rival Jack Coombs. He missed a shutout when Frank Baker lined a home run over the right-field fence. In Boston, Johnson got his first shutout of the season, winning 3-0. However, just as he reached a winning groove, the needle jumped. He struggled to a 7-6 win on May 6 after complaining he did not feel well before the game. In his next start, as the team began a road trip in Chicago, an obviously ill Johnson gave up four hits and a walk, and the White Sox scored four runs in the first inning. He retired only one batter. Paul W. Eaton failed to give a diagnosis in his team reports to *The Sporting Life*, only observing that Johnson had to rest to regain his form.

Ten days later, Johnson was called on to halt a Detroit rally in the ninth inning. Washington's lead had disappeared, and the score was 8-8 as Ty Cobb came to bat. Johnson had relieved with the bases full and retired two batters without a run scoring. Now came Cobb. An account of the game says that Cobb "pranced and danced around the plate like a hen on a hot rock." Johnson, distracted by Cobb's antics, walked in the winning run. Two days later, Walter Johnson finally won another game, 6-2. The rocky road trip was over, and Washington's second-division fate settled. Yet, even back in Washington, Johnson lost his next two starts and dropped his record to 4-5. He won the next two, shutting out the only team with a worse record than the Senators—the St. Louis Browns, 13-0.

In Philadelphia his teammates made four errors in one inning as the A's scored three times without a hit and without the ball leaving the infield. Johnson's own wild throw cost him his next start, 3-2. In reporting the team's misfortunes in *The Sporting Life*, Paul W. Eaton wrote, "The move from Philadelphia [to New York] was like a jump from Scylla to Charybdis." Presumably, metaphors based on Greek mythology were not wasted on Eaton's readers. Johnson finally stopped Washington's eight-game losing streak, this time beating

John Quinn of the Highlanders, 5-2. On July 1, in a game in which Eddie Collins dislocated an elbow in a collision with Danny Murphy, Johnson gave up seven runs in the sixth inning, most of them unearned. The team made five errors in the game, another loss to Jack Coombs. After the July 4 doubleheaders, Washington was in seventh place with only St. Louis below them. Philadelphia led Detroit by half a game for the league lead. Moving to Boston, Johnson homered into the center-field bleachers and won to even his record at 8-8 at the season's midpoint. The Washington Nationals next swung through the West, with only Johnson's four victories to offset 16 losses by the floundering team.

July 24, an open date for all teams, had been designated for a special memorial game to be played in honor of Addie Joss. The best players of the league came together to form one of the greatest All-Star teams ever assembled. They played the Cleveland Indians in a fund-raising game to benefit the widow and children of the immensely popular Joss. In addition to being the league's premier pitcher, he had the same personal attributes the baseball world was discovering in Walter Johnson.

When Johnson won his first major league game, Addie Joss watched as his Cleveland teammates were overwhelmed by the phenom. Joss, who led the league with 27 victories in 1907, commented: "That young fellow is another Cy Young. I never saw a kid with more than he displayed. Of course, he is still green, but when he has a little experience he should be one of the greatest pitchers that ever broke into the game. He has terrific speed and a motion which does not put much strain on his arm. And all this will improve as he goes along."

Joss had sized up Walter Johnson, whose sidearm motion was similar to his, perfectly. The comparison with Cy Young was particularly appropriate in terms of the All-Star Memorial Game. Now 44 years old, Young was at the end of his career and would be released before the 1911 season ended. Even if he was past his prime, Cy Young was the right choice to start the game for Cleveland. It might have been more appropriate had Walter Johnson, whom Joss called "another Cy Young," opened for the All-Stars. Perhaps however, Jim McAleer, who managed the collection of top players, felt it better politics to give the starting assignment to Johnson's rival, Smokey Joe Wood. When Johnson took over in the fourth inning, with Gabby Street behind the bat, he pitched three scoreless innings.

For once, Walter Johnson was backed by a team of peers. Ty Cobb,

Sam Crawford, and Tris Speaker covered the outfield. Frank "Home Run" Baker, Bobby Wallace, Eddie Collins, and Prince Hal Chase formed the infield. Except for Chase, whose penchant for crookedness eventually got him banished from baseball, the starters are all long-established in baseball's Hall of Fame in Cooperstown, New York.

Cleveland's lineup included its manager, Larry Lajoie, and a rookie, Joe Jackson, dropped by Connie Mack. The new Cleveland star was battling Ty Cobb for the batting championship, with both soaring well over .400. The final score of the memorial game was 5-3, won by the All-Stars, who hammered out 15 hits. Speaker and Milan shared center field and had two hits apiece. Also with two hits were Collins and Cobb, who played in a borrowed Cleveland outfit. Prince Hal Chase led all batters with three hits and handled 18 chances flawlessly. He played with characteristic grace. Expert baseball opinion held that Chase was the finest fielding first baseman who ever played.

It was a gala occasion, and 15,270 fans were entertained by the antics of Johnson's fun-loving teammate Germany Schaefer on the coaching lines. The proceeds added up to $12,914 for the widow and children of Addie Joss, who had pitched only nine seasons before his early death at 32. He had been so dominant that he was elected to Cooperstown by special waiver of the 10-year rule.

While the team was on its long road trip, great progress had been made rebuilding the new National Park. The stands were now roofed, but the players were more interested in changes that affected them. The old clubhouse in center field was gone, and the players now dressed under the grandstand in a locker room three times the size of the old one. The player's facilities were modeled after those in the new Shibe Park in Philadelphia. The A's new home was the first concrete stadium built and the forerunner of modern ballparks. There was an underground passage between the player's bench and their clubhouse. They could avoid passing the often resentful spectators after a game. There were now five showers where there had only been two. The umpires had their own dressing room and shower next to the players.

After losing his first start in the new ballpark to Detroit, Walter Johnson ran off 10 straight victories, although the team still struggled in second division.

Washington started its final road trip, and Johnson shut out the Browns and saved another game in St. Louis. He won in Chicago, drubbed Detroit, 16-2, and was so sparing with his pitches in defeating Cleveland, 2-1, that he threw only 72 pitches. This beat Christy Mathewson's feat of using only 75 pitches in a game. Only 15 of Johnson's 72 pitches were called balls. Next, Johnson reached the 20-win mark. He hit two doubles while beating the Highlanders in New York, 11-1. On Labor Day in Philadelphia, Johnson pinch-hit in the ninth inning to drive in the tying run and then took over the pitching. He held the A's, who were headed for another championship, scoreless for three innings to win his 10th in a row.

Back in Washington, Johnson pitched well, struck out eight and got two of Washington's five hits, but he lost to New York, 5-2. Johnson beat Boston when they came to town and before the Red Sox left, they had a new owner and Johnson would soon have a new manager. Jim McAleer became half owner of Boston, although he continued to manage Washington until the season ended.

Johnson's remaining games gave him a possible chance to influence the batting race between Ty Cobb and Joe Jackson. Cobb carried a substantial lead over his new rival, colorfully nicknamed "Shoeless Joe." Jackson would become the first American Leaguer to fail to win a batting title while topping .400. Although Jackson hit .408, Ty Cobb had his personal career high, batting .420. One of Cobb's self-serving fictions told in his later years was that he had psyched Jackson out of the championship. Cobb claimed that when the two met in a season-ending series, Jackson had folded when Cobb coldly ignored the unsophisticated rookie. Cobb sneered that Jackson was so upset that he blew the championship. Hurrah for the master psychologist Cobb? No. It's another fable from the past that has become embedded among the legends of the game. It was also unworthy of Grantland Rice, in his autobiography *The Tumult and the Shouting*, to relate this spurious tale. He did so as one Southern aristocrat supporting another. Jackson's illiteracy had been an affront to the educated Rice. His forte as a writer was to compose memorable leads although not the one which gave Johnson his nickname, "the Big Train." Research he left to others. In the 1911 batting race, Cobb held an uncatchable lead in the last week. In the three-game set, he was actually out-hit by Jackson. Cobb then sat out the final three games as needless insurance that his 16-point lead would hold up.

Walter Johnson did not have an adverse effect on either Cobb or Jackson. Sam Crawford's recollection of Johnson's mastery over Cobb was far off the mark in 1911. Cobb had 11 hits in 22 times at bat against Johnson for a .500 average. Jackson's 19 at-bats produced eight base hits for a .421 average which included a double, triple, and home run. Although Walter Johnson held all opposing batters to a .238 season average, the league's two top batters hit him harder than they hit the rest of the league's pitchers.

Walter Johnson had improved his record to 25-13, although his team had repeated its seventh-place finish. Despite his early-season illness, he pitched 323 innings, third most in the league. His strikeout total, 207, was also third best behind Ed Walsh with 255 and Joe Wood with 231. His 1.89 ERA was second to Vean Gregg's 1.81. Johnson tied Eddie Plank with six shutouts and led the league with 36 complete games. It had been a splendid season for the young pitcher and, as Addie Joss had predicted, he improved as he went along.

The National League schedule again ended a week later than the American League's, with the New York Giants qualifying to meet the Philadelphia Athletics in the World Series. The pre-series games against a group of star players from the rest of the league had put the A's in fine form to beat the Chicago Cubs the year before. What's more, it made money as fans came to see the best players against the best team.

The same idea was repeated to prepare the 1911 A's. It worked just as well, as this time Connie Mack's team beat John McGraw's Giants in six games. The All-Stars were again managed by Jim McAleer, who used his best players as a nucleus: Walter Johnson, with Gabby Street to catch him, Clyde Milan, Kid Elberfeld, George McBride, and Doc Gessler. Germany Schaefer was a clowning coach and fill-in player. The drawing cards were Ty Cobb, Larry Gardner, and Hal Chase.

Four games were played, with George Mullin, Ray Collins, Walter Johnson, and Smokey Joe Wood each starting a game. The first two were played in Washington and drew only a combined attendance of 6,000. The games in Richmond, Virginia, where the fans were less accustomed to seeing such stars, drew 15,000. The series was split with Johnson and Wood losing their starts. The players shared in the gate receipts, and each got a gold watch and a diamond stickpin.

During the winter, Washington would hire a new manager, Clark Griffith, to fill the vacancy caused by Jim McAleer's departure. Known as "the Old Fox," the wily Griffith would greatly influence Walter Johnson's career and life.

7
Clark Griffith
Takes Over

IN 1912 THE TITANIC was launched. Built to be unsinkable, the huge ocean liner struck an iceberg on its maiden voyage and sank. That same year the Washington franchise rose from the depths of the American League under the new leadership of Clark Calvin Griffith, who would become Walter Johnson's mentor and closest lifetime companion and friend. They came from the same self-reliant pioneer stock. Both were driven by a fierce determination to succeed. Unlike the robust, 200-pound Johnson, Griffith was only 5-foot-6½ and barely topped 150 pounds. Although he was a leading pitcher in both the National and American Leagues, he never had a Johnson-like blazing fastball. Griffith's Hall of Fame credentials, 240 wins and 144 losses, were achieved by guile. He threw six different pitches, among them what he claimed was the first screwball. Even as a youngster, breaking in with Cap Anson's Chicago White Stockings, he was dubbed "the Old Fox." His first full major league season was 1894. Among his incidental assignments that year was to toss down the ball Pop Schriver caught at the foot of the Washington Monument.

Walter Johnson and Clark Griffith had more in common than being right-handed pitchers. Johnson's favorite off-season activity was hunting. He did it for sport. Griffith, as a 10-year-old, had actually helped support his family, tucked away in the rural recesses of backwoods Missouri, as a professional hunter and trapper.

When the Griffiths moved to Bloomington, Illinois, where the family's provisions could be bought at the local grocery store and meat market, young Clark Griffith discovered baseball. He also learned he was exceptionally skilled at the game. Local teams would recruit him to pitch, and he usually was the best hitter as well. He was only 18 when he signed his first professional contract, with Milwaukee. In 1893 he won 30 games, losing 18, with the Oakland Oaks of the

California League. He had known Joe Shea, who had tipped off Joe Cantillon about Walter Johnson. Even more, when the Oaks could not meet the payroll, Clark Griffith and several teammates turned vaude-villians. They played San Francisco's Barbary Coast circuit, which included Cantillon's saloon. Such was the small world of baseball when men like Clark Griffith gave it the form it held for many years.

Griffith was to create a family business with the Washington franchise. It survived until his adopted son, Calvin Griffith, sold the team early in 1984. The third-generation owner was overwhelmed by the modern forces of marketing and merchandising after the team had been transplanted to Minnesota. The ties that bound baseball men together in Clark Griffith's time now linked speculative financiers, corporation lawyers, and ego-driven men with the money to buy power. These nouveau riche franchise owners did not want to simply support the sport. They wanted to possess it. They basked in a lime-light that was reflected from playing fields and shone into the owner's luxury box.

However, in 1912 it was all only beginning. There was a new spring training site, Charlottesville, Virginia. It was closer to Washington than Atlanta, and the weather was understood to be mild most of the time. The University of Virginia's baseball team would provide opposition for early training games. For cultural excursions, the home of Thomas Jefferson, who had founded the university, was nearby at Monticello. Griffith, the new manager, just into his 40s, was a hands-on leader. He quickly disposed of much of the woeful roster he inherited, keeping the handful of good ballplayers. They were led, of course, by Walter Johnson and included Clyde Milan and George McBride, but not Gabby Street. The widely held opinion was that only Gabby Street could handle Walter Johnson's pitches. What Griffith knew was that Street was having difficulty handling anyone's pitches. He had been badly slowed by inflammatory rheumatism, and although he continued to catch for many years with minor league teams, he no longer had the agility Griffith wanted. Griffith much preferred a pair of catchers, Eddie Ainsmith and Bull Henry, whom McAleer had used lightly behind Street. Ainsmith, badly underrated by those whose opinions are formed entirely by statistical tabulations, became Johnson's regular catcher. Looking back over his career after he retired from competition, Walter Johnson assessed those who had caught him through 20 seasons: "I guess that Ainsmith may have a slight edge on the others," he hedged, not wanting to offend Street and others. "Eddie was a peppery catcher who chattered to the batters almost incessantly and also helped me out of many a tough spot."

Griffith put together a ball club which made an amazing transformation from next-to-last in 1911 to next-to-first in 1912. The team's second-place finish with players, other than Johnson, who were not regarded as tops at their positions, was one of the great form reversals in baseball's history.

Griffith brought with him two men who helped transform baseball Nick Altrock, a faded pitcher with the Chicago White Sox. He was a combination comedian and skilled pitching coach. He teamed first with Germany Schaefer and later with Al Schacht in comedy coaching acts, some of which Max Patkin preserved in his own clown act into the 1990s. However, Altrock's chief contribution was to turn a losing pitching staff into a winning one. Bob Groom improved from 13-17 to 24-13. In 1909 he had led the league with 105 walks and lost 26 games, 19 of them reportedly in a row. Long after Groom's death, a search of the actual box scores reduced his string of losses to a face-saving 17.

Long Tom Hughes, whose main claim to fame had been to stop a team of runaway horses charging down Broadway with several New York City debutantes shrieking in a carriage, went from 11-17 to 13-10. Carl Cashion, a 2-3 rookie, bloomed into a 10-6 fourth-starter. Walter Johnson, while appreciating whatever pitching technique he could learn from Griffith and Altrock, had simply gotten better. He improved on his 1911 record of 25-13 with his first 30-game season, winning 32 and losing 12.

Clark Griffith also brought with him his former trainer, Mike Martin. When Manager Griffith was fired by the Tammany Hall politicos whose micro-management ultimatums wrecked the New York Highlanders, Mike Martin was booted out too. He went to Cincinnati with Griffith, where they worked under the far more benign ownership of Garry Herrmann. Mike Martin had come off the streets of New York City to survive and rise in the manner of an Horatio Alger hero. He had been a delivery boy, fighting other kids for routes. He had trained bike riders when six-day marathons had been popular, had trained boxers, and had worked for the period's most renowned conditioner, Mike Murphy, at the University of Pennsylvania. He had trained rowers and track men at the New York Athletic Club. He was literally Griffith's strong right arm and would be so throughout Walter Johnson's long career. He never claimed credit for the speed in Johnson's throwing arm, but Johnson gave public endorsement for its durability later in ads for "Mike Martin's Liniment." He went along with the implied promise that the trainer's formula would, if not turn a weak arm into one as strong as Johnson's, at least insure one without an ache or pain.

It was time to raise the curtain on the new team in Washington. At last, the team would be led by a winning manager. Clark Griffith was a close ally of Ban Johnson and a key player in forming the American League. He had been an active organizer of ballplayers seeking a minimum salary of $3,000 at the time the new league was formed. Griffith delivered nearly 40 players from the National League, and Ban Johnson repaid him with the role of playing manager of the Chicago White Sox. Griffith rewarded the owner, Charles Comiskey, with the first American League pennant. Not only did Griffith provide the field leadership, he also led the league in pitching with a 24-7 record and a .774 winning percentage. Griffith's reward, after a fourth-place finish the next year, was to be sent to New York City. He was asked to build the franchise into the powerhouse the league's prestige required.

In 1904, Griffith came within a ninth-inning wild pitch by Jack Chesbro of giving New York its first pennant. He had been pressured by the Tammany leaders from their field box to overuse Chesbro. "Happy Jack" is in the Baseball Hall of Fame largely for what he did in that overworked 1904 season. He pitched 454.2 innings and started 51 games, one every third day. He won 41 games and lost only 12. But the last game he lost also cost the pennant when his tired arm wild-pitched the winning run home.

Griffith had eased the strain on Chesbro the next two seasons by developing the role of the relief pitcher. Although Chesbro started 38 games in 1905, he only had to finish 24 of them. In 1906 he made a league-leading 42 starts but was relieved in 18 of them. This preserved a 24-16 record. The same sense of how to handle players was to be Griffith's trademark in Washington, too.

Griffith brought in sure-handed fly chasers Danny Moeller and Howard Shanks to flank Milan in center. The speedy holdover outfielder would take Ty Cobb's stolen-base crown away from the Georgian in 1912. Except for George McBride at shortstop, the infield had been porous and weak-hitting. Eddie Foster, a defensive star who also hit well, took over the hot corner. Gabby Street was traded to New York for Jack Knight, a proven second baseman. Although

Knight flopped, Ray Morgan, up from the minors, more than filled the bill. Germany Schaefer remained as an all-purpose utility man. After the season was underway, Griffith solved the team's first-base problem by buying Chick Gandil from the International League. The future leader of the Chicago White Sox conspiracy to sell out the 1919 World Series to gamblers, hit with power and was outstanding on defense, leading the league with a .990 fielding percentage. Although far from a star-studded lineup, the same regulars kept the team in contention for four years. They would be better known now had they not run head-on into the dynastic Philadelphia A's and the Boston Red Sox in the same period. Boston would win pennants in 1912 and 1915, and Philadelphia, which had won in 1910 and 1911, also won in 1913 and 1914.

One of the most repeated Johnson stories is told to illustrate the great care he took not to injure batters with his pitches. The convincing example, as confirmed in interviews he gave later in life, was to confess to the only time he deliberately took aim at a batter's head. The mild-mannered Johnson had been exploited by hitters like Ty Cobb who dared injury by crowding the plate. Cobb bragged that he gained an edge against Johnson by taking away the inside half of the plate, safely assuming Johnson would keep the ball away from him. Others, either foolhardy or desperate enough to try anything against Johnson, would stand with their toes touching the plate and try to slice an outside pitch to the opposite field.

Johnson was persuaded by the hard-nosed Mike Martin to act in his own interest, and Home Run Baker was chosen for the demonstration. "He's been murdering you for years," pointed out Martin. Johnson agreed to aim a fastball at Baker's head. When he drove the A's slugger into the dirt, he rushed to apologize. Both players were shaken by the near miss. It was the only time, according to Johnson, that he ever deliberately threw a bean ball pitch. Some of the myth-makers adorned the story by stating admiringly that although he hit a record 206 batters in his career, Johnson never hit any in the head. Not true. In 1912 he accidentally nailed a scrapper named Jack Martin, who played for the New York Highlanders. Martin failed to get his head out of the way of an errant pitch. His upper jaw was fractured but he survived. In fact, when he died at 93 he was New York's oldest former player, and he took bows at old-timers' games at Yankee Stadium as late as 1979.

Johnson met Clark Griffith for the first time when he arrived in

Charlottesville. Griffith had managed New York in 1907, and his team had been shut out, 2-0, in the only game Johnson pitched against the Highlanders. In 1908, Griffith had been deposed as manager before Johnson had pitched his famous three shutouts in four days against New York. As Johnson was already signed to a three-year contract, he and Griffith did not have pre–training camp contact. Perhaps it was just as well; Griffith, lured by the offer of stock in the team, was drawing $7,000—the same salary as Johnson.

8

1912
—The Season of Streaks

NINETEEN TWELVE was a season of streaks. First, in the National League, Rube Marquard got off to a flying start on April 11 and did not stop winning games consecutively until July 8. By the time he was stopped, he had won 19 games without a loss.

Marquard had come to stardom in 1911, having lived down the scurrilous nickname "the $11,000 Lemon." John McGraw had tacked on an extra grand when buying the 18-year-old pitcher's contract from Indianapolis at the end of the 1908 season. It would be good publicity, reasoned the Giant manager, to top the $10,000 once paid for Mike "King" Kelly in the 19th century. The promotional ploy backfired and the disappointed press dubbed Marquard "the $11,000 Lemon." He had first been nicknamed "Rube" in expectation he would emulate another lefthander, Rube Waddell. In 1912, he did what Waddell never did: he ran off 19 wins in a row before a scoring interpretation stopped him. Marquard and Giant fans would argue in vain against the decision which stopped his streak. The baseball establishment is reluctant to undo a wrong, no matter how unjust. Even before Marquard's streak was cut off at 19, fans were arguing he should have been given another victory along the way. Early in his streak, Marquard relieved Jeff Tesreau with the Giants behind, 3-2. They rallied to win, 4-3, but, as the starter had pitched effectively enough, in the opinion of the official scorer, Tesreau was given the victory.

Then, to Marquard's greater dismay, his streak ended when he was charged with a loss in a game in which he relieved with runners on base. It was believed by scorers in 1912 that it was more onerous to let a batter drive in a winning run than to have put the scoring runner on base. That's what happened to Marquard on July 8. He gave up the hit that scored a runner he had inherited, and his streak ended.

A few days earlier, on July 3, Walter Johnson brought his record to

14-7 with a victory that launched his own string of consecutive wins that, like Marquard's, eventually ended with a relief loss. Similarly, Johnson would take the fall for allowing the preceding pitcher's runner to score. At the time, the rule in both leagues said the pitcher who was on the mound when the winning run scored was charged with the loss. Even so, Marquard's record has never been equaled, and Johnson's, although tied the same season and twice since, is the American League record.

Let's go back to the start of the season for Washington and take things as they come. Walter Johnson was the opening day pitcher, facing the defending World Champion Philadelphia Athletics in Shibe Park on April 11. This might have been the game Johnson dusted off Home Run Baker. None of the references to it, including Johnson's own admission of the event, give the date when it happened. A missed batter, unlike a hit one, is not registered in the box score. Johnson was a bit off form, possibly shaken by the near miss of Baker, and lost to Jack Coombs, 4-2, walking three and allowing six hits. He struck out four.

Next, Walter Johnson, with his former battery mate Gabby Street, now catching Jack Quinn of the New York Highlanders, showed he could change backstops and still pitch shutouts. He outdueled the spitballing John Picus Quinn, 1-0. Quinn, who was three years older than Johnson, was still pitching in the big leagues in 1933, just short of his 50th birthday.

Washington's home opener with Philadelphia was played on April 19. This time, the presidential box was occupied only by the vice president, James Sherman. President Taft was leading a nation mourning the sinking of the Titanic. The steamship had gone down on April 15 with the loss of 1,503 lives, among them Archie Butt, an aide to Taft, who had urged the president to take time off to enjoy baseball. Taft missed seeing Walter Johnson pitch another opening day shutout, 6-0. The new manager, Clark Griffith, had his team off and running.

After the home opener, Johnson continued to pitch in great form. The team went to Boston and he won there, 5-2, missing a shutout when Eddie Ainsmith's two passed balls allowed the Red Sox to score separate unearned runs. Back in Washington, Johnson threw another shutout, blanking the Highlanders, 2-0. Then, while leading Boston, 5-0, he eased up and the Red Sox scored a ninth-inning run.

On June 8 another inside pitch got away from Johnson and broke Lee Tannehill's wrist. It ended a 10-year career for the player, who had been the White Sox third baseman since 1903. In that game,

Johnson gave up the only home runs he allowed all season. Harry Lord and Ping Bodie each homered with a runner on base. It was the first time Johnson had been hit hard that season. He gave up six in five innings and left the game. Damaging Tannehill, who threw up his hand to deflect a pitch coming at his head, very likely unsettled the fastball pitcher.

Johnson was back in stride when Cleveland came to town, pitching his fourth shutout of the young season, 8-0, on May 11. He breezed past the St. Louis Browns, 6-2, before losing a 2-0 shutout to Wild Bill Donovan. It was Donovan's only decision and, except for appearing once in 1918, his last major league start. Ty Cobb was out of the lineup, suspended for having climbed into the stands after a heckling fan. Johnson's consolation prize was $50 he won when he hit a double off the Bull Durham sign.

His next game, at New York, was the one when Walter Johnson hit Jack Martin. For the first time, a ball that got away skulled an opponent. It was something that Johnson feared, but he also accepted it as a circumstance under which baseball is played. Clearly, skulling Martin did unnerve him in this game, as he lost, 6-3. Johnson pitched again against New York before the team left town, winning 8-3 on May 28.

In Boston, Johnson struck out 13 in a shutout in the afternoon game of a two-admission Memorial Day doubleheader. When the teams broke for lunch, and so that the Boston owners could empty the park and then sell more tickets, Washington's record was 17-21. Johnson was 9-4. The team was in the familiar surroundings of second division. However, Johnson's win set them off on a fabulous streak that caught the imagination of baseball fans everywhere. Clark Griffith's new team was on its way.

Johnson won, 3-2, in St. Louis and, in Chicago, he homered off Ed Walsh and pitched four innings of relief. Two days later he beat the White Sox, 7-1. The team rolled on, into Detroit where, on June 12, Johnson chalked up number 13 in the team's winning streak as well as his own 13th victory. He missed a shutout on a misjudged fly ball, a passed ball, and an error, but won, 5-1.

Walter Johnson missed the next two weeks, not pitching again until the team was back in Washington. This time Johnson was laid low by tonsillitis. It seemed almost an occupational disease for ballplayers. His new teammate, Chick Gandil, complained of swollen tonsils too. Gandil stayed in the lineup, but Johnson lost at least three starts from a season in which he won 33 games. Johnson was sent back to Washington for treatment but decided against having the tonsils out. When the rest of the team returned to the city on June 18, President Taft was in a box seat leading the cheers of most of the leaders of the U. S. government. The team's winning string was extended to 17 but ended the next day. Meanwhile, Johnson was still unable to pitch, not getting back into action until the Red Sox came to town for a double-header on June 26. Boston, which pulled away from Washington throughout the season, pitched its young ace, Smokey Joe Wood, in the second game. Wood and Johnson were to hook up later in an even more memorable duel, but this one went to Wood, 3-0, on a three-hitter. Johnson only allowed four hits and struck out 10 batters. However, Tris Speaker's triple drove in all the runs Smokey Joe needed to win.

Johnson lost his next two decisions, failing in relief in a 10-inning game with the A's on June 28, and losing, 2-1, the next day. Then, on July 3, in New York, Walter Johnson began his own personal winning streak. In the second game of a doubleheader, with Washington ahead 9-1 after six innings, manager Clark Griffith, as he often did with Johnson, excused him for the rest of the afternoon. The easy win brought Johnson's record to 14-7 at the season's midpoint.

It was good that Griffith had given his star pitcher a breather. Two days later he entered a game with the Highlanders with one out in the fourth inning and the score tied. The teams battled for 16 innings before Johnson added another victory to his record. A point of marginal interest is that Paul Otis, one of only four major leaguers to reach a 100th birthday, claimed his only big league base hit in this game. Otis cackled to curious interviewers when he became the oldest ex–major leaguer that it had come off Walter Johnson. Otis recalled it as a screaming line drive over second base. It was a clean hit in Otis' memory and looked like one in the box score. Actually, it was a blooper that bounced off George McBride's glove. Three of the Washington papers covering the game charged McBride with an error. Only the *Herald*, whose reporter was the official scorer of the game, gave Paul Otis the only major league hit he managed in 20 at-bats. Another footnote from this game comes from the play-by-play account of the fourth inning when Johnson entered the game. A run was in, two runners were on base, and there was one out. Johnson fanned the opposing pitcher, Jack Warhop, and *then hit Bert Daniels in the back of the head to load the bases.* We have the second career beaning of a batter, although apparently a glancing blow. Then came the Otis pop fly behind third base which McBride dropped with two runs scoring. From then on, Walter Johnson allowed only two hits until Washington won in the 16th inning.

Another of baseball's four centenarians, John Francis Daley, contributed to Walter Johnson's lore when the St. Louis Browns came to town on July 20. The phrase "You can't hit what you can't see" has been connected to Johnson's fastball but attribution has been guesswork. Norman Macht, chairman of SABR's Oral History Committee, has identified the true phrase maker. Macht taped an interview with the ex–big leaguer with a keen memory soon after Daley's 100th birthday. He was thinking back 75 years to when, as a 25-year-old, he played 18 games for the Browns in his only major league season.

Here's an excerpt from Macht's taped interview:

On July 20 in my third big league game, I batted seventh and played shortstop. Long Tom Hughes is pitching for the Senators. In the top of the ninth we tied the score on a couple of walks and a hit. It's three to three, there's two men on base and two outs. The Washington manager, Clark Griffith, this is 1912, brings in a relief pitcher, Walter Johnson. And I'm up. The count goes to three and two. I foul off a couple into the dugout. The next pitch I never saw. All I hear is what sounds like the ball hitting the catcher's mitt. Strike three.

George Stovall, the Browns' manager, is standing by the dugout. I guess I have a dazed sort of look.

"What's the matter, kid?" he says.

"You can't hit what you can't see," I tell him.

The writers used to sit down at field level in the first row. The next day, one of them who overheard me writes about "the kid who couldn't see."

A couple of years ago some other fellow claimed he was the originator of that phrase. I told him I'm the one who did it and he could look it up.

We looked it up and every detail in Daley's account rings true.

The string of victories grew with Johnson doubling in relief roles as well as taking his regular turn. On August 20, in the first game of a doubleheader, under odd circumstances, Johnson broke Happy Jack

Chesbro's record of 14 straight wins set in his fabulous 1904 season. Johnson was not the starting pitcher. He worked 8⅔ innings of relief. Griffith had maneuvered to match his ace against Vean Gregg, Cleveland's brilliant young lefthander. He wrote the name Lefty Schegg into the starting lineup, intending to replace him with Johnson before he threw a pitch. Griffith's maneuver with Johnson would take place as soon as Gregg took the mound to start the game. However, umpire Tommy Connolly insisted Schegg pitch to one batter before Johnson could take over. Schegg got the first batter, Joe Ryan, on a line drive to second baseman Ray Morgan.

About Schegg: He was a lefthander Griffith found pitching for a famous baseball touring club of that era, the Nebraska Indians. Schegg was not an Indian. His name was not even Schegg. He was Gilbert Eugene Price and used his real name for many years in the minor leagues. After his one batter debut, he made one other relief appearance before he disappeared, another of Griffith's pitching disappointments.

After the ersatz Indian departed, Johnson was waved into the game and beat Gregg, 4-2. Washington's own rising pitching star, Carl Cashion, pitched the second game, called after six innings to allow Cleveland to catch a train, and he had to settle for an abbreviated no-hitter.

Walter Johnson added number 16 to his new record with an easy verdict over Detroit, 8-1, on August 23. Then, with Marquard's 19-game string in the National League still ahead, Johnson's skein was snapped on the 26th. Two days earlier the popular president of the Washington baseball club, Thomas Clarence Noyes, had died of pneumonia. Whether this impacted Johnson and his teammates, and to what degree, the death of Noyes seems to have interrupted the momentum Johnson and the ball club had underway.

The same rule interpretation that had stopped Marquard, brought down Johnson in the game of the 26th. Johnson failed to head off a Browns rally when he entered the game with one out in the seventh inning. Before he got the side out, a go-ahead run was scored by a base runner starter Tom Hughes had left behind. As with Marquard, the scoring rule in use in 1912 put the blame on the pitcher on the mound when the winning run was scored. Although Johnson pitched scoreless ball in the eighth and ninth innings, Washington could not score either. An appeal was made to league president Ban Johnson, but he stood fast. The rule was upheld.

Walter Johnson did not fall apart in dejection; tough losses never untracked him. However, he lost his next two decisions, 3-2 and 9-7 (in 10 innings), while heading for one of the most dramatic pitching confrontations ever arranged by a fortuitous schedule and a coincidence only a writer of boys' baseball fiction would dare to invent.

While Walter Johnson was methodically stretching his string of victories, his great rival, Smokey Joe Wood, was doing the same. When Johnson's streak was stopped at 16, Wood's had reached 13. What better scenario than to have Walter Johnson himself defend the new American League record he had just set?

Washington arrived in Boston on September 4 with only a slight chance of overtaking the league-leading Red Sox. They immediately lost more ground when Ray Collins beat them, 6-2, and the next day they lost to Buck O'Brien, a 20-game winner in 1912, 4-3. Then came the showdown date, September 6.

Many years later, Joe Wood would tell interviewers that he had pitched out of turn, risking his winning streak to face Johnson. Early biographers of the Big Train had also romanticized that he had obligingly moved his starting turn up a day to insure a big crowd. Actually, both men were pitching with the same amount of rest. Both had last pitched on September 2. Johnson had lost that high-scoring 10-inning game to Philadelphia, and Wood had shut out New York, 1-0. The deeper pitching staff of the Red Sox might not have required Wood to pitch on three days' rest, but it was hardly a heroic sacrifice. Like Johnson, Wood was a fierce competitor and welcomed the challenge.

The newly opened Fenway Park could not hold the crowds that came out even on a weekday afternoon. Thirty thousand fans were crammed in, standing behind ropes in the outfield. This turned pop flies into two-base hits when balls reached the standing spectators, as one of them did in the sixth inning. Tris Speaker lofted a ground rule double into the crowd in left field. Duffy Lewis, the next batter, hit a line drive down the right-field line, just inside the rope holding back the crowd in foul territory. Danny Moeller pulled up short and stabbed at the ball. It ticked off the end of his glove for a single, and Speaker scored the only run of the game.

Walter Johnson, who never blamed anyone for anything, had no criticism of Danny Moeller. Perhaps Johnson was even more forgiving of the fly chaser who was known as "Daredevil Danny." Moeller not only made diving catches but he constantly dislocated his left shoulder. It happened once when President Taft was at a game with his military aide and army surgeon, Maj. T. L. Rhoades. Taft got a medical opinion that Moeller should have an operation. Meaning no disrespect, "Daredevil Danny" declined and let trainer Mike Martin continue to snap his shoulder back into its socket.

Washington had runners in scoring position in the sixth, eighth, and ninth innings, but Joe Wood had all his smoke that day. He struck out nine batters, and the shutout was one of 10 he pitched that year. Although Johnson had failed to derail Wood's drive for the record, Smokey Joe was destined only to tie Johnson's 16-straight. He won his 15th with the help of Charles "Sea Lion" Hall in relief against Chicago. Wood then beat St. Louis, 2-1, in a game stopped by darkness after eight innings, to tie Johnson's record. However, that is as far as his skein would go. The best of pitchers occasionally have an off day. Against Detroit on September 20, Joe Wood was far less effective than usual. He was wild, at one point walking four batters in a row, giving up seven hits, and losing, 6-4. Even at that, the two runs which beat him were unearned.

The American League record co-held by Walter Johnson and Smokey Joe Wood has since been tied twice. Lefty Grove of the 1931 Philadelphia A's and Lynwood "Schoolboy" Rowe of the 1934 Detroit Tigers equaled it. Rube Marquard's National League mark is unmatched since it was set in that streaky year, 1912.

The most startling of historian Frank Williams' discoveries while reviewing Walter Johnson's career from the actual score sheets, is that he was never credited with one of the victories in his 16-game streak. The glaring oversight had puzzled historians trying to reconcile Johnson's individual game-by-game win totals with the year-end number printed in the record books. The discrepancy was explained in the 1993 SABR publication *Baseball Records Update*. The game which caused the confusion was played on August 5 in Chicago. It came during Johnson's 16-game consecutive winning streak. *It was counted as part of that string by the press and acknowledged by President Ban Johnson.* Yet it was not tallied with Johnson's season's totals by the American League office. The game of August 5 had been credited to the starter, Carl Cashion, on the official score sheet. In the opinion of the scorer assigned by the league to keep the box score, Cashion was the winner. No one else had thought so. The other accounts of the game gave the win to Johnson, because he was entitled to it *under the prevailing rules*. Johnson had come into the game in relief with the score tied, 7-7. He pitched the final two and one-third innings, holding the White Sox scoreless and driving in the winning run in the 10th inning himself.

Chalk it up to clerical error in a league office that was probably understaffed. A great many mistakes are still listed in the baseball encyclopedias, which are taken as holy writ by figure zealots determined to quantify margins of excellence. In 1917, the reigning guru of stats, Al Munro Elias, published Walter Johnson's record up to that time. It shows his won-lost record for 1912 against all opponents, and this adds up to 33. The August 5 win over Chicago is included. Incidentally, this gives Walter Johnson a share of yet another still-existing record. His nine wins over Chicago ties the record for most games won from one team in a single season.

In the final weeks of the 1912 season Washington struggled to finish in second place ahead of Connie Mack's World Champion Athletics. After Walter Johnson had held the A's at bay for two and two-thirds innings in a 3-3 tie on September 26, Washington pushed back into second place the next day. Eddie Plank pitched all 19 innings before losing, 5-4. Bob Groom pitched the first nine innings for Washington and then Walter Johnson took over. He and Plank matched zeros until Washington broke the tie in the top of the 19th inning. Johnson had pitched 10 scoreless innings.

The team finished the season, playing away from home almost the entire month of September, a game ahead of the A's. Counting their sorry years in the National League before they were dropped in 1900 when the senior circuit was reduced to eight teams, 1912 marked the first time a Washington team had finished in first division in 40 years. Their season ended in New York with Walter Johnson winning what now must be recognized as his 33rd victory, 4-3. It was a banner year for Johnson. He regained the strikeout leadership with 303, starting a run of eight straight seasons in which he led the league in strikeouts. His 1.39 ERA led the league but, although another win has been found to add to his total, even at 33 it is one less than Smokey Joe Wood's 34 wins for the pennant-winning Red Sox.

Walter Johnson did not head for Kansas as soon as the season was over. There was money to be made by pitching exhibition games, several matching him against the Brooklyn Dodger star, Nap Rucker. A fine lefthander, Rucker was beloved in Brooklyn for being the one hope against an otherwise almost certainty of defeat. He was doomed to star for a succession of second-division clubs. In this, he was much as Johnson had been before the coming of Clark Griffith and the team's rise into contention. Unfortunately for Rucker, by the time Wilbert Robinson turned around the fortunes of the Dodgers with a pennant in 1916, Nap's arm was worn out.

Johnson and Rucker went to Bridgeport, Connecticut, to take part in a timing experiment of their fastballs. They were tested at the Remington Arms U.M.C. Company, with equipment developed to measure the velocity of bullets. Johnson took his first throw while still wearing his suit coat. Then he took it off and let fly with a pitch that was calculated at 122 feet a second. That converts to 82 miles per hour. All the test proved conclusively was that Johnson was faster than Rucker. Of course, anyone could have told that from their records, loyal Brooklyn fans excepted.

Coffeyville welcomed their town's baseball hero home with the first "Walter Johnson Day." These became annual occasions with the towns-people overflowing the rickety stands at Forest Park. Walter pitched for the town team and, for the inaugural game, the Redmen of Wagoner, Oklahoma, furnished the opposition. In the first five innings, Walter Johnson struck out 13 of 15 batters. It ended his year's work.

Soon after Walter Johnson reached Coffeyville, his Cole touring car arrived. He co-owned it with Zeb Milan, and it was his turn to use it between seasons. Made by the Cole Motor Company of Indianapolis, Indiana, the Cole had narrowly missed qualifying for the first Indianapolis Speedway 500-mile race the year before. It fell just short of averaging 75 miles per hour in the trial runs. However, such speeds were impractical for either the boulevards of Washington, D. C., or the dirt roads around Coffeyville.

With his younger brother Earl's help, Johnson put the car in running order. They drove out to the farm to take their mother and the other Johnson children for a spin. As they passed along the dirt roads, neighborhood boys were invited to pile in the open-topped touring car. Walter Johnson's automobile opened a wider social circle. Although friendly and smiling, he had kept mostly to himself during his first winters in Coffeyville. Now he began to get around town and make more friends. There was also one other matter to look after. He finally had his tonsils removed.

9

The Cinderella Team Misses the Ball

WASHINGTON'S SURPRISING LEAP from seventh to second place under Clark Griffith's first year of leadership raised everyone's expectations for 1913. The players who assembled in Charlottesville, Virginia, were much the same cast that Griffith had put together the previous year. Now, however, "the Cinderella Team" was intact for Opening Day. Chick Gandil, also sans troublesome tonsils, would be at first base the full season. Ray Morgan had steadied himself after an in and out start as a batter and would be a solid player at second base. George McBride was reappointed captain, and his glove work was unexcelled by any shortstop in the league. Kid Foster at third base was a defensive demon. Beyond that, he was the kind of offensive weapon that a smart manager like Clark Griffith utilized well. SABRmetricians would dismiss Foster as lacking power. He owns the longest streak without hitting a home run in major league history. He went to bat 3,278 times without a four-bagger. His specialty was the hit-and-run play. Ty Cobb described him as the best at that skill in baseball. Given Griffith's style of play and his batting position behind the new stolen-base champ Clyde "Zeb" Milan, Foster was truly a secret weapon.

In the outfield Hank Shanks, another batter without power, made timely hits and game-saving catches. Flanking Milan on the other side was Daredevil Dan Moeller, another with a deceptively low batting average whose penchant was scoring runs. Despite a lifetime batting average of .243, he averaged better than 80 runs scored a season. And, his trick shoulder had healed during the winter. Milan's speed kept the ball from going up the alleys to the distant fences of the spacious ballparks of 1913. He got leg hits and had line-drive power and was an ideal player at the top of the batting order.

John "Bull" Henry was a superlative catcher with an adequate batting record for his position. He caught most of the games, although Eddie Ainsmith was confirmed as Walter Johnson's regular catcher. The earlier belief that Johnson's fastball could only be held by Gabby Street had been disproved. Street had passed out of the big leagues during 1912. He had finished the season with Providence in the International League. In 1913 he would be with Chattanooga of the Southern Association. However, the resilient Gabby created a long managerial career, with time out for World War One combat heroics. He later led the St. Louis Cardinals to a pennant in 1930 and again in 1931 when they also won the World Championship.

Walter Johnson had no peers, unfortunately, on the pitching staff. The others, carried over from 1912, might as well have placed paper bags over their heads and taken turns in starting the games Johnson did not.

Griffith rented two side-by-side houses for the 36 players he brought to camp. One was owned by the Delta Chi fraternity, whose brothers would be away on spring break. The players took their meals at Mrs. Sauer's boarding house. Griffith made optimistic spring predictions. He had the usual prospects with promising futures, but it was the established players on whom he would depend. Walter Johnson, with a year left on his three-year $7,000-annual deal, was spared the hassle of negotiation. Johnson's idea of his worth to the team was driven by his desire to build up the value of his property in Coffeyville. Johnson would, characteristically, convert extra income into livestock or equipment for the farm. One inducement he always spurned was the easy pickings of the vaudeville circuit. His teammate Germany Schaefer was a veteran performer who entertained audiences with comic routines. However, there was also a market for superstars willing to stand stage center and answer questions about baseball. Despite his interest in making side money, the shy and honest Johnson was tongue-tied at the idea of being a public exhibit.

A source of income for famous baseball players was the bylined reporting of the World Series and whatever else their ghostwriters could pontificate about. Mathewson, Cobb, Chance, Evers, and others were frequently in print. When Johnson's byline headed an infrequent story, the piece was written for him by Ralph McMillan, a Washington, D.C., sportswriter.

Endorsements were not yet a substantial source of extra income, although a new national soft drink company, Coca-Cola, featured ballplayers in their ads. In addition to assuring the fans that Coca-Cola was refreshing, Ty Cobb parlayed his connection into a fortune by investing in the company's stock. Johnson's quest for extra income was in response to a personal time clock that was running. It reminded the 25-year-old Johnson that it was time to marry and start a family.

Before the players moved on to Charlottesville, they assembled in the nation's capital. Johnson and the others watched the Inaugural Parade of President Woodrow Wilson before taking a train to their spring training site. Woodrow Wilson would prove an even more enthusiastic baseball fan than President William Howard Taft. He had managed an undergraduate team at Princeton, and his wife, Ellen, was reported to be capable of keeping a scorecard account of a game.

Spring training followed a regime Griffith held to for many years. Intersquad games, playfully umpired by Nick Altrock and Germany Schaefer, got winter kinks out of the athletes. Then came games with stronger opponents, first minor league teams and then big league out-fits, which led to Opening Day. Walter Johnson's pace was similarly stepped up as the start of the season approached. One sidelight report-ed before the team broke camp at Charlottesville was a claim for a new fungo hitting record by Walter Johnson. He lofted a ball that landed 381 feet, 8 inches away.

A matchup of two great pitchers took place on March 29, when the Philadelphia Phillies stopped at Washington for an exhibition game. Johnson was in top form, striking out eight and pitching six scoreless innings. Grover Cleveland Alexander, who had been ineffective all spring, was reported to be in poor health. The score, a 12-1 drubbing of the Phillies, seemed to confirm this.

A hoped-for face-off with Christy Mathewson did not come about. The Giants' manager, John McGraw, decided bigger crowds would come to see Matty and Johnson pitch separately than would be drawn to a man-to-man matchup. Johnson beat the Giants, 3-2, holding them to two hits in six scoreless innings. The next day Mathewson beat Washington. The two superstars would eventually meet in 1913, but far from the major league scene.

The season's opening game had now become institutionalized by the promotion-minded Clark Griffith. Although the custom had start-ed with President Taft's inaugural toss in 1910, before Griffith arrived in Washington, he had ceremoniously presented the new president with a gold pass. Griffith impressed upon Wilson that throwing out the first ball was almost as necessary to confirm his presidency as tak-ing the oath of office.

President Wilson—who was to become something of a good luck

charm for the ball club which almost always won when he was in the park—saw the first game New York played as the Yankees. The new owners had dropped the Highlanders name but not yet adopted pin-stripes. More importantly, President Wilson was also present for the start of one of Walter Johnson's most remarkable feats, pitching 55.2 consecutive scoreless innings. Johnson's record lasted until Don Drysdale, pitching for the Los Angeles Dodgers in 1968, racked up 58.2 innings of scoreless pitching. Subsequently, another Los Angeles Dodger, Orel Hershiser, knocked Drysdale out of the record book by pitching 59 consecutive scoreless innings in 1988.

Johnson's shutout string would have been an inning longer and started from the first inning of the season had it not been for a Chick Gandil misplay. In the first inning the Yankees scored a tainted run that was regarded as an error by those keeping box scores for three of Washington's newspapers. Mrs. Wilson might have scored it an error, too. Only the ubiquitous reporter from the *Washington Herald*, who had given Paul Otis his lone major league base hit the year before, differed. The scorer, whose decisions were forever preserved as "official," said the run was earned and absolved Gandil of an error everyone else blamed on him.

Another spring cold and wet weather kept Johnson idle for nine days, and then he shut out the Yankees in New York, 3-0, on six hits. He struck out eight. The team returned to the capital for a series with the Boston Red Sox. Johnson shut them out too, 6-0, on April 23 and saved the game on the 25th with a scoreless ninth-inning rescue. The next day an electrifying news item appeared in the Boston papers. It was datelined April 26, Cambridge, Massachusetts:

> Walter Johnson, pitcher of the Washington Nationals is soon to marry Miss Anna B. Scully of Cambridge, according to an announcement made here today. The date of the wedding is not given out, but Johnson is said to have asked for two weeks' leave of absence following the series between the Red Sox and the Senators here next week. Miss Scully is 19 years old.

The image of Walter Johnson dallying with the affections of a teenager is contrary to the upstanding, clean-living, honorable stalwart we know him to be. Was Miss Scully a 1913 baseball groupie? Had she gone to Washington when the Red Sox traveled there? A subsequent explanation from an admiring Johnson biographer, Vincent X. Flaherty, assured his readers that Johnson was innocent of misleading Miss Scully or of jilting her. It was all a misunderstanding, we are told. Walter, a shy companion to Milan and other teammates, had met a group of Boston belles at a social gathering the previous season. Glances across the room indicated a mutual show of interest. Johnson's pals joshed him about the pretty young girl who was giving him the eye. Milan, a far more sophisticated bachelor than his roommate, Johnson, aided this flirtation by telling Anna Scully that Walter thought she was mighty pretty, too.

In her girlish and inexperienced way, the Cambridge girl mistook this for true ardor and told her parents she was going to marry the Washington pitcher. The matter disappeared from the newspapers, and Johnson managed to survive the facts and implications of his fling, however innocent, with Anna Scully. It might even have enhanced his status with the young lady he *had* been seeing, Hazel Roberts. Miss Roberts was the attractive socialite daughter of Congressman Edwin Ewing Roberts. He was Nevada's lone delegate to the House of Representatives and, with his wife and only child, Hazel, lived at the Dewey, a residential hotel, while in Washington. So did Zeb Milan and Walter Johnson, who shared an apartment. Eddie Ainsmith and other bachelors on the team also lived at the Dewey, which was within walking distance of the ballpark. Hazel and Walter had noticed each other across the lobby, but Walter was shy and Hazel was limited by the social customs of the day.

When Congressman Roberts introduced himself to Washington's most famous athlete and formally presented his daughter, Hazel Lee Roberts, the ice was broken. Milan made sure it stayed thawed. His own matrimonial plans were set for a wedding after the season. He urged his best friend to court Hazel and helped Johnson disavow intentions of any sort toward Miss Scully, the Irish lass in Boston.

Roberts invited Johnson to dinner with his family in their apartment and had no objection to the young ballplayer taking his daughter on rides along the Potomac. Hazel was the belle of the ball at Washington society's Sunday tea dances, where Johnson would be a wallflower. As the tall, attractive, poised daughter of a member of Congress, Hazel Lee Roberts was at the center of Washington's social whirl. However, when Walter got behind the wheel of the sporty two-seater Cole Eight he owned with Milan, much of his shyness was shed in the slipstream of racing along at 25 miles per hour. The young couple continued to see each other throughout the 1913 season. They exchanged letters when Congress adjourned and Congressman Roberts went home to his constituents. Roberts was impressed, of course, with Walter Johnson's pitching accomplishments. His rock-solid American roots also assured the congressman that if the young man became a suitor, he would be a suitable one.

The Johnsons traced back to Nathaniel and Anna Johnson, Walter's great-grandparents, who came from England and settled in Ohio when it was still "Indian Country." Their son, John H. Johnson, married a Scotch-Irish lass named Phoebe, and they produced Frank Edwin Johnson, Walter's father, who was born at Kingscreek, Ohio, October 17, 1861. As both were from the same Anglo-Saxon, Protestant, white, work-ethic, conservative mold, the congressman and the pitcher found the other's values admirable. Anna Scully would have been up against stiff-necked resistance had she actually led her Walter to the altar. The Boston Irish were only a generation removed from signs posted by the ruling classes that said, "No Irish Need Apply." That went for jobs, housing, and marriage licenses for interfaith weddings, as well.

Johnson's family tree had solid roots. His origins were steeped in American values. The way Walter Johnson's parents had met, when wagon trains carrying their families arrived at a crossroad in Humboldt, Kansas, was both fortuitous and typical of the time and place. America was a growing country where a man could make his fortune by his own efforts. Minnie Olive Perry, born in Indiana, was part of Com. Oliver Hazard Perry's extended family if you stretched it back several generations. This linked Johnson's mother to the hero of the Battle of Lake Erie. A will to win was a family heritage. Her parents had been a determined couple, seeking to wrest a future from a farm in central Indiana. Her father, John L. Perry, was a Civil War veteran who had fought at Antietam and Bull Run. Shot from his horse, he was captured and spent the rest of the war in Libby Prison at Richmond, Virginia.

When the Perry's farm in Indiana failed, the family took Horace Greeley's advice and headed west. Going in the same direction were the Johnsons, who left the unpromising soil of western Pennsylvania behind. They had previously been disappointed in Ohio, where Frank had been born. In 1885, both sides of Walter Johnson's family were searching for somewhere with more rewarding prospects. The families traveled west with wagon trains whose trails crossed in Kansas.

Minnie Perry met Frank Edwin Johnson, the eldest son of the western-bound Johnsons at a dance. At 18, she was three years younger than her dancing partner. Romance aside, they did not exactly whirl off into a storybook marriage. In the hard-pressed times, their pairing was far from that of a dashing prince charming and princess-in-waiting. Minnie was bigger than her man. She was a strong, wide-shouldered woman who looked as though she would live to be a hundred, and eventually, did.

Frank Johnson had sloping shoulders and extra-long arms, physical characteristics he passed on to his son Walter. He was hardworking, ambitious, and an undaunted breadwinner. When the wagon trains rolled on, Frank and Minnie Johnson stayed behind to homestead a farm near Humbolt, Kansas. It was "Little House on the Prairie" country where the Laura Ingalls Wilder stories are set. Their farm was just over the border from Missouri, with the Oklahoma Territory to the south. A bare living could be wrested from the soil, provided a twister did not blow it away and the livestock lasted through the hard winters.

Frank Johnson was a man who could always make a living, however hard he had to work to do so. The Johnsons raised crops and children. Although all United States census figures for 1890 later were inadvertently destroyed, the 1900 federal head count shows that Frank Johnson's family had four children to report to the government nose-counters. Effie, the first child and only daughter at the time, was a 14-year-old teenager. Walter was 12, with brothers Leslie, 10, and Earl, six. Blanche, the family's youngest daughter would be added to the family before they pulled up roots and moved to California in 1902. Once there, Walter Johnson's final sibling, Chester, was born. While in Kansas, the children attended the Crescent Valley School in Allen County until the Johnsons sold off their holdings and headed west again. Walter, the oldest son, was entering his teens when that happened, and he could tell Hazel Roberts his own story from that point on.

10
Walter Johnson's
Greatest Season

THE COURTSHIP of Hazel Lee Roberts moved at as fast a pace as the shy young Washington pitcher could manage. He had only half as much time as other suitors, as the ball club was on the road as much as they were at home. And, as the hot summer approached, Congress pushed toward adjournment. Walter Johnson's modesty inhibited him. Hazel would have to draw him out about his teen years and how he became a baseball player in California. Probably he told her what became a staple in accounts of his early years, that he had never played baseball until his family moved west. In Kansas, the prairies were too wide to get enough boys together to form a team. In California it was different.

Walter was about the biggest kid in his high school class. Because of his size, it was decided he would be a catcher. He was willing and, although he was obviously out of position, his throws to the bases were so hard and accurate he soon was on the pitcher's mound. The new problem was the school did not have anyone able to catch him. That was remedied when Johnson was recruited by teams with more capable players, and soon he was pitching against grown men. The rest, if Hazel cared to drag it out of him, was history.

It would help bridge Walter's diffidence about girls to learn that Hazel captained the basketball team at state champion Carson City High School. Athletic but girl-shy boys fantasize about playing catch with a date. At least they did when Frank Merriwell and the Rover Boys were young.

As their interest in each other deepened, Walter could confide in Hazel of his loneliness and fear as a teenager when he was cut loose by the ball club in Tacoma. His account of his time in Weiser probably left out many details of life in that rough-and-ready town. Still, Hazel had grown up in Carson City, Nevada, and it had its own recent traditions of frontier rowdyism. She may have told him how her family, or her father, at least, arrived in Carson City. The congressman, born in California, was an enthusiastic sports follower. With other young friends, he went to Nevada to see the famous heavyweight championship fight between Gentleman Jim Corbett and Ruby Robert Fitzsimmons in Carson City. Fitzsimmons knocked out Roberts' fellow San Franciscan, Corbett, on St. Patrick's Day of 1897; Roberts probably did not drink to the result, but he liked his prospects in the boom town so much that he stayed there.

Walter Johnson, the celebrity ballplayer, was at heart a farmer. It was in his blood. His father had never been happy away from the fields and livestock, the barns and silos, of a farm. Johnson, the eldest son, was as much a man of the soil as any forebear back to his yeoman ancestors in England. Hazel Lee Roberts, in contrast, was a District of Columbia debutante. She was the prettiest girl at society balls and courted by rising government men as well as swains back home. It was tough competition, but unlike in baseball where the other side tried to defeat you, Hazel's acceptance of him showed she, too, cared. Maybe it was a case of opposites attracting opposites, but it was more than a passing fancy for both.

The team departed on a long trip which would take Johnson out of the city for the month of May. Included was a stop in Boston. With Milan's help, Johnson had squared himself with Hazel over the Anna Scully imbroglio. He hoped the matter would not have a Boston flare-up. As it happened, no irate man announcing himself as Mr. Scully came pounding on Johnson's hotel room door. None of little Anna's brothers waited at the player's entrance to Fenway Park or sat in the bleachers with shotguns across their laps.

Walter Johnson had arrived with his shutout string intact, having won a strikeout-laden duel, 2-0, from Eddie Plank in Philadelphia. Johnson fanned 10 batters and Plank a dozen. Both of Walter Johnson's Boston mound appearances were in relief and extended his shutout inning string while adding to his win total. He was nearing 50 runless innings as Washington's long road trip wended its way west.

Walter, an avid letter writer, could describe the places he saw. He and Milan regularly visited galleries, museums, and most places listed in guidebooks. Walter Johnson, while far from being a touring aesthete, had a natural curiosity about places his baseball travels took him. Letters on hotel stationery were filled with descriptions of where he had been. It was also a chance for Walter Johnson to write to Hazel

70

about his life before he met her. After the Johnsons settled in the small southern California community of Olinda, he went to high school in nearby Fullerton. In present times, Olinda does not exist; it has been swallowed up in the urban sprawl of the Los Angeles area.

Walter Johnson had done more in high school than play baseball. He was part of a class of 50 young men and women. His letters to Hazel would tell of the tug of war between his belief in himself as an athlete and his family's conservative insistence that he continue his education. They expected him to become a mathematics teacher and were pleased when he enrolled in a business college to study book-keeping.

Meanwhile, Walter Johnson was having the greatest season of his pitching career. There were clippings to send from the newspapers reporting his unbroken success. His scoreless inning streak, however, was ended in St. Louis by his usual nemesis, the Browns. They had ended his 16-game winning streak the year before. Clark Griffith, reminiscing with friends after Johnson's death, remembered the streak ending this way: "The last six innings of the streak, he had St. Louis shut out, but we scored six runs and I said to myself, 'Good night, here it goes.' I knew he'd coast on that lead and I'd advertised him in Detroit where we were going next and Cobb had been promising to score on him and I knew we'd get a crowd up there.

"Sure enough, he threw a nothing ball to Gloomy Gus Williams, who hit a triple. Joe Gedeon tripped Williams at second, fell on him, hollered for the ball and tagged him, but Billy Evans sent Williams on to third for interference and he scored on a fly."

Griffith's memory for details was probably right, and the facts fit except that the streak-ending run was scored in the fourth inning. After two more innings, Johnson was excused for the rest of the day with a 6-1 lead.

In Detroit, Ty Cobb made good his promise to score on Johnson, although the edge was off the drama of a personal duel. Cobb stole home to avoid a shutout, as Johnson won a close 2-1 game. A Sunday crowd of 24,466, the largest in the team's history, watched the duel between the two great stars.

Johnson, who had not lost a game yet in 1913, won his 10th straight game, in relief, from Cleveland. Buff Williams, a utility player, pinch-hit a home run to tie the score in the top of the ninth inning, and Johnson kept it that way for two more innings until his teammates got two runs in the 10th. The next day, May 22, Walter Johnson was beaten for the first time, 5-0, by spitballer Bill Steen. Joe Jackson's throw to nail Zeb Milan at the plate drew special comment. However, most writers marveled over Johnson's great start.

Walter Johnson got right back on the winning track when the team reached Philadelphia, where the A's were trying to regain their place in baseball history. Their loss of the 1912 pennant had interrupted a run of championships, and they were determined to get back on top. However, they were no match for Johnson, either the pitcher or batter. He won, 9-2, both A's runs being unearned, and had three hits himself, one a home run.

Washington was back home for Memorial Day, and it can be assumed that Hazel and her father sat under an umbrella while a pregame shower limited Johnson's warm-up. Harry Hooper, leading off for Boston, hit the first pitch out of the ballpark and the familiar specter of the 1-0 loss spoiled the homecoming holiday. When Philadelphia came to town, another old-time foe, Home Run Baker, reprised his act and beat Johnson, 4-3. However, St. Louis went down 1-0 and Detroit fell 3-0. Chicago was easy, 8-3, but Cleveland lefthander Vean Gregg turned the shutout tables on Johnson, 4-0, on June 18.

Gregg might have benefited from the good luck charm of the team's mascot. Larry, a bull terrier, belonged to Indian outfielder Jack Graney and traveled with the team. Larry had trotted along with the players to the White House that morning. The team was to meet President Wilson, a.k.a. "the Nationals' Good Luck Charm." At first the bulldog excitedly chased squirrels across the lawn, but he fell in line when the players entered the president's office.

Larry was a clever dog and did many tricks on the ball field. Even before Frisbees had been invented, he could leap in the air and grab a softly tossed baseball in his jaws. He leapfrogged over players, chased intruding dogs and cats off the field, and was a fierce protector of the players' gloves when they were left on the field between innings. However, he disdained such routine dog tricks as "shaking hands." That was for house pets. Yet, here he was in line with the players to do that very thing with the president of the United States. There was no protocol to guide him. No dog had ever been formally presented to the nation's leader.

The president gingerly shook hands with the players, fearing the hand that held the pen that signed the bills might be crushed. He would gladly settle for patting Larry on the head, but was wary.

President Wilson knew Larry's role as Cleveland's good luck dog conflicted with his own record as the Nationals' good luck person. The team never lost when he was at a game. He commented about the Cleveland mascot, saying, "I recognize your dog; my daughters have told me about him."

Diplomatically, President Wilson changed his plans for the day. He told the players he was sorry he could not get to the afternoon's game as he had planned. Wilson was too good a politician to risk a conflict of interest with representatives from such a large constituency. Ohio had many electoral votes. The District of Columbia residents could not even vote. That afternoon, President Wilson signed papers in his office, and Larry the Cleveland mascot provided uncontested good luck for his team. Probably Vean Gregg would have beaten Walter Johnson on merit alone that day. Yet, who is to say.

With the Indians and their mascot gone, Johnson won his 15th game, beating New York with another shutout, 6-0. When he only lasted three innings on June 25 as the front-running A's scored four quick runs, *it was the only time in the 1913 season that he was knocked out of the box.* Two days later he snapped back to beat Connie Mack's team, 2-0. It was his eighth shutout and the season was only half over.

The July 4 holiday weekend was spent in Beantown, and if the Scullys were at Fenway Park, they probably switched to the Boston Braves after what Johnson did to the Red Sox. He began by relieving Bob Groom, who was hooked up with Joe Wood in a 1-1 game in the eighth inning. Johnson matched his rival, Smokey Joe, with zeros until Washington scored twice in the 11th. On July 3, Walter Johnson pitched a 15-inning shutout against the Red Sox, winning 1-0. In the ninth inning the hometown fans were frustrated when, with the bases loaded, two runners were thrown out at the plate and Johnson fanned the final batter. By mid-season Washington was in close contention with Philadelphia and Boston, almost entirely because of Johnson's 18-5 record. He was on a pace to win 36 games.

Washington headed west from Boston, and Walter Johnson continued his exceptional season with a two-hit shutout in Detroit. His new string of scoreless innings reached 37 before Cleveland broke the spell, although Johnson won the game, 5-4. When the team reached St. Louis, the Midwest was suffering through a sweltering heat wave. On July 16, Johnson won a game in relief and two days later, with temperatures over 100 degrees, won again with a four-inning rescue job. He held the Browns at bay until his team scored three runs in the 12th inning. Johnson was starting in turn and relieving frequently. He was keeping Washington in the pennant race almost single-handedly.

11
Another Duel
with Smokey Joe

THE HEAT WAVE followed the team from St. Louis to Chicago. Here, at least, the waters of Lake Michigan offered hope of a cooling swim. The Nationals stayed at the Chicago Beach Hotel, where the waves of the lake were more inviting than the muddy waters of the Mississippi at St. Louis. After Sunday's game of the 20th, the players headed for the beach outside their hotel. The next day the Washington newspapers carried this alarming news: "Narrow Escape From Death Of Five Players."

The news accounts told how Walter Johnson and four teammates had barely made it to shore after being caught in a strong undertow. Joe Gedeon, a rookie utility infielder, was seriously injured when he was lifted by a huge breaker and flung against the pilings of a pier. Gedeon had been trying to rescue a boy who was clinging to a rope in the heavy sea. While catcher Bull Henry landed the boy, Johnson, infielder Frank LaPorte, and catcher Eddie Ainsmith brought Gedeon to safety. They then went to the rescue of another swimmer. They brought the floundering man a lifeline and, with the aid of life preservers, got him pulled to the beach. After that the ballplayers had their own strenuous struggle with the undertow before they finally staggered out of the turbulent lake. The team also lost Hank Shanks for several weeks. He was entertaining the hotel guests by doing back flips off the pier and landed in shallow water, severely spraining an ankle. Clark Griffith declared the beach off-limits to players for anything more dangerous than sunbathing. There were showers and tubs for those who wanted to cool off.

The next day, while the fans back in Washington were reading of the narrow escape of the players, Walter Johnson was routinely pitching another ball game. The day after the beach incident, he defeated the White Sox, 2-1, holding them to four hits in a needlessly close game. Washington made 11 hits, had four walks, stole two bases, and benefited from five White Sox errors. Still, they only gave Johnson two runs to work with. .

Joe Boehling, Griffith's rookie find for the pitching staff, was having a sensational season. He ended the road trip by winning his 11th straight game, 7-1, from Chicago. Another pitcher whose work was promising, Joe Engel, opened the home stand when the Nationals got back to Washington. It was a carnage-filled game. In the fourth inning Sam Agnew, a young St. Louis catcher, was hit under the eye and his cheekbone fractured by an Engel pitch. Agnew was taken to the Georgetown University Hospital for more than a week's stay. When Tom Hughes could not stop the Browns' rally, Walter Johnson replaced him and found another way to get into the record book. The game went 15 innings, an 8-8 tie, before it was called because of darkness. The game took 3:35 to play. In the 11.1 innings he pitched, Johnson struck out 15 batters. It is still in the record book as the most batters fanned in a relief role. The St. Louis pitcher, Carl Weilman, struck out six times, and Johnson four times. Johnson came out of the game with more than honors. He also limped off with a spike wound in his foot and missed his next turn.

August 2 was turning into an annual celebration by the local fans. It was the anniversary of Walter Johnson's first appearance in a Washington uniform. Before the sixth anniversary game, a silver trophy cup, three-feet high and stuffed with $1,148 in currency chipped in by the fans, was presented to him. President Woodrow Wilson led the applause of 17,000 fans. Walter Johnson accepted graciously and showed his appreciation by beating Detroit, the same team that he had faced in his debut game. He had been idle for eight days, and his spiked ankle was not fully healed. However, this time the 3-2 score was in Washington's favor.

The home stand continued into August with Johnson extending his winning streak but pitching somewhat gingerly. He came out of one game early because he had a comfortable lead and Griffith wanted to rest him. When the team left on another trip to the western American League cities, Johnson remained idle for a week. He resumed pitching in Detroit and again was excused early, leading 9-2 after seven innings. *The Sporting Life* dispatch said, "Johnson is suffering from a lame arm and his shoulder pains him when he throws the ball. He contracted his problem after the 15-inning game [when he struck out 15 batters in relief]. Johnson thinks the trouble comes from a cold."

On August 24, Johnson's arm was in fine shape again as he won his 14th game in a row, 2-1. He was within two victories of tying the record he and Joe Wood had set the previous year. The way Johnson was going, the betting favored him doing it. He shared a training tip with newspaper readers that delivered a mixed message to youth. The report began with this observation: "Walter Johnson is pitching himself to glory on a diet of pudding, sherbet, cake and iced tea." The great Senator pitcher discoursed scientifically on the whys and wherefores of his midday meal. "I don't believe in eating much before going out to the ballpark. Overloading the stomach is bad for a ballplayer. I like pudding and cake, particularly on a day I am going to pitch. Sherbet or ice cream is soothing to the stomach and so is iced tea. Then when I come back to the hotel I eat my heartiest meal of the day."

Johnson took his fitness beliefs to Boston for a publicized rematch with Smokey Joe Wood. Their 1912 roles were reversed. This time it was Wood who had to stop Johnson. If the Washington pitcher won, he would be only a victory short of tying the record they shared. If he tied it, his next win would break it.

The game went 11 innings, with Johnson losing another 1-0 game. This loss pained him more than any of the 26 games he lost this way. Afterward he said, "I doubt if I ever pitched a better game in my life. In 10 innings, only one Boston player reached first base and he got there on a scratch hit. In the 11th a hit, an error and another hit gave Boston the winning run." It was unearned, of course.

Smokey Joe Wood said of his rival, "Johnson has it on me. He has the advantage of being taller and having longer arms which aid him in his speed. Johnson doesn't exert himself as do other pitchers, including myself, and when he wants to cut loose he has all his power at his command."

As it turned out, Johnson would not have tied the record in his next start. He wobbled his way to a 10-inning loss to the Philadelphia Athletics, 6-5. He helped himself with a home run but gave up 10 hits, and all the A's runs were earned. After two scoreless non-decision relief appearances, Walter Johnson reached the 30-victory level. It came in the nightcap of a pair of games in New York after he had saved the opener. Johnson won his 30th game with style, this time coming out ahead in a 1-0 game. Dan Moeller singled to lead off the ninth inning. He stole second, went to third on an error, and scored on a sacrifice fly.

Johnson kept Washington in the pennant race, but the Philadelphia A's retained their lead even though he won all his remaining games. Washington's second-place finish placed them ahead of Cleveland and Boston. In games with Connie Mack's champions, Johnson won four times, three of the victories being shutouts. The A's defeated him three times, once in extra innings, once by one run, and they knocked him out of the box the only time that happened all season.

September 29 was George McBride Day. The team captain only batted a characteristic .218, but he also had a spectacular .960 fielding average. Playing on rough surfaces, with a small glove, he excelled when the league had many outstanding shortstops. The others, who included Buck Weaver, Ray Chapman, Roger Peckinpaugh, Donie Bush, and Jack Barry, collectively averaged .935. September 29 honored McBride, but the playing honors went, as usual, to Walter Johnson. He won his final game with a characteristic 1-0 squeaker. It was his 36th victory and 11th shutout of the season. He had lost only seven games. In the stretch from June 27 to September 29, he won 20 games and lost only two. Those defeats were by one-run margins and came in extra-inning games. Johnson reasonably could have won 22 straight and been stopped only by the end of the season.

It would have been best for Walter Johnson's statistics had the season ended with the September 29 game. However, the season had almost another week to run its course. Washington had been eliminated from the pennant chase with Philadelphia holding a $6\frac{1}{2}$ game margin at the finish. The season came to a close with the Boston Red Sox in town for a meaningless game. It was played as a farce intended to entertain the fans, including the 6,000 servicemen from military bases in the Washington area. The soldiers brought their own band and the selections were intended to be humorous. Germany Schaefer was in his element and danced mock waltzes while the band played selections by Strauss.

Clark Griffith made out his lineup card with tongue-in-cheek carelessness. He led off with a 17-year-old Cuban rookie, Merito Acosta. Schaefer batted third and opened in right field. He rotated positions freely during the game. Sometimes he abandoned the outfield and hovered between first and second base. He shifted to center field, took over at second base, and even pitched.

The soldiers and sailors demanded Walter Johnson, and they got him. However, they expected to see him pitch. The starting assignment went to an Ozark giant, the 6-foot-$3\frac{1}{2}$ Mutt Williams. It was his debut game, and the only one he ever won. Johnson played center field, except for a brief mound appearance in the final inning of the game. Washington's early "safe lead" of 10-3 was almost wiped out by Boston's ninth-inning surge when they scored six runs. These tallies came more from Washington's foolishness than the Red Sox' efforts. Manager Clark Griffith, 43, pitched an inning to his coach, 44-year-old former catcher, Jack Ryan. Players on both teams played out of position, deliberately let balls roll through their legs, muffed fly balls on purpose, and created a scorekeeper's nightmare.

Eventually, the scorer got his revenge. It was the same misguided reporter who had several times rendered exclusive opinions on controversial plays during the season. This time, however, he simply entered in the official box score details that were unarguably true. Yes, Walter Johnson pitched. He faced two batters and lobbed up fat pitches which were turned into base hits. Both runners scored and were charged to Johnson's record. That was the price Walter Johnson paid for an afternoon's frolic. He never knew the ultimate cost of his folly. Long after Walter Johnson had died, with the best single-season ERA of all time for pitchers with more than 300 innings pitched (1.09 in 1913) among his records, the official score sheets were reviewed.

When the league records were tallied after the 1913 season, the league statistician paid no attention to Johnson's pitching stint in the farce game. Perhaps it was not even a deliberate oversight and the runs were simply unnoticed in the scrambled entries in the box score. According to the records compiled then, Johnson had pitched 346 innings and given up 42 earned runs. Those numbers produce a 1.09 ERA. Add two more earned runs, and the ERA rises to 1.14. What's so bad about that? It is two points higher than the 1.12 ERA Bob Gibson later registered in the run-depressed 1968 season.

Of the two statistical bibles, *Total Baseball* shows Johnson's 1913 ERA as 1.13. Macmillan's *Baseball Encyclopedia* has not changed this stat since it appeared in their monumental first edition in 1969. It was 1.09 then, and they still held to that figure in the 1993 eighth edition. As with the "missing" 33rd Johnson victory in 1912, Macmillan is faced with a decision which involves the integrity of the statistics of baseball. It is good to have competition, but this is a drawback when each reference source holds its own opinions and interpretations. Hopefully, a stat-by-stat reconciliation will take place, perhaps arbitrated by the Society for American Baseball Research.

Another honor was voted to Walter Johnson by the sportswriters who helped the Chalmers Motor Company award their automobile prizes. In the Most Valuable Player contest, Johnson was the leading vote-getter, topping Joe Jackson of Cleveland, 54 votes to 43. In the previous year's balloting, his 32 (or 33) victories had landed him in third place behind Tris Speaker and Ed Walsh. The Chalmers Company had abandoned giving its prize on the basis of the highest batting average after the debacle of the 1910 contest between Cobb and Lajoie. That season had ended with a splurge of bunted base hits by the popular Frenchman in an attempt to deny Cobb the title.

Walter Johnson remained behind when his Washington teammates dispersed at the end of the season. Both leagues now finished at the same time and the World Series began as soon as the regular league seasons ended, so there would be no more exhibitions to prepare the American League winner for the World Series. Johnson had a different post-season agenda this year.

Walter Johnson and Zeb Milan attended World Series games in New York and Philadelphia, where the Chalmers car was awarded. Johnson waved to the fans and expertly drove his prize of the field. He considered himself a good driver. Johnson and Milan owned a Cole Eight, which they bought in 1911. The car sold for $1,500 and it made sense to share the expense. Also, it lacked a self-starter, so one partner was needed to crank the motor. Johnson and Milan may have taken turns shipping it home to use between seasons. Johnson had used it in Coffeyville the winter before. It is likely that this time Johnson had the Chalmers sent to Coffeyville while Milan, who was getting married, drove the Cole back to Tennessee. Unlike the Cole, which required cranking to start, the Chalmers Motor Company began providing self-starters in 1912. The model awarded to Johnson had that feature and was the first of a new line of six-cylinder models.

The Chalmers winner had acquired the nickname "Barney" because of his driving. When he gave a ride to Germany Schaefer, his teammate claimed Johnson drove like Barney Oldfield the "mile a minute" racing driver. After he had been stopped and ticketed by the capital police for driving at the breakneck speed of 25 miles per hour, his other teammates also began calling him Barney.

Nineteen thirteen turned out to be the greatest individual season Walter Johnson would ever have. He had brought his team close to a pennant, six and a half games behind Connie Mack's dynastic Athletics. In future seasons, Johnson would lead in many departments, particularly strikeouts, but he would never again lead in all the categories he topped with the figures he posted in 1913. He led with 36 wins. Against seven losses, they produced a league-leading .837 percentage. His 1.09 ERA, even after it is raised to 1.14 for his goofy contributions to the last game of the season, is still a league-leading stat (and still the American League record). He led everyone with 29 complete games, and had been lifted early in some situations where he had a commanding lead. His 346 innings pitched testified to his "iron man" stamina. The 243 strikeouts were evidence of his power and the 11 shutouts of his mastery. Indeed, 1913 was Johnson's greatest individual season. More successes and team championships were in the future, but he would never again put up the kind of numbers he posted in 1913. And, he wasn't done pitching for the year yet.

12

The Red Ant Derails the Big Train

WALTER JOHNSON agreed to play a post-season game promoted by Dave Driscoll, a New York City sports promoter. Johnson made a Sunday afternoon appearance in Schenectady, New York, two days before the World Series began. He pitched for a team billed as Walter Johnson's All-Americans. The advance promotion hinted at a supporting cast of other big league players. Instead, Driscoll had rounded up a collection of New York area semipros and minor league performers. The team was put in charge of Fred Jacklitsch, who, after 13 years in the major leagues, had managed and caught for Rochester in the International League in 1913.

The game was a promoter's dream, matching Walter Johnson, the greatest white pitcher, and Frank Wickware, considered by many to be the greatest black pitcher in baseball. The scene also turned into a nightmare that almost got the principals arrested and put the estimated 7,000 overflow crowd in serious danger. Johnson's team was booked to play the Mohawk Giants, one of the great black teams of the time. They served Schenectady as a "hometown team" and played white teams from other upstate New York towns as well as touring black teams, such as the nationally famous Leland Giants, Rube Foster's team in Chicago, and the East-dominating New York Lincoln Giants.

Frank Wickware made his Negro League debut in 1910 with Chicago's Leland Giants. In the short and erratic schedule, Wickware was 6-0. Manager Rube Foster, who is a member of the Baseball Hall of Fame, was 2-0, and Smokey Joe Williams was 3-1. In 1913, Wickware joined the independent Mohawk Giants. Most of the players also came from out of town, black professionals looking for a way to make money playing baseball. The team played on weekends and holidays. Men with job skills and a suitable servile workplace attitude could combine baseball for pay with a regular paycheck.

Although the players were required to clown their way through ball games, they were also expected to win. They achieved a 1913 record of 51 wins against 22 losses with two ties. They began their season beating Montreal of the International League and ended it with a victory over Walter Johnson. They were good. They were also very unhappy. The players claimed they had not been paid for six weeks and, after the ballpark was filled, they struck. The games of the Mohawk Giants were played at Island Park, aptly named because it was in the middle of a river. Spectators bought their tickets at booths on the Schenectady side and then crossed over a pontoon bridge.

While the day was sunny and calm, the agitated players were not. The pontoon bridge seemed frail as the irate Mohawk Giants, led by a bat-brandishing Frank Wickware, thudded across it. They were headed for the box office, where the team's owner, Bill Wernecke, was tossing 50-cent pieces into a satchel. He acknowledged being behind on the player's wages but claimed this was necessary to keep the team intact and in town until Walter Johnson's team showed up to generate a good payday for all. As soon as the game was over, everyone would be paid off, he promised. The players did not believe him. They feared Wernecke had other plans and his own idea about what "getaway day" meant at the close of the season.

For once there was a cop when one was needed. Sheriff J. Ackerman Gill took charge and solved the impasse. He contacted Alfred Nicholau, a silent partner in the Mohawk Giants, who produced $500 to at least partially settle the player's claims for back wages. Meanwhile, Wernecke was hugging his black satchel with the day's ticket sales inside.

At this point, Dave Driscoll demanded the visitor's share of the gate receipts. He pulled his team off the field. He acknowledged he had received the $500 guarantee—most of it needed to pay Walter Johnson—before the players left New York, but said he was also entitled to a share of the gate receipts. Sheriff Gill was a man for the occasion. With spectators nervously starting back across the bridge in fear of an ensuing riot and trying to get a refund on their way to safety, the sheriff pulled his watch on Driscoll. He ordered him to get his players on the field and the game underway in five minutes. Otherwise, Sheriff Gill would confiscate the gate receipts and refund the customers their money as they left.

Finally the game began, and it lived up to everyone's expectations. Walter Johnson was effortlessly at his best. The first eight pitches were strikes. The ninth pitch retired the side on a soft fly ball to center. Walter Johnson, who held the record for the fewest balls thrown in a game, was in a hurry to get the game finished. He struck out the side on 11 pitches in the third inning. The game had been delayed, and the autumn sun was about to set. Concern that an incomplete game might jeopardize the payoff hurried Walter Johnson. He was a purposeful man when such interests were at stake.

In the fourth inning, the Mohawk Giants scored a run on a fly ball double that fell into the overflow crowd encroaching on left field. A stolen base and a sacrifice fly put the Mohawk Giants ahead. In the fifth inning, Johnson again struck out the side in order, using only 15 pitches.

Meanwhile, "the Red Ant," as Frank Wickware was called for reasons which are unfathomable from this distance in time, struggled but kept Johnson's team scoreless. Walter Johnson hit doubles in his two times at bat, but his mates only managed three hits, none with a runner in scoring position. The All-Americans failed to score off Wickware in the sixth and, with darkness closing in, the game was called without complaint. The fans had seen the great Walter Johnson and marveled at his speed and ability. They could argue all winter whether Frank Wickware was as good as Johnson or better.

It would be interesting to know if Wickware and Johnson had talked with each other. They were neighbors back in Kansas. Johnson now lived in Coffeyville, and Wickware had been born there. Johnson and Wickware were from metaphorically different sides of the Atcheson, Topeka, and Sante Fe tracks that divided Coffeyville socially. Both were big men, six-feet tall and weighing 200 pounds or more. Both had great fastballs and were master craftsmen on the mound. They could hit and hit with power. They fielded everything in reach. They only differed in one defining way. Johnson's ability got him to the major leagues, and Wickware's color kept him out.

The Walter Johnson All-Americans took the train back to New York City, where on Monday he watched the opening game of the World Series and on Tuesday checked into Shibe Park in Philadelphia for game two and the presentation of his Chalmers automobile. He saw Christy Mathewson of the New York Giants shut out Eddie Plank and the Philadelphia Athletics, 3-0. It was the only game John McGraw's team would win. Plank reversed the tables, 3-1, when he and Matty met in the series-ending fifth game.

Zeb Milan, who accompanied Johnson to the game, was headed

home to Tennessee. On November 19th he would marry Margaret Bowers. They had met eight years earlier when he played independent baseball in Clarksville, Texas. Milan may have believed in long engagements for himself, but he wanted his best friend, Walter Johnson, to be a more expeditious suitor. He urged him not to let Hazel Roberts get away.

Walter Johnson had another baseball appearance to make in 1913. A world tour, the most ambitious ever, was announced in August. The Chicago White Sox and the New York Giants would travel westward to circle the globe. It would have a missionary purpose. America was determined to make converts to its National Game. In 1874, A. G. Spalding had led two teams of players abroad to show the British what the colonists had done with the game of rounders. An even more extensive tour took place in 1888 when Cap Anson's Chicago White Stockings toured with a team of players from the National League and American Association led by John Montgomery Ward. For the past six years, Charles Comiskey, the White Sox owner, and John J. McGraw had been discussing the possibility of a world tour on a truly grand scale. By 1913 they were ready, even if some of their players were not.

The promise of an all-expense-paid first-class trip, with wives included, to Japan, China, the Philippines, Australia, the Suez Canal, Egypt, Italy, Austria, France, Germany, and Great Britain, including Scotland and Ireland, excited most of the players, but not all.

Even John McGraw's domineering personality could not induce all his regulars to make the trip. Only a few pitchers would be needed once they were abroad. However, extra pitching would be needed as the teams played their way across the country. Christy Mathewson and Jess Tesreau, along with a few lesser lights, would get them to their point of debarkation, Vancouver, B.C. They could spare Rube Marquard to the vaudeville circuit, where he took second billing to his wife, headliner Blossom Seeley.

The biggest drawing card of the Giants, except for Christy Mathewson, was Jim Thorpe, the fabled Indian athlete who had dominated the 1912 Olympics. His amateur's medals were later taken from him for the then-heinous sin of playing sports for pay. While on summer vacation from the Carlisle Indian School, he had played for a team in a North Carolina piney tar circuit. In our present time, when world-class athletes have agents and can hardly fit another sponsor's patch onto their uniforms, it may be difficult to consider how class separated amateurs from professionals. It sullied the honor of the stiff-necked simon-pures who controlled amateur athletics if a working-class person crashed their elite domain. They were shocked to learn that the man who would be voted the greatest American athlete of the 20th century, had been paid beer money to play in an out-of-the-way whistle-stop league. Thorpe had to give back his medals. However, in 1913 he was making an honest dollar playing the outfield for McGraw. He did not play it as well as others on the team and had an exploitable weakness against curve ball pitching, but he was a gate attraction.

Jim Thorpe welcomed the around-the-world trip. It would be his honeymoon excursion. Shortly after he had signed with the Giants that spring, he married Iva Miller, an attractive coed he had met at Carlisle. On their first date, Iva had told Thorpe she was a Cherokee, but when he proposed, she admitted she was just another girl from immigrant stock. Her father was a hotel man in Muskogee, Oklahoma, and she attended an Indian school there before transferring to Carlisle. Her sister was a teacher there and a cut-rate tuition tempted her to pass as an American Indian.

Thorpe, whose own parentage included a spot of Scot, some Irish, and a medley of other nationalities, although heavily offset with Sauk bloodlines, said he was not prejudiced in such matters. Particularly when Iva Miller was the prettiest girl in school.

The Thorpes were not the only newlyweds along on the trip. Larry Doyle, the Giants' captain, had left the ranks of bachelors during the pennant race. In all, there were six pairs of newlyweds among the 11 couples in the around-the-world party. The train that carried the travelers across the United States was called "the Honeymoon Express."

The Giants had filled their ranks with several stars from other National League teams. Lee Magee, as wild a card as ever plagued management, was a switch-hitting outfielder from the Cardinals. The Phillies sent third baseman Hans Lobert and shortstop Mickey Doolan. Also added to the cast was the colorful Mike Donlin, absent from the major leagues in 1913 but intent on a comeback with the Giants. He had alternated careers with them. After finishing second to Honus Wagner in three batting races in a row, he had dropped out of baseball to tour as an entertainer with his wife, Mabel Hite. Like Rube Marquard's wife, Blossom Seeley, she was a vaudeville headliner.

The White Sox had added the crowd-pleasing Germany Schaefer as well as Sam Crawford, Walter Johnson's favorite opponent. Wahoo Sam was slowing up and had moved to first base, but this hardly left a gap in the outfield. The Boston Red Sox star, Tris Speaker, would cover center field and as much of left and right as might be required. Red Faber and Doc White were the ranking Chicago pitchers.

Walter Johnson welcomed the invitation to join the troupe, even if only for a few days. The original plan was to have him meet Christy Mathewson in a matchup of superstar pitchers in Joplin, Missouri, on October 27. However, there was a bigger ballpark in Tulsa, Oklahoma, a sleeper jump farther west, and the meeting between the titans of their time finally took place there. Johnson arrived for the Joplin game from Muskogee, Oklahoma. A tour game there had been snowed out.

Not to totally disappoint the ticket buyers in Joplin, Walter Johnson opened the game for the White Sox. Bunny Hearn, a lightly used pitcher who would be dropped from the tour as excess ballast when the group sailed from Vancouver, B.C., was the Giants' starter. The *Joplin News* explained Mathewson's absence, saying he had pitched too often on the tour to-date and was tired. The 5,000 fans who had braved cold weather watched a slugfest on a muddy field. Snow from the night before had to be cleared away before the game could be played.

Although the fans did not get the pitching duel of the century which had been promised, they saw a maximum of hitting as the Giants beat the White Sox, 13-12. Jim Thorpe made a late-inning appearance as a first base coach, and the newspaper reported, "The crowd rose to its feet and cheered the big athlete." The account of the game said about Johnson, who pitched two scoreless innings and gave up two runs in the third, one unearned: "He did not exert himself to any great extent but the fans saw the great American League star in action and were satisfied."

When Walter Johnson went to the plate for his first turn at bat, the game was interrupted while two local politicans presented him with a watch. A short speech lauded Johnson as the greatest pitcher in the world, while dark looks were directed at Christy Mathewson. Matty sat huddled under several sweaters, watching from the dugout. Then, Johnson doffed his hat to the crowd, bowed, and struck out.

After the game, the players and their entourage boarded their special train and departed for Tulsa, the next stop on their cross-country tour.

13
Johnson and
Mathewson Meet

ULSA HAD SET ASIDE Tuesday, October 28, 1913 as a red-letter day in the city's history. The banks closed at noon, and the visiting big league players paraded from the business district to South Main Street Park, 10 blocks away. The Fifth Artillery Band led the way, and Company L, Ninth U.S. Infantry of Fort Logan H. Root, Arkansas, fell in behind. Oklahoma's governor Lee Cruce and his daughter rode by in an open touring car. A small fleet of automobiles chugged out Main Street, and thousands of people, many with children whose schools had been closed for the visit by the ballplayers, waved pennants. Most of the cheering spectators went along to the ballpark, too.

For days, the *Tulsa Daily World* had warmed up the community for the festive occasion. The Sunday edition carried a quarter-page announcement in large display type: "WORLD'S GREATEST BALL STARS IN ACTION—New York Giants vs. Chicago White Sox." A boxed inset promised: "Christy Mathewson and Walter Johnson Will Be in the Box." The game was scheduled for 3 P.M.

Actually, the game got underway earlier than advertised. There had to be a change in plans. An extra edition of the *Tulsa Daily World* explained the reason. The headlines, spread the width of the front page, read: "ONE KILLED—50 INJURED." Beneath this, large type announced, "Bleachers Collapse During World's Series Game at Tulsa With Disastrous Result. Weakened Structure Crumbles Like Kindling!" In a commendable job of spot news coverage, the dispatch from the ballpark described a tragedy that might even have been worse, although one man was dead. Pvt. Chester Taylor, a soldier from Fort Root whose company had been crossing under the bleachers when they collapsed without sound or warning, had been crushed to death. The carnage was devastating. People were dug out of the rubble with broken limbs and head wounds and were hysterical from shock. A joyfully anticipated event suddenly turned tragic when a too-rickety, unroofed bleacher section gave way. A facing range of wooden plank seats in left field had remained standing, but the occupants scrambled to the playing field.

In front of the main grandstand, the Fifth Artillery Band kept playing martial airs, and the governor and his party tried to calm the patrons who remained in their seats.

Meanwhile, the wounded were bundled into automobiles pressed into duty as ambulances, and the town's supply of emergency vehicles rushed to the ballpark. Although hurriedly written for the extra edition, the reporter filled in small details. He described a mother, whose son had a bleeding cut on his head, carrying the boy in her arms to a doctor's office in town. He observed that one man was found with a nail driven through his nose. The news account ended, "The ball game started at 1:45 o'clock and the majority of the people on the grounds stayed to see it." Apparently, batting and infield practice were dispensed with, and the starting time was moved ahead to adjust to the situation and divert the crowd.

While the police, National Guard, and firemen sorted out the casualties, the players had warmed up in front of the grandstand. The spectators were torn between admiring the star players they had come to see and watching their injured neighbors being carried away. As soon as the field was cleared, the teams took their positions. Bill Klem, the home plate umpire, announced the batteries: Walter Johnson and Ray Schalk for Chicago, and Christy Mathewson and Chief Meyers for New York. The crown roared its appreciation and expectation. Johnson had replaced Mathewson as the "greatest pitcher in the world," but Matty was still near his top form. He had led his league with a 2.09 ERA and had a 25-11 won-lost record. He had pitched 301 innings. These were impressive stats, although not as overwhelming as they once had been and not as dominant as Johnson's for 1913. However, Matty was 33, eight years older than Johnson. The baton of pitching leadership was changing hands. When the two were photographed before the game, Johnson wearing his Washington uniform, they clasped hands symbolically. The two shared the moment. Despite the distraction of the calamity, they had finally met.

For three innings both men held their opponents scoreless. Matty weakened first, being hit hard in the fourth inning as the White Sox scored twice. Hooks Wiltse could not stem the tide in relief and four more runs were scored in the fifth inning. Meanwhile, Walter Johnson was methodically mowing down the Giants batters. He pitched a shutout, striking out eight and walking one.

The White Sox piled up 16 hits. Three double plays kept the game reasonably close. Buck Weaver, leading off, was five-for-five with a pair of doubles. Tris Speaker and Sam Crawford each had three hits. Jim Thorpe, who played right field, singled in two times at bat and drew Johnson's only walk.

The catastrophic collapse of the stands, the death of a soldier, and the hospitalization of dozens of others, took the edge off the gaiety the people of Tulsa had expected. The players were transported back to the hotel, where they showered and changed. The governor's reception was abbreviated, speeches forgone, and a sobered troupe of players climbed aboard their special railroad cars and headed west. Walter Johnson said goodbye. He would see the American Leaguers in the spring. He would never again pitch against Christy Mathewson, but he would have a long association with John McGraw. Johnson's train ran east, taking him back to his farm in Coffeyville. He had one more game to pitch before he could finally rest on his laurels.

The folks in Coffeyville had arranged a second Walter Johnson Day on October 30. Just as the match between Johnson and Christy Mathewson had stirred the fans in Tulsa, Coffeyville had a compelling contest of its own. This time they matched one local hero against another. Larry Cheney, who had led the National League with 26 wins as a rookie with the Cubs the year before, now made his off-season home in Coffeyville. He lived with his sister and her husband, Frank Long, on a farm outside the town. Cheney would match his craftsmanship against Johnson's speed. Earlier in his career he had been badly injured when a line drive back at the box was deflected by the hand he flung across his face. The fingers, badly broken, had been poorly set. Subsequently, much like Three Finger Brown, he found his warped digits enabled him to throw strangely breaking curve balls.

Coming on the heels of the Mathewson-Johnson contest in Tulsa two days earlier, the game between two local teams, each with a major league star pitching, stirred regional enthusiasms. Challenged, both pitchers bore down all the way with the game ending, diplomatically, in a scoreless tie.

Nineteen thirteen was Johnson's "career year." Although modest about his achievements, Walter Johnson was always aware of them and their significance in salary negotiations. He had settled too cheaply, he knew, when he had accepted the three-year deal at $7,000 a season. But he would get a new contract for 1914, and he expected it would pay him what a back-to-back 30-plus winner was worth. Griffith had tried to sign Johnson for the coming season before he departed for Kansas, but it was left to be settled later. A long Kansas winter lay ahead, but beyond it waited a marriage and the turmoil which engulfed him when another effort to start a new league succeeded and he became its best-known captive in a bitter war with organized baseball.

14
Walter Weds the Congressman's Daughter

W HEN THE WHITE SOX AND GIANTS ended their around-the-world trip in New York City, they were welcomed as returning heroes. They went ashore for a gala celebration and testimonial dinner. They also landed in a maelstrom of contract challenges. While they had been circling the globe, team owners had been circling the wagons against a rapidly emerging threat to form a third major league.

Unlike the shoestring promoter D.A. Fletcher, whose ambitions four years earlier were unsupported by backers with hard cash, James A. Gilmore, a resourceful organizer, was supported by men of substance. Robert B. Ward, head of a baking empire, Harry F. Sinclair, an oilman with a Rockefeller touch, Phil Ball, whose ice supply business provided unmeltable millions, and others like them, wanted to own a big league ball club. When the present market of 16 teams seemed closed to them, they acted to create their own supply. There were places, such as Buffalo, Baltimore, Indianapolis, and Kansas City, that were eager for major league status. Larger cities with one team or two, offered the possibility that they could accommodate one more. Brooklyn, Pittsburgh, Chicago, and St. Louis could provide fans who were looking for more action or were dissatisfied with what they were getting.

The fledgling league had big name targets, Tris Speaker, Eddie Collins, and Walter Johnson being among the most viable. Speaker would parlay a potential offering from a well-heeled outlaw operator into a new Red Sox contract for $15,000. This so overburdened the Boston team's payroll that Speaker was sold to Cleveland after another season.

Collins became an expendable asset to Connie Mack when the fans, somehow grown jaded by the A's winning four pennants in five years, stopped coming to ball games. Right after winning the 1914 pennant, Connie Mack sold Eddie Collins to the White Sox for $50,000. This put cash in the bank and lowered Philadelphia's payroll. Charley Comiskey, determined to hang on to his new superstar, paid Collins far more handsomely than other members of the team. This undercut morale and was a factor in the eventual sellout of the World Series by the 1919 White Sox.

Walter Johnson approached the coming 1914 season thoughtfully. His money was invested in his new farm and its stock. He hoped for a marriage and wondered about his prospects. As the reigning "King of the Mound" he sat atop the baseball world because of his 1913 achievements. Could he be sure he would stay there? How could he turn his situation into the best financial advantage?

As winter turned into spring, Johnson was still unsigned. No one from the Federal League had contacted him with a tempting offer. Yet he was as willing to be seduced as he had been in 1910. His attitude toward baseball as a profession was unchanged. He owed his loyalty to the team for which he played. But he was not obliged to extend that relationship if a better offer could be found. He was tied to Washington by a one-sided arrangement, and if someone else replaced it with one that paid better, he had to think of himself first. Now, he believed, that future might also include a family.

Clark Griffith was a nervous shepherd anxious to get his flock under contract before the raiders of the Federal League carried off his players. Walter Johnson's salary was a major part of the payroll. It was critical to get his ace pitcher satisfied and signed. The three-year contract, paying $7,000 a season, had ended. It had proved to be a bargain for the Nationals. This time, Walter Johnson wanted a better return for his work. Griffith and Johnson settled on a $10,000 salary and a bonus of $2,000 for signing.

Walter Johnson headed into the 1914 season with his life divided into separate roles. He was earning top dollar for pitchers in his league. Only Christy Mathewson was paid more, and his reign had been longer. Johnson's farm property was established. His father could oversee operations and hired men would do the work while he was away working at his own trade. Johnson also invested in America's growth industry, the automobile, by operating a garage in Coffeyville.

His life off the field centered on Congressman Roberts' daughter. Hazel would be in Washington for much of the summer. Johnson would adjust to losing Zeb Milan, married during the off-season, as a housemate. They would still room together on road trips, but Johnson took a smaller apartment and lived alone. He hoped it would not be for long.

Hazel Roberts and her parents had moved out of the Dewey. The congressman had been reelected and the family leased a house at 1408 Monroe Street. There was a front parlor where Walter could sit with Hazel and continue his courtship. He was the sole owner of a new Chalmers automobile and could take her for drives. As spring training ended, the cherry trees were blossoming along the Potomac. Taking a girl to an ice cream parlor was Johnson's idea of a great date. His life-long search for the perfect flavor could be continued while Hazel sipped the new fountain concoction, Coca-Cola.

But first, there was the baseball season. That's the way Walter Johnson made his living. Two weeks before the season opened, the sad but not surprising news that Rube Waddell had died at age 37 reached the baseball public. Walter Johnson, who would never break the Rube's single-season strikeout record, was 12 years younger. He was the antithesis of the eccentric lefthander who had wasted his life and his opportunities. Even the saintly Connie Mack had to wash his hands of him. This cost Waddell the chance to pitch in a World Series, something that Walter Johnson was determined to achieve.

The A's ran off a string of pennants without Waddell, while he pitched for other teams which also soon tired of his antics. Even in 1905, when he pitched Philadelphia to a pennant, Waddell missed the World Series. Just before he had his chance to match himself against Christy Mathewson and the New York Giants, he took on a teammate in a friendly wrestling match on a train platform. While changing trains in Providence, Rhode Island, the other players had dented his out-of-season straw skimmer, which fashion dictated was not to be worn after Labor Day. Waddell, immune to fashion's dictates, had fallen on his shoulder and his already impaired pitching arm became useless. Waddell had been regarded by Walter Johnson as the best pitcher he had ever seen.

Washington opened its season in Boston and Walter Johnson picked up where he had left off, with a 3-0 victory over the Red Sox. Boston now had an Irish mayor. Mayor Fitzgerald had broken the hold on city hall of the Boston Brahmins, the aristocrats who ruled New England. "Honey Fitz" Fitzgerald was the silver-tongued Celt whose daughter, Rose, became the mother of John Fitzgerald Kennedy, first Catholic President of the United States.

A record crowd of 25,000 filled the new Fenway Park. No Green Monster loomed in left field. It was a spacious arena, whose outfield was patrolled by the greatest defensive trio, old-timers insist, ever to chase down fly balls: Duffy Lewis, Tris Speaker, and Harry Hooper.

When Washington moved down to New York City, the headline across the top of the sports page of the *New York Times* reprised, in a way, that which had run in the *Tulsa World* the previous fall. Baseball's two greatest pitching heroes were linked in the headline: "Brooklyn Drives Mathewson Off The Mound—Walter Johnson Defeats The Yankees." Succinctly, the headline suggested the passing of one superstar and confirmed the rising eminence of another. Johnson, although allowing only four hits, was wilder than expected. He walked five and had two wild pitches. One of these allowed New York's only run to score, as Washington won, 2-1.

The scene was set for Washington's home opener. President Wilson, the team's good luck charm, had to waive making the customary first pitch. There was big trouble in Mexico. An impudent bandit, Pancho Villa, was raiding across the border into Texas, and tactics somehow called for landing the U.S. Marines in Vera Cruz. As in more recent interventions to maintain America's economic interests, soldiers, sailors, and Marines were killed in these excursions. Wilson, as commander in chief, was busy at the White House. Walter Johnson could have used the chief executive's good luck presence. This time, the wrong Johnson won the opener.

The Red Sox unveiled "their Johnson," a rookie making his first start. A. Rankin Johnson, a Texan, pitched more like Walter Johnson than he did. Boston's Johnson limited Washington to four hits, and the shutout roles were reversed. The Red Sox spoiled Washington's home opener, 5-0. A very competitive rivalry developed between the two Johnsons, although Washington was about the only team A. Rankin Johnson could beat consistently. Another of the pitching Johnsons was also in the day's news.

Chief Johnson, whose rookie year in Cincinnati had promised a significant career with the Reds, had jumped to the outlaw league. Garry Herrmann, the Cincinnati owner, was not amused that a player he had under contract chose to ignore this. Herrmann had Chicago deputies serve papers on Chief in the dugout between innings. Shades of Dred Scott! Chief Johnson with enough Native American blood to participate in casino ownership had he lived into the 1990s, broke his bonds with organized baseball for a short career in the outlaw Federal League.

Walter Johnson lost a pair of one-run decisions in Philadelphia. It was a typical Johnson loss, 2-1, on April 28th. Both of the A's runs were unearned as Johnson's teammates made three errors. On May 1, Johnson made an appearance in relief, but instead of saving a victory, he gave up three runs in the ninth inning.

Things snapped back to normal when the New York Yankees came to Washington. In reporting the game back to its readers, the *New York Times* referred to Johnson as "the King of the Mound," as well he was that day. Not only did he pitch another shutout, he retired the first 19 batters in order. An error in the seventh inning allowed the first runner to reach base, and a single stopped the hitless string.

When Philadelphia came to town, Johnson again flopped in relief. He gave up six runs to lose a 9-3 lead. Only a triple play pulled off by Bull Henry and Chick Gandil in the top of the ninth saved Johnson a loss. He kept the A's from scoring in the 10th and, after Washington was retired, the game was stopped due to darkness, a 9-9 tie. Milan's four-for-four day, with a home run, helped Johnson win from the White Sox, 3-2, and he pitched successive victories over the Cleveland Indians.

When Detroit arrived to end Washington's long home stand, Johnson had a rare chance to coast. With a 10-1 lead, Manager Griffith removed his ace pitcher after seven innings. The Tigers' run scored on Zeb Milan's error. Washington had moved to within half of a game of the league-leading Detroit team.

The Senators returned to Boston and A. Rankin Johnson was waiting for them. Walter Johnson reversed the roles this time. However, he barely won, 1-0. Before the Senators left town, another matchup of the two Johnsons was scheduled, both men pitching on two days' rest. Now it was Boston's Johnson who reversed the roles, with Washington's Johnson winning, 1-0. Walter Johnson's throwing error gave Boston its only run.

Walter Johnson had three hits, including a double and triple, while beating the St. Louis Browns, but fell victim to shutouts in his next two starts. Washington made only one hit off Joe Benz in Chicago and were shutout again next in Cleveland. Walter Johnson lost, 4-2, in a rain-soaked game at Detroit. It was an ominous foretelling of what would be Johnson's most devastating defeat in the rain-plagued 1925 World Series. The newspaper comment was, "The slippery ball seemed to bother Johnson." The account of the game went on to say, "On more than one occasion Washington outfielders slipped while attempting to cut off drives." It was Johnson's third straight loss and, more significantly, his seventh loss of the season. His record was an unspectacular 9-7. He had lost as many games by mid-June as he had all the previous year.

Before the Johnson-Cobb competition could pick up again in Detroit, the Georgia Peach broke his hand in a tawdry demonstration that he was as aggressive off the field as on it. Cobb's wife had bought a piece of fish past its prime at a local market. When Ty Cobb strode into the store to demand a refund or fresher replacement, an argument began. Cobb pulled a revolver to enforce his complaint and a butcher's clerk, Harold Harding, disarmed him. In the fight, Cobb broke his thumb. He later avoided a jail sentence by paying a $50 fine, but he was out of the Tigers' lineup for two weeks. At the ballpark, Johnson took over the attack. He hit a grand slam home run over the left-field wall, in a muscle-flexing 7-3 victory. It was a strong note on which to end a long absence from Hazel Roberts.

June 24 would ever be a red-letter day for Walter Johnson. In the afternoon the Nationals won a doubleheader. They were generally called the Senators on the road, but the local papers persisted in the older name. Johnson pitched the second game and beat Philadelphia, the league leaders, 2-1. Hazel Lee Roberts was at the game. It was the last event she would attend by giving her maiden name at the pass gate. During the game newsboys raced through the stands hawking ink-fresh "Extras" with the news that Walter Johnson would be married that evening. He had shyly told his teammates about his plan or at least confirmed what his blabber-mouthed best man, Zeb Milan, had leaked out. The press thought it important enough to print special editions. As word rippled through the 12,000 spectators in the stands, there was spontaneous cheering. Hazel, in a field box, and Walter, on the mound, were given the well-wishes of the fans.

The wedding, despite the newsworthiness of its principals, was a quiet one. Hazel Lee Roberts became Mrs. Walter Perry Johnson in a ceremony performed by the Rev. Forrest J. Prettyman in the front parlor of the bride's home. He was the chaplain of the United States Senate. The bride, reported the *Washington Star*, wore a wedding gown of creamy lace covering cream taffeta silk. Her hat was made entirely of feathers, with a large white bird perched in front. We are not told what Johnson wore—probably a dazed look. Although Hazel and Walter had been going steady, there had been no formal engagement. Hazel got her wedding band in a Methodist ring ceremony. The small wedding party went outside to acknowledge the good wishes of neighbors and fans who had come by for the event. The couple went to Atlantic City for a short honeymoon. Walter couldn't get his big Chalmers automobile started, and a neighbor gave the bridal pair a lift.

Three days after the wedding Johnson was back at work. He lost to Philadelphia, 4-2, in a strange way. It was another game played in the rain. When the new bridegroom began by walking two batters and the A's clustered their hits for four quick runs, know-it-alls in the press box nudged each other. They began to compose leads that would support their assumption that Walter Johnson had overextended himself on his brief honeymoon. However, Johnson hit his stride and shut out the A's in the remaining seven innings.

There was another agenda being played out. The previous day Ollie Chill, a first-year umpire, had forfeited the game to Philadelphia because Washington's players had been overly critical of his decisions. Chill was quite short, and Washington's catchers were six-footers weighing over 200 pounds. Catchers at that time did not squat low, they stooped high. It was pointed out that Chill, when working the plate, had to guess the location on pitches he could not see. The Senators said he guessed wrong too often. When he abruptly stopped play, he only made friends with the home team. Even the A's supporters felt cheated out of watching the game they had paid to see. Chill got the cold shoulder, as it were, even from Ban Johnson, the American League president. He upheld the young umpire's decision but groused, "I thought we had overcome such things."

Clark Griffith had protested the forfeited game and ill will ran rampant. At an opportune moment while Johnson was on the mound, Chick Gandil threw a ball at Umpire Chill. Although he missed, giving as his alibi that Chill was a small target, the ump thumbed him out of the game. Rain interrupted the contest, but Chief Bender never let the Senators get back into it when play started again. The final score was 4-2, and Johnson headed back to Washington for a long home stand.

The weeks the team would be in Washington would give the newlyweds a chance to settle into family life. The Johnsons rented a house at 1840 Biltmore Street. The man of the house went off to work every day, and his bride pasted the evidence in the family scrapbook.

Starting on June 30, Walter Johnson ran off the first of five straight victories while enjoying the comforts of home. The string began with a relief win, 2-1, when Johnson blanked the New York Yankees for three innings until Washington scored in the 11th. Boston arrived with "their Johnson" primed for a July 3 holiday encounter. It was a rout. Walter Johnson possibly had enough from his upstart namesake. Clark Griffith rewarded his Johnson by sending him home early, with a 12-0 lead after seven innings.

July 4 is the traditional time to examine the league standings and invoke the less than inviolate rule that the team which leads the league at that midway date usually wins the pennant. Washington was in third place, four games behind Philadelphia, with Detroit in between them. The adage would hold true in the American League for another Connie Mack championship. In the other league, the New York Giants, who led everyone, led the Boston Braves most of all. They were dead last, 17 games behind the high-flying men of John McGraw. What happened is another story for another time, but it is why the Boston team has ever since been known as "the Miracle Braves."

The Red Sox sent "their Johnson" back to try again, and A. Rankin almost succeeded. George McBride stole home against the Boston rookie for the only run of the game. Clark Griffith saved Walter Johnson further exertion the next time out—as he liked to do when Washington built up a safe lead—after five innings when he led St. Louis, 8-0. Another Walter Johnson shutout, a three-hitter against Detroit followed. Ty Cobb was still out of the lineup, his broken thumb unhealed. The Tigers, who had been on the heels of the Athletics when Cobb brawled with the butcher boy, began to slip in the standings.

Cleveland came to town and brought their good luck mascot with them. "Larry" entertained the crowd before the game and invoked his mystic powers during it. Two unearned runs tipped the scales against Walter Johnson, 3-1. Cleveland left and Walter Johnson closed the long July home stand by shutting out Chicago, 4-0.

Over the span of another long road trip, Walter Johnson won only three of seven decisions. Other matters were on his mind. The Federal League was nipping at the heels of organized baseball. Hal Chase had jumped. He, too, while playing for the Buffalo Feds, was served papers during a game and was escorted off the field by bailiffs. Bob Groom, who had been a close friend of Johnson's, had jumped the Senators at the start of the 1914 season for a better offer from the St. Louis Feds.

As the road trip was winding down, Washington reached New York. In a first-person article, "Why I Signed With The Federals," which appeared the following April in *Baseball Magazine*, Johnson said the first contact by the Federal League came at that time in mid-August. Johnson said in his article that he was approached "last summer in July," but the team did not play in New York during that month.

According to Johnson, he was told that Robert B. Ward wished to see him. Ward was the principal backer of the league, sponsoring not only his own team in Brooklyn, but helping bail out other franchises. He even picked up the tab for the Fed's only minor league, the outlawed Continental League of New England. In exchange, Ward got to have a major league club named for his product. Ward's Tip Top Bread was a market leader, and the Brooklyn team was called, "the Tip Tops." Even in the present-day's sellout to commercial interests, no owner has had the commercial chutzpah to put his brand name on a team. We have not had the St. Louis Buds or, and this is reaching, the Chicago Tribunes.

Johnson said he was picked up in a limo at his hotel late in the evening and driven a long distance to Ward's estate. He arrived at midnight, and the men talked inconclusively with no firm offer being made. Johnson went back to his hotel impressed with the substance of Ward's opulent lifestyle. Surely, when he got back to Washington it was a major topic to share with his wife. In all the assessments of Johnson's team loyalty or lack of it, none of those who commented seemed to weigh the effect of his new responsibilities on Walter Johnson. He took all his marriage vows very seriously, including "for richer or poorer." Hazel's family was affluent, and Johnson was determined to keep her in the style to which she was accustomed.

Whether the meeting with Robert B. Ward took place before Johnson pitched against the Yankees is not known. It would be interesting to know, as he lost his August 17 start, 4-3, when he wild-pitched home the winning run. Had he been out too late the night before conspiring with the Federal League's representative?

Back in Washington, Walter Johnson had a stretch of games which might have put anyone's new marriage to a severe test. Hazel Johnson coped with a husband who had a sure win over the Browns rained out after he had pitched four scoreless innings. He lost 2-1 games to Detroit and Chicago in succession, and wasted a 10-inning 4-4 tie game before the team went to New York. There, he had to go 13 innings before beating the Yankees, 4-1. This is another game where Walter Johnson took charge of his team's offense, too. The New York reporters commented admiringly about his curve ball. One of the constant negative themes about Johnson was that while he had a spectacular fastball, he had only a dinky curve. That's not the way his contemporaries saw it. He was repeatedly praised for his curve ball and pitching savvy. He knew how to pitch and did not just blow batters away with speed. In the 13-inning game, Johnson scored the first Washington run. In the fourth inning he singled, stole second, and slid home in a cloud of dust on Foster's single. In the 13th inning, Johnson singled with the bases full to drive in the go-ahead run. Then, of course, he made it stand up, retiring the Yankees in the home half of the inning. He allowed only four hits in the 13-inning contest.

The team returned to Washington, and Hazel saw her husband batted out of the box for the first and only time in a home game that season. The high-flying A's hit him hard, and he took an early shower in the fourth inning. When the Red Sox came in to close the team's final long home stay, Johnson was in good form, giving only three hits in the six scoreless innings he pitched before Griffith felt the lead was big enough to send in someone else to take over.

The road trip was literally something to write home about, although the Senators had fallen out of contention. Johnson began by shutting out St. Louis, 1-0. In Chicago, on September 21, despite allowing only six hits in a 13-inning game which the Senators finally won for Johnson with a late rally, 6-1, a false negative charge was entered against Walter Johnson in the record book. Eighty years later it is still there. *The Sporting News* has assumed the role of keeper of baseball's records, and they have never corrected the mistaken entry against Walter Johnson. Each edition continues to report him guilty of making four wild pitches in the fourth inning of the September 21 game. The Al Kermisch "truth squad" has not broken through the stonewalling that takes place when incorrect entries are proven wrong. Kermisch published the correction in SABR's *Baseball Research Journal*, giving the play-by-play account of the fourth inning when the four wild pitches were supposed to have occurred. Quoting from the evening edition of the *Chicago Daily News* on September 21, 1914, Kermisch cites: "Collins dropped a single in short left-center. Daly was called out on strikes. Collins stole second. Foster threw out Schalk. Collins scored on a wild pitch, tying the count. Roth grounded out, Morgan to Gandil. One run, one hit *and one wild pitch.*"

Johnson won again in extra innings at Detroit, a 10-inning affair that the Senators won, 6-2, with a four-run rally. Back to Washington as the season was closing down, the Athletics again edged Johnson in another 10-inning game, 3-2. The season came to a close with a final visit to Boston. There was no "their Johnson" to send against Walter Johnson. A. Rankin Johnson had jumped to the Feds. He finished the 1914 season with the Chifeds.

15

The Jump to
the Federal League

URING THE FINAL WEEKS of the 1914 season, breadwinning was as much on Walter Johnson's mind as winning baseball games. He continued to discuss his salary expectations with Clark Griffith. The manager knew of Johnson's meeting with Robert B. Ward. The always up-front Johnson had openly discussed the temptation of the new league. Griffith had moved up the usual contract negotiating time with the players he wanted to keep for the next season. He struck the despised "10-day clause" from all contracts. This was a provision that the team could terminate a player's contract for any reason, or even without one, 10 days after announcing the cut. It was a potential liability in a court case brought by a former player. However, the ubiquitous reserve clause giving the ballplayer's team exclusive claim on his future services remained. Johnson's resentment, unanimously shared with other professional ballplayers, was particularly bitter.

The old wound of the fine he had been assessed in 1908 for a postseason appearance against the independent Logan Squares in Chicago was reopened. Instead of being offered as compensation for a unsettled injustice, a check for $50 sent to him by league president Ban Johnson was unexplained. The even-tempered Johnson was angered. Was it a coincidence that the money was suddenly reimbursed while he was negotiating a new contract? The incident cost the American League Johnson's unswerving loyalty. He was ready to swerve.

When the season ended, Walter Johnson waited in Washington to continue his salary discussion with Clark Griffith. It was put off, briefly as it turned out, until after the World Series. After the Miracle Braves of Boston romped over Connie Mack's Athletics in four straight, the two men tried to reach a solution.

The amount of $20,000 a season was in Walter Johnson's mind. Even if it was inflated, for bargaining purposes it was in line with the numbers rumored to be available from the Feds, who were dangling $18,000 in front of him. Johnson was willing to negotiate. There were advantages to remaining in Washington. However, Clark Griffith did not have the final say. Benjamin Minor, Jr., the club president, had to approve any salary Griffith offered. He and Griffith had different perceptions of the continued threat of the new league. The 1914 season had been a financial disaster for most of the outlaw franchises. Only the almost bottomless resources of the well-heeled franchise owners had kept them afloat. However, rich people do not remain wealthy by sticking to losing propositions. Minor believed, as did other owners, that the Federal League would fold over the winter. Griffith was unwilling to risk losing Walter Johnson on that assumption. Finally, unsigned, the pitcher and his new wife left for Kansas and their Coffeyville farm. Hazel had never seen it, and Walter's parents had not yet met their daughter-in-law. The welcome mat was out in Coffeyville, and from all reports, Minnie Johnson and Hazel hit it off fine right from the start.

For Hazel, an only child, meeting a farmhouse full of in-laws could have been a culture shock. However, her devotion to her husband and her natural friendliness made it an easy transition. Hazel Johnson was now a farmer's wife and expected to learn the lifestyle that went with the role. Among other matters, she learned more about her husband's boyhood life. There were events to be remembered that he had been too shy or diffident to tell her about. He probably squirmed when his brother Earl told the family anecdote about Walter and the wolves. He had been about 12 when he led his young brother and little sister on a trek across distant fields. When they spotted a wolf, the children tracked it to its lair. The wolf disappeared among rocks, and the children discovered a tunnel, down into which Walter wiggled his way. He hauled out five pups for them to play with, never realizing that had the dens been connected, the mother wolf would have torn him to pieces.

Another incident Walter Johnson was not allowed to live down had happened after the family moved back to Kansas. His favorite sport, coon hunting, had almost cost him his life. Earl Johnson told how one wintry night, the hunting party was crossing an iced-over pond in the dark when it gave way and Walter Johnson had fallen into the freezing water. Wearing heavy hunting garb, he floundered to stay afloat. It was minutes before the others could find a tree branch long enough to reach him. He grasped the end of the limb and was hauled to safety. A lesser man, Earl pointed out to his sister-in-law, would not have been able to stay afloat or survive the numbing icy plunge.

Hazel Johnson got to see her husband pitch another ball game. The third-annual Walter Johnson Day baseball game was played at Forest Park on October 28. Once again, nearby local pride was at stake in choosing Johnson's mound opponent. Mutt Williams was imported from just across the Oklahoma border. A mountain of a man, at 6-foot-3½ and well over 200 pounds, he had briefly been Walter Johnson's teammate. He won his only start in 1913, in the "farce game" which ended the season and added points to Johnson's ERA. But he had failed to survive in 1914, pitching in only a few early-season games before returning to a minor league career. Mutt Williams pitched for the nearby Nowata's town team, and the game ended 10-5 in Walter Johnson's favor.

The baseball fans in town had followed their townsman's season. The Coffeyville *Journal* kept track of his games. The town's sports took pride in his 28 wins but wondered why he had lost 18 times. Billy Evans, the tireless Johnson observer, summed it up in *The Sporting News*. His article was headed: "What's The Matter With Walter Johnson?" The subhead gave Evans' conclusion: "He Asserts Constant Use Of Twisters Will Injure Any Pitcher." As is often the circumstance, the headline writer had not read the copy carefully. Although Evans puzzled over Johnson's form reversal and observed he had switched from constant fastballs to more curves and slow balls, he let Johnson make his own case.

Johnson, probably wondering why he had to defend a season's performance when he led the league in wins, games, complete games, strikeouts, and shutouts, pointed to the number of low-score games he had lost. He insisted he felt in great shape, had no sore arm, but that his mates had been unlucky behind him. As a side note, Evans, who must have been paid for the length of his pieces and not the breadth of their wisdom, recalled, as he inevitably did, umpiring Johnson's debut game. He had the score wrong, but the point was made that the rookie relied only on speed and almost beat a team which feasted on fastball pitching. Evans also dropped in a remembered observation made by Cy Young of Johnson during his rookie season. "Why that fellow is faster than Rusie," said the veteran whose career straddles the change from the 19th century to the 20th. "He gets up speed without any exertion. Those long, sweeping arms enable him to get a world of stuff on the ball." Cy had predicted a long career for Johnson.

October lengthened into November, and the unsettled future nagged at Walter Johnson. He wanted the best income he could arrange for as long as it could be kept coming. In addition, he needed some serious money right away. A farmer is always one natural disaster away from calamity. Life on the Kansas plains was not guaranteed to be safe from natural or man-made hazards. Johnson wanted to build stronger outbuildings, improve the breed of his livestock and have a nest egg against adversity. In addition, his brother Leslie was financially strapped by his faltering automobile business.

Griffith had to put Johnson off while he and President Minor debated the strength of the Federal League. Also, the Feds had dented the box offices where they shared a city with a club in organized baseball or were near enough to draw away customers. The Fed's Baltimore franchise encroached on Washington's territory. Competition is not always good for business, as baseball promoters learned.

In Chicago, the Federal League's Whales, with a northside location, had survived. They were the property of Charles Weeghman, an entrepreneur in food and transportation. He owned restaurants and taxi cabs. His pockets were not deep, but his drive was always in high. A legacy he left when the inevitable collapse of the Federal League came after the 1915 season, was Wrigley Field. It is on the same site and foundations as the ballpark where the Chicago Whales played.

Charles Weeghman wrote to Walter Johnson and proposed that if he was serious about improving his fortunes in baseball, he should come to Chicago and talk it over. Johnson replied that farm business kept him too occupied to make the trip. Weeghman dispatched his manager, Joe Tinker, to Coffeyville to negotiate with the pitcher. Quicker than a ball could be relayed via the doggerel trio, "Tinker to Evers to Chance," a proposition was worked out. The Chicago team of the Federal League would pay Johnson $20,000 a season for three years. What's more, they would advance him $6,000 on his first year's salary *and pay him a bonus of $10,000 to sign a contract.* That was a lot of up-front money, and baseball's premier pitcher was tempted. The Feds desperately needed some big name players. In 1914 they had few box-office drawing cards. Hal Chase, the Prince of Darkness, and Joe Tinker were well known. Benny Kauff and a very young Edd Roush gained stature as they led Indianapolis to the pennant, although too few people paid to see them do it. The team was moved to Newark for 1915.

Fielder Jones, a very respected former player and manager who had taken over the last-place Federal League team in St. Louis late in the season, had an owner, Phil Ball, who was ready to splurge. Jones was given the courtesy of a visit to Coffeyville. He offered $20,000 a season, but nothing was said about a bonus or salary advance. At that point, Johnson later said, he was confident Washington eventually would agree to a salary somewhere around $18,000. Johnson wanted to stay with the team. He was satisfied with life on the Potomac and, more importantly, Hazel was literally at home there. She was established with friends and social activities, and her parents would live there as long as her father kept getting reelected to Congress. In the give-and-take of negotiation, it was a factor. Fielder Jones' offer was a nonstarter. If Walter Johnson was to go anywhere, it would be to the Windy City.

Then the mailman delivered a letter which lit the fuse under Walter Johnson. It had been written and dated in Washington, D.C., on November 28, a Saturday. Benjamin Minor, Jr., the team president and an attorney, had written a cold, take-it-or-leave-it letter. It blamed Johnson for having a poor season; he won only 28 games. This virtually destroyed the team's chances for the future as Ben Minor viewed it. Instead of offering an increase in the range where Griffith had been talking, the ultimatum was to sign a new contract for $12,500 a year. If Johnson did not accept, the club would invoke its right to impose the same terms that had prevailed in 1914. In other words, $10,000 and forget any extras.

An angry Walter Johnson reacted by telling Charles Weeghman that he accepted the offer of the Chicago Federal League team. Weeghman immediately wired the bonus money, $10,000, and another $6,000 salary advance. Johnson was his. It was a bombshell that rocked the baseball world.

Clark Griffith was stunned. He had learned of Minor's letter too late to stop it, but had sent one of his own pleading with Walter Johnson not to be offended by the president's letter. Matters could be mended, Griffith's letter assured his star pitcher. Johnson later explained, "If I had received that letter in the morning, instead of the afternoon, I would at least have put off signing with the Federal League."

Walter Johnson's recollections of past events were never precise. He surely never deliberately lied, but in some cases, particularly in explaining his jump to the Feds and his jump back again, he was at least ingenuous. It does not seem possible for Minor's letter of

November 28 to have traveled by post from Washington to Coffeyville and a deal be worked out with Chicago and announced on December 4. It had to be a standing offer, already understood by both parties, for Johnson to accept so soon after getting President Minor's letter.

The news that the beloved pitcher, Walter Johnson, had abandoned his fans in Washington caused bitter reaction. It was not forgotten that Johnson had told the press during the baseball season, when the Federal League was trying to lure established stars from their teams, that he would jump to the Feds if they offered him more than Washington was willing to pay. Baseball fans of that time believed that an athlete would always be loyal to his team. Johnson's understanding of team loyalty was the same as it had been in 1910 when D.A. Fletcher was blowing smoke about a new league. He had not changed. In Johnson's view, once signed he would be 100 percent committed to his team. But, if someone made a better offer for the next season, he would put the well-being of himself and his family first.

There were letters of rage in the sporting press. If there had been call-in "talk shows" on Marconi's new invention, people would have flooded them with bitter complaints about Walter Johnson's treachery. Angry people said they would never again go to a ball game when Walter Johnson was going to pitch.

Whether or not Clark Griffith was truly outraged, he was deeply hurt. Not only did he feel betrayed that Johnson had not contacted him after getting Minor's letter, but his own future was threatened. Griffith was more than a bench manager. He had continually invested his money in the club's stock and had borrowed to do this. Without Walter Johnson, the team would not be a contender. In November, a petition to overturn the ban on Sunday baseball had been thrown out of court. Not being able to play at home on the Sabbath cut 11 good paydays from the schedule. It meant extra travel and weekend exhibition hops. The reason Manager Griffith pulled Walter Johnson out of lopsided ball games early was so he could start him again sooner. The crowd was always larger when Walter Johnson was scheduled to pitch.

Clark Griffith was not about to give up. He had some legal underpinning, although it was shaky. It depended on a favorable interpretation in court of the very provision which had caused Johnson to jump. Eventually, the Supreme Court would grant organized baseball immunity from antitrust laws, but in 1914 the reserve clause was a vulnerable proviso to risk. Still, it provided some basis for hope that Walter Johnson would at least not be allowed to pitch for his new owners.

Griffith would rather let lawyer-owner Ben Minor pursue that trail. He knew that money would be a better argument with Walter Johnson. He got Minor to agree to match the Chicago salary. However, the Washington president said he could not also reimburse Charles Weeghman for the cash bonus he had paid to Johnson.

Clark Griffith needed to get to Johnson and asked Fred Clarke, the Pittsburgh manager who was his friend and also a Kansas farmer, to help. Clarke, still being a good sport about letting the teenage Johnson end up with Washington, was willing to help them try to get him back. He approached Johnson. Would the pitcher meet with Griffith? Johnson agreed, and a meeting was arranged in Kansas City. Griffith knew he might talk Johnson into calling off his deal in Chicago, but he still lacked the cash to repay the up-front money Weeghman had already paid to Johnson, most of which had already been invested in farm improvements and used to pay debts.

Griffith appealed to Ban Johnson to use league funds to buy back Walter Johnson. More austere than astute, the frosty founder of the American League refused to help. Desperate, Griffith knew one baseball man who had $10,000 and a reason to fear Johnson's jump to the Feds. Charley Comiskey had made his fortune in baseball. Griffith pointed out that if Walter Johnson was pitching for the Whales over on the northside the same day the White Sox were playing on the southside, Comiskey's gate receipts would be off considerably. The Chicago owner did not like it, but agreed with the Old Fox's logic. That took care of that aspect. Johnson could keep the $10,000 he got from Weeghman, and the Chicago Whales would be reimbursed. The $6,000 salary advance could be worked out. Maybe, Griffith thought, he could get Minor to do the same; prepay Johnson part of his 1915 earnings in advance, or Johnson could make restitution out of his salary from Washington if he could not repay it all at once.

Griffith's real task was to convince Johnson he was more obliged to help Washington than to hurt it by helping Chicago. Johnson said he liked and approved of Weeghman, Tinker, and company, and he did not want to dash their hopes and plans. On the other hand, he could see how his defection would all but destroy Griffith, the man who had become his friend after taking over as manager. They were as close as an employer and employee could be. As Johnson said later, "I had got in a position where whatever I did was wrong."

Reluctantly, Walter Johnson disengaged from the Chicago arrangement. The Federal League said they would take the case to court. It was not a comfortable position for Walter Johnson. And, the fans had turned against him.

Griffith talked Walter Johnson into accepting a three-year guaranteed contract for $12,5000 a season. This was far less than Weeghman's Chicago Whales had offered, but Washington was far more likely to be in business for the next three seasons. Also, there was a war on. There were rumors of shortened seasons, maybe none at all. And besides, the arrangement let him keep the $10,000 signing bonus.

If Walter Johnson was trying to impress his new bride with his fiscal acumen, he could point out that he had ended up with better than a 50 percent salary boost, and a $10,000 cash bonus as well. His politician father-in-law, Congressman Roberts, would admire that kind of wheeling and dealing. However, Walter Johnson was not a wheeler and dealer. He had stumbled into his financial windfall and would regard the loss of the fans' affections as not worth the money he had pocketed.

As it turned out, Johnson was never taken to court over the matter, and the fans, happy to have a winner back, resumed their idolatry. His baseball spikes might be worn over feet of clay, but in a place like Washington, D.C., ethically he stood tall among the politicians and powerbrokers.

In exchange for an opportunity to present his version of the flip-flop with the Feds, Walter Johnson allowed his privacy to be invaded. He was not a recluse, but he was a shy and very private person. His home was his castle and the drawbridge was only lowered by special invitation. F.C. Lane, the editor of *Baseball Magazine*, filled an interesting niche in the coverage of baseball. J.G. Taylor Spink, nephew of Alfred Spink, who had founded *The Sporting News* in 1888, had become its editor in 1914. With *The Sporting Life* giving over half of its content to shooting and hunting, Spinks' publication was justified in calling itself, "The Bible of Baseball." The focus was on box scores and spot news. F.C. Lane's monthly publication was produced at a more leisurely pace and served up interviews, profiles, and opinion pieces.

Whether Lane mostly wanted to do an "at home" article about the newly wedded Walter Johnson or get the real slant about the Federal League situation, two separate pieces appeared in the April 1915 issue of his magazine. One was headed, "Why I Signed With The Federal League," and the other, "At Coffeyville with Walter Johnson." The first appeared over the facsimile signature of Walter Johnson, and the other was bylined F.C. Lane. It is most likely that both pieces were written by Lane, composing the article attributed to Johnson from notes he had made while visiting Coffeyville. Lane was an unusual literary personage. He had known almost nothing about baseball before becoming editor of the magazine. However, he became expert at reporting the affairs of the game and produced excellent interviews. Then, after 20 years, when the magazine began to crumble faster than its cheaply printed pages, F.C. Lane began a new writing career. Already in his 60s, he produced a series of travel books, circling the globe seven times with his wife in search of topics and authenticity. He turned out dozens of texts which were staples of the trade for years, some even outliving him when he died in 1984, at age 98.

Lane gives us a first-hand description of life on the Johnson farm. He offers little about his hostess except to say she was a charming young lady and to quote her as saying, "I never knew much about baseball before I met Walter but no one is more interested in it now than I am." Lane observes that Hazel "seems well content with the peaceful solitude and easy abundance of a Kansas farm. Far different from the maze of political intrigue at Washington, or the towering mountains and arid wastes of Nevada, she admits a fondness for her new home."

From Lane's interview with Frank and Minnie Johnson, we learn that they did not know about their son's marriage until they read about it in the paper. A letter telling them of the upcoming wedding reached them late, being delayed when a bellhop, to whom Johnson gave the letter for mailing, carried it around in his pocket for three days before he remembered to mail it.

Frank Johnson told Lane he had played town ball, a progenitor of today's game, as a boy in Ohio shortly after the Civil War. The article is long and well illustrated with photographs. These show the Holstein bull "Jerry" and some of the $600 Holstein cows that Johnson later sold off to square accounts with Weeghman for his salary advance. The family album provided a number of pictures of Walter Johnson's parents and brothers and sisters. His favorite dog, a collie, is posed with Blanche, Johnson's youngest sister.

"Five horses and a brace of mules do the heavy work on the farm," Johnson told Lane. "I have about half the land under cultivation. My father looks after most of the work with such help as he can get." The farm's principal crop was grain and alfalfa. There was a large silo, described as "one of the best in the state," indicating Johnson's determination to build solidly to protect his future. There were hens, but the turkeys had been sold mostly for the Christmas trade. The visit was probably made in January or early February.

Lane describes the parlor having "a huge silver trophy cup nearly filled with an accumulation of pictures, newspaper clippings, testimonials, mementos of all kinds." "In a neat case," Lane observed, "is a baseball autographed by President Taft, a warm admirer of Johnson."

F.C. Lane's train had been met by Walter Johnson, who drove him to the farm over four miles of muddy roads. For the return trip, the roads were now judged as too muddy to risk one of the garage's cars getting stuck. A horse and buggy was summoned, with a colored boy to drive it. Lane works in some stereotypical dialog and demeaning assumptions, presumably to amuse the readers of *Baseball Magazine*. There is an account of a frantic rush to the depot to catch the day's last train. It is a scenario for a Mack Sennett silent-screen comedy, as F.C. Lane barely catches his train. As the sun slowly sets over Coffeyville, F.C. Lane, the future travel writer, has provided baseball readers with a view of Johnson's life and his philosophies of living on a Kansas farm just before the First World War disrupted that way of life permanently.

16
The Head of
a Growing Family

WALTER JOHNSON put the turbulence of his Federal League misadventures behind him by settling his obligation to Charles Weeghman. He sold a herd of steers from his Coffeyville farm for $6,000 and reimbursed the Chicago Whales for the salary advance they had paid him. A statement found among the American League notes in *The Sporting Life* sounds more like the forthright Johnson than the understanding from other accounts that Charley Comiskey's till was tapped to settle all obligations.

Johnson also began the season under a dire cloud of assumption by Christy Mathewson. The Giants superstar was quoted widely for his views about baseball matters. Matty, speaking through the Wheeler Syndicate, expressed a doomsayer's view: "I doubt if he [Johnson] plays much ball with anyone next summer." Matty claimed his contacts with the Federal League told him that Johnson's abrogation of his contract would be the focus of the outlaw league's legal appeals. Like most sports page pontification—then or now—Matty's forecast proved wrong.

Walter Johnson headed for Washington's spring training camp in Charlottesville, Virginia. He reported to Clark Griffith on March 14, and it was observed that the big hurler was a bit underweight. The usual Johnson springtime cold was soon reported. Another piece of training camp news certainly did not impact the abstemious pitcher. Clark Griffith banned cigarette smoking. Players, whether puffing the dandified "tailor-mades" from Sweet Caporal or rolling their own from a Bull Durham sack, would be hit with $25 fines for lighting up. Cigars and pipes were not included in the ban nor were chaws of tobacco. The players were free to squirt tobacco juice into cuspidors or spit at outdoor targets.

Clark Griffith had failed to persuade league president Ban Johnson to make Opening Day a Washington fixture. The benefit to the league and the national pastime of having the president of the United States ceremoniously throw out the first ball, had been passed up in favor of standardization and nonfavoritism by the stern American League leader. However, for 1915 it was Washington's turn to open the season at home. President Woodrow Wilson's bereavement following the death of his wife on August 6 the previous year had caused him to pass up all late-season ball games in 1914. However, for the 1915 inaugural, he was on hand to do his top-hatted duty, and Walter Johnson obliged the team's "good luck charm" with another opening day shutout. He allowed the New York Yankees only two hits and coasted to a 7-0 win.

One of baseball's darker figures cast a shadow of coming events in Johnson's next start, against Boston. Carl Mays made his major league debut in a 4-2 loss to Johnson. Mays' underhand pitch was hard to follow, and his attitude toward the risk of hitting batters was the opposite of Johnson's. Mays asserted that the plate belonged to the pitcher. Any batter encroaching on that area became a target. Mays eventually would throw the only fatal pitch in major league history. Had Walter Johnson been as uncaring as Mays, it is likely that he would have claimed a victim long before the submariner did.

Although Johnson's pitching was outstanding, the team stumbled early. In four starts, from April 24 through May 9, his teammates gave Johnson only one run. They were shut out three times, although Johnson allowed only five earned runs over four games. The only game he salvaged was a 1-0 victory over the A's. He got the least support in a 1-0 loss to Detroit when the Senators were blanked on a one-hitter by Ray Dubuc. Then Eddie Cicotte beat Johnson, 4-3, to drop him below .500 with four losses against three wins. It was the only time that season that Johnson would have a losing record. He won six of his next seven starts and then tacked on three straight shutouts to bring him to a 12-5 mark by the end of June.

During that winning spurt, Johnson's bat helped his cause. In Cleveland he amazed the natives by belting a pitch over the left-field fence. League Park was now five years old and Johnson's was the first ball to clear the barrier. It was measured at 400 feet to the point were the ball landed. Johnson also tripled in the game and was called out at the plate trying to stretch it into a home run. Johnson homered again in his next game, this time impressing the Tiger fans in Detroit. He always hit well in the Detroit ballpark.

Johnson was even more devastating to the Tigers on his next visit. On June 19 he missed hitting for the cycle. A home run was all that was lacking as he singled, doubled, and tripled. He left the game early with a 7-0 lead after seven innings and Doc Ayers came in to complete the shutout. According to the scoring rules of the time, Johnson was credited with a shutout and it was counted among the 113 career shutouts he claimed when he retired. However, along with two other similar incomplete scoreless games, it was later removed from his shutout credits. This lowered his record to a seemingly permanent 110 shutouts. Like the point of whether he won 416 or 417 games, how many shutouts he pitched is primarily of statistical interest. By any measure, 110 career shutouts is astounding.

Next, Johnson added a pair of regulation-length shutouts, blanking Boston 5-0 and Philadelphia 2-0. He was getting much better support. In the win over Boston, Chick Gandil, who had stabilized the Senators' infield, stole four bases, including a theft of home.

A greater joy came to the summertime Washington residence of Walter and Hazel Johnson. *The Sporting Life* coyly reported: "A brand new twirler arrived in Washington, D.C., July 1. He weighs eight and a half pounds. The stork dropped him at 8:30 that night at the home of Walter Johnson, the famous pitcher of the Washington team. Both mother and son are doing nicely. Walter married a daughter of Representative Roberts, of Nevada, last August." It had really been the previous June, but either way the margin was safe enough to avoid raised eyebrows.

When Washington went to New York for an Independence Day doubleheader, the Senators reverted to their usual level of play behind Johnson. July 4 fell on Sunday, a nonplaying day in New York City. On July 3, Johnson saved the adjusted holiday opener for Washington by striking out two of three batters in a ninth-inning rescue. In the nightcap, although he allowed only one earned run, Washington made seven errors to kick away the ball game, 4-1.

It was not until Walter Johnson, Jr., was two weeks old that his absent daddy could arrange to bring home a game-winning ball. The team had gone from New York to Boston and Chicago and then St. Louis before the new father won a game. He had managed a 1-1 rain-ended five-inning tie with Chicago and also earned a dramatic save against the White Sox. Johnson came in with the bases loaded in the eighth inning and one out. A double play ended the inning, and the White Sox went out in quick order in the ninth. In St. Louis, Johnson batted sixth in the lineup and had one hit. It did not help. The Senators were shut out, 3-0. Then the next day, July 19, in Cleveland, Walter Johnson won an unusual contest.

The game has been warped into one of those recurring anecdotes involving the storybook pitcher. In the telling, and retelling, it has been used to explain the abject fear Johnson's fastball instilled in batters. Like so many of the apocryphal stories associated with famous people, its original version is difficult to pin down. We can believe that someone must have passed up an opportunity to take a third strike from the fireballing Johnson and said, in effect, they would be just as happy to settle for fanning on two pitches. Go back far enough and someone probably defaulted on a final chance at a fastball from Hoss Radbourn or Amos Rusie in the 19th century.

Billy Evans was a very close observer of Walter Johnson's career as well as a part of it. He never stopped reminding readers that he had been the home plate umpire for Johnson's debut game. As a columnist for *The Sporting News*, he attributed the remark about defaulting on a Johnson third strike to Ray Chapman, saying it took place in 1915 at Cleveland. Evans remembered that after taking two strikes, Chapman tossed aside his bat and told the home plate umpire, "I don't want the third strike, Johnson's too fast." The July 19 game is the only one which matches Evans' details. It is the single game played that season between Washington and Cleveland which he umpired with Johnson on the mound in a game played in Cleveland's League Park. The story had been echoed since by other overwhelmed batters, such as when Leo Durocher faced the untested high school fastballer Bob Feller in an exhibition game. The particulars of Evans' account all fit together, but the moral applied to them does not match the circumstances. Rather than wanting to avoid the inherent dangers of Johnson's fastball, Chapman simply wanted to get through with a game that had been incredibly out of kilter from the start.

For example, in the first inning Washington stole eight bases. Steve O'Neill, rated one of the best, was the catcher. The game was so lopsided that the fun-loving Nick Altrock, the team's 39-year-old pitching coach, replaced Johnson in the seventh inning with the score at 8-0. The out-of-hand game ended with a score of 11-4. This particular game, though, hardly qualifies as an example of Johnson's devastating strikeout prowess, particularly as *he had no strikeouts at all in the game*. The scorer charged Chapman with a strikeout for failing to finish his time at bat, but he did not credit it to Johnson.

It makes a good story, even if it is not based on a batter's fear of a Johnson fastball. However, the same quotation was also attributed to Joe Gedeon, a former Johnson teammate and a principal in the swimming accident at the Chicago beach. Gedeon played most of his career with the Yankees and Browns, finishing in 1920. Shirley Povich retold the story in his column "This Morning..." in the *Washington Post*, January 25, 1956. Evans had just died and Povich was telling his Washington readers about him. On balance, it seems more likely Povich's memory lapsed and, with a deadline to meet, he did not put the incident in the cross hairs of a researcher's sights. Then again, like tales which are more likely apocryphal than not, maybe it was someone other than Chapman or Gedeon. Ping Bodie, a baseball character whose gift for memorable observations, perhaps all of which were made up for him, has also been named in the telling of the anecdote.

Moving on to Detroit where the long road trip would end, Ray Dubuc, something of a nemesis for Johnson, again shut out the Senators, this time 2-0. The next day, Walter Johnson finally closed the road trip with a save. Again an anecdotal tale fails to match the reality of the game's box score. The admiring writer, Shirley Povich, who left no coincidence undeveloped if it added to Walter Johnson's luster, described the rescue this way: "Johnson, off the bench, took six warm-up pitches and struck out the next three batters, Donie Bush, Marty Kavanaugh and Ossie Vitt, with the bases full." That's not quite accurate. The box score, while crediting the three strikeouts, also shows that Johnson faced four batters and hit one of them.

Finally, the proud new father got back to his family with only a 3-4 road trip to tell Walter Jr. about. However, once back home, Johnson produced a game worthy of any son's approval. On July 29, Cleveland came to Washington and started a rookie named Roy Walker, who took Johnson to the 10th inning of a 1-1 tie. Then Johnson ended the game in time for dinner. He hit a drive off the center-field wall that scored George McBride from first base. Although only credited with a double, it was claimed that Johnson would have had an inside-the-park home run had not the winning run already scored. Johnson's swat came on his fourth time at bat against Walker, after the rookie had previously fanned him three times.

On August 2, the eighth anniversary of his debut game, Johnson easily defeated St. Louis, 5-1. It brought his season's record to 17-9. It was his 195th career win, an average of well over 20 games won a year. However, Walter Johnson's games were not always a steady progression of evenly pitched innings. On August 6, he struggled through a hot-and-cold demonstration to an 8-6 victory over the White Sox. He reached the eighth inning with a tidy 2-0 lead, only to give up six runs in the eighth and lose the lead. Then, in the home half of the inning, Washington came back with its own six-run rally to regain the lead, 8-6. That is the way the game ended. In the ninth inning, Johnson recovered his form and held the lead, fanning the side and making Eddie Collins his final victim.

Detroit came to Washington for the last series of the Senators' home stand, and the thing Johnson dreaded most happened again. This time it was the Tigers' peppery third baseman Ossie Vitt who crowded both the plate and his luck. Leading off the game, he caught an inside pitch in the head. It immediately raised an ugly bump and also unnerved the speedball pitcher. George Moriarty, who was in professional baseball as a player, umpire, and manager for 50 years, replaced Vitt, who was carried off the field. Moriarty was in his final season as a player. His grandson, actor Michael Moriarty, collects anecdotes about his celebrated forebear. The pugnacious Moriarty heckled Johnson throughout the game, and the shaken pitcher lost his composure. The Tigers won, 8-2, with 11 hits, two walks, and, of course, one hit batter.

Then it was time for another of the extended road trips teams traveled in that era. In Boston, Johnson met up with a red-hot Red Sox rookie named Babe Ruth. It was the first of many games the two would play against each other, first as rival pitchers and, eventually, when the Babe had become the Home Run King, as opponents in their pitcher-batter roles. This time, Ruth, pitching in his first full season, won 4-3.

In Detroit, Johnson won easily, 8-1. It was another game with an unusual event. Washington scored a run without being charged a time at bat. Gandil and Acosta walked, Williams sacrificed, and McBride scored Gandil with a sacrifice fly before careless base running by Acosta made the third out. Johnson's victory ended a nine-game Tiger winning streak.

Johnson, who was often involved in extra-inning games, to a large extent because his team scored so few runs for him, became involved in an unusual 14-inning game in Chicago. On August 25, he came in to hold the score at 4-4 in the 13th inning. Then, in the top of the 14th, Johnson started a three-run rally with a single and nailed down the game by holding the White Sox runless in the bottom half of the inning. It was the third consecutive extra-inning game for the White Sox. They had just played two 16-inning games and, following this 14-inning affair, were involved in another extended game, which Johnson saved in relief.

A new star began to rise in the American League in 1915. A graduate of the University of Michigan, George Sisler had joined his former college coach, Branch Rickey, who managed the St. Louis Browns. He would become the greatest player ever in the history of that usually woeful franchise. He broke in as a pitcher, and on August 29, took on Walter Johnson in a pitching duel, which Sisler won, 2-1, when the Browns scored a pair of unearned runs.

The Senators returned to Washington to finish out the season, playing almost all their September games at home. It was a happy month for the young Johnson family. Father was home every night and when at work, he never lost a game. Johnson swept through the balance of the schedule, winning seven games in a row. He capped the season's 27-13 record by beating Boston, 3-1. His old rival, Smokey Joe Wood, and the new one, Babe Ruth, were combined against him in the season's finale. With eight more strikeouts, he pushed his strikeout total to 203 to lead the league again.

Walter Johnson's 27 wins were the most in the league, as were his 39 starts and 35 complete games. Two of his incomplete games came when he left with huge leads. The other two games he did not finish were the one when Washington made seven errors behind him, and the game in which he had beaned leadoff batter Ossie Vitt. Johnson, never missing a turn, pitched 337 innings. Although only 8.2 innings were pitched in relief, two of Johnson's victories were earned that way, and he had four saves. He led the league in shutouts, with seven.

The Cinderella Team of 1912 still had Walter Johnson as its Prince Charming, but after finishing second twice and then third, Washington had slipped to fourth. Clark Griffith began to recruit players who would eventually pull Cinderella's coach all the way to the palace.

On August 7, a rookie pitcher mopped up a game already lost to the White Sox. He would fail as a pitcher, but as an outfielder, Sam Rice became the greatest the Senators would ever have. In Rice's debut game, the short-handed Senators had a right fielder named Walter Johnson who had one hit in three trips.

On September 20, Chick Gandil was replaced at first base by an even better first baseman and a far more sterling character, Joe Judge,

119

who would be Washington's first baseman for 18 years. He would become Walter Johnson's roommate after Clyde Milan's own starring career ended.

Walter and Hazel Johnson vacated their rented home in Washington and went back to their farm in Coffeyville, Kansas. His prize herd of steers had been sold, but there were puppies for his son, Walter Jr., to grow up with. Walter Johnson was a fine father. As his family grew, he would teach his sons to hunt and fish, and pamper his daughters. Education would be a priority. He told reporters, "Our children will be given the best education they can get. I was not fortunate enough to go to college but my children will if that is their ambition." Asked whether Walter Jr. would be encouraged to be a ballplayer, Johnson said he would help his son but not push him. As it turned out, Walter Jr., and the two brothers he would eventually have, loved baseball. None would become successful, although Walter Jr. briefly played professionally.

As usual, Johnson responded to an invitation to pitch a post-season game. The Coffeyville rooters did not scout up a game for the annual Walter Johnson Day. However, on October 24, two other communities imported star pitchers to uphold civic pride. Webb City, Missouri recruited Walter Johnson from over the state line, whereas Pittsburgh, Kansas, put their hopes and money on Rube Foster of the Boston Red Sox. He had just won two games from the Philadelphia Phillies in the 1915 World Series. After eight scoreless innings, Johnson, idle for almost a month, weakened and lost, 3-0. Then it was back to his farm and the autumn harvest, where he put in a winter of chores that would keep him in shape for the next baseball season.

17

A Plague of
One-Run Losses

THE BALL CLUB that Clark Griffith put together as a first-year manager in 1912 unraveled in 1916. Although the cogs had been slipping for several years, few new parts replaced them. Griffith sold Chick Gandil to Cleveland for $7,000 and turned the first base job over to Joe Judge. The rookie was not quite ready, and the money received for Gandil did not buy players of value. A continuing stream of "wannabes" and off-brand prospects, from semipro and college ranks, passed through. Victory depended too often on Walter Johnson alone. A tall, slender Texan, Bert Gallia had emerged from the ranks of Griffith's pitching prospects in 1915 and would help Johnson keep the Senators out of the basement. What really prevented the Senators from carrying Walter Johnson down to the ignominy of last place, was the Philadelphia Athletics. Connie Mack sold off his best players, and their replacements lost 117 games while winning only 36. How bad were they? The 1962 New York Mets, considered the most pathetic team in more recent times, lost 75 percent of the time. The A's were even worse, losing 76.5 percent of their games.

Spring training in Charlottesville was less fun-filled. Germany Schaefer had broken up his act with Nick Altrock to join the Feds the year before. When the Federal League capitulated during the winter, Germany caught on with the New York Yankees as a coach and sideline comic.

Johnson made his first spring exhibition appearance against Brooklyn and pitched four scoreless innings. The lone hit was by Casey Stengel. Johnson's final tune-up was against the Philadelphia Phillies, the previous year's National League Champions. Grover Cleveland Alexander was in fine form this time, and he and Walter Johnson matched zeros as starting pitchers for three innings. Alex gave up two hits and Johnson none. Both struck out one batter.

Ban Johnson was still adamant about starting the season in Washington with the president of the United States in a key role. As a result, Walter Johnson had to take his opening day specialty to New York. Zeb Milan started the season with a lead-off home run, but the score became tied in the ninth when umpire Brick Owens called Lee Magee safe on a play he afterward admitted he missed. It was not until 11 innings had been played that Johnson had an opening day victory, 3-2. He struck out 10 and allowed only five hits. The schedule makers then gave Johnson another opener as Boston began its season with Johnson facing Babe Ruth. The day belonged to the Babe. It was the first Red Sox game without Tris Speaker, sold during the winter to Cleveland. Johnson lasted just six innings, while Ruth sailed along to a 5-1 victory. By now he was the class of left-handed pitchers in the American League. He ran off eight straight victories at the start of the season, and his 1.75 ERA would be the league's best in 1916. He and Walter Johnson would meet five times during the season, with the Babe winning four of the games.

Washington's own opener did not take place until April 20, eight days into the season. Someone goofed and the game began at 2 P.M. instead of the usual 3 P.M. Nine thousand disturbed ticket holders, arriving in mid-game, demanded refunds and got them. It was Johnson's third opening day assignment in a row, and, with Woodrow Wilson in his customary role, but playing to a smaller audience than usual, the Senators coasted to a 12-4 victory over New York. Before the Yankees left town, Johnson beat them again, 8-2. He shut out Boston, then went to Philadelphia where he split two decisions but, more interestingly, pitched his fourth game in a row without walking a batter. In fact, except for the easy home opener when he gave up four walks, he did not give a base on balls in six of his first seven starts.

In a long May home stand, Walter Johnson lost only once, winning three complete games and relieving in two games that ended in ties, once because of darkness after 14 innings and once, after Washington tied the score in the ninth, to catch a train. During the span, Washington made an overnight hop to Cleveland and back again for a Sunday game won by Walter Johnson who doubled home the winning run in the ninth. Washington was still denied home games by Sunday "blue laws" in the nation's capital. A rising tide of righteousness pressed a restrictive national agenda on Congress. Prohibition of alcohol was demanded by the Anti-Saloon League. Johnson's father-in-law, reflecting the views of his Carson City constituents, stood firm.

"A barrel of booze and a dipper on every corner," counterproposed the Nevada lawmaker.

Washington began June in Boston, where Babe Ruth and Walter Johnson met again. To improve his batting order, Griffith had Johnson hit sixth, but he went zero-for-four. Bill Carrigan, Boston's manager, was more traditional and confined Ruth to the pitcher's place at the bottom of the lineup. The Babe blanked the Senators, 1-0, on three hits. Johnson gave up four, and they each struck out six batters.

Washington's visit to Chicago coincided with the Republican National Convention, and Johnson's in-laws were there. Congressman Roberts was a delegate from Nevada and would help nominate Charles Evans Hughes for president. Johnson was to pitch a game against Ed Walsh, who was attempting to win a job with his former team. His spitball was no longer puzzling hitters. However, Johnson had to pass up the game. He had been up all night caring for his father-in-law, who had been taken ill at the convention.

Walter Johnson was pitching well enough to win almost every game had there been any hitting behind him. Griffith continued to put him high up in the batting order, but Johnson, too, was in a batting slump. Walter Johnson made his last start on the road trip in Boston, winning comfortably over the league leaders, 6-2. However, before the series in Beantown (a more than apt name under the circumstances) was over, Carl Mays had touched off a riot. Clark Griffith took a dim view of anyone deliberately throwing at his batters. His best weapon for retaliation was no help. Everyone knew about Walter Johnson's fear of injuring a batter. He had only thrown one for the team in his career and that, aimed at Frank Baker, had scared him out of doing it again. "If you think a pitcher has deliberately hit you, go after him. Throw the bat at him," Griffith told his warriors.

Bill "Rough" Carrigan's Red Sox pitchers had been pitching aggressively—Ruth and Mays in particular. When Mays bounced a ball off George McBride's head, the Senators captain flung his bat at him. Sam Agnew, once hospitalized by a Washington pitch when with St. Louis, was now the Boston catcher. In the bench-erupting brawl, Agnew leveled Clark Griffith with a punch to the jaw. The police arrested Agnew and the league suspended him. A week later he paid a $50 fine and was reinstated. Nothing seems to have been done about the instigator, Mays. He went on with his reign of terror. Not even after he had killed Ray Chapman did he relinquish his belief that home plate belonged to him, and the hell with anyone who stuck his head out over it.

On the season-dividing Fourth of July holiday, Washington was barely in first division, and Red Sox, White Sox, and Indians were pulling away. Getting back home to Washington did not improve Walter Johnson's luck. On July 3, Ray Caldwell of the New York Yankees held Washington to three hits, one by Johnson, in an 11-inning shutout loss. Johnson gave up only five hits and the only run was unearned. Then his mates made seven errors in a 5-0 loss that dropped Washington to fifth place. They gradually slipped lower the last half of the season. Walter Johnson, 13-9 at this point, lost one more game than he won over the final months. He won 25 for the year, but he lost 20.

It was a frustrating season for the King of the Mound. His throne was not resting on a firm foundation. One-run games were the norm. From July 22 to August 15 nine of the games he pitched were decided by one run. The last game of this stretch was a 13-inning duel with Babe Ruth that the Red Sox southpaw won, 1-0.

Walter Johnson settled down for the final weeks of the season with Hazel and Walter Jr. waiting for him each day to come home from work. He won his 20th game from St. Louis on August 19, 5-3, then won three more in a row. Two were shutouts, including a one-hitter against New York in a game where he homered for a 2-0 margin. He gave up only one earned run in this spurt. Then Babe Ruth beat him again in another pitchers' duel, 2-1. Washington's home season closed with another Johnson and Ruth meeting. Ruth took a 2-0 lead into the ninth when Washington tied the score. Carl Mays relieved Ruth with no one out and seemed a winner when Boston scored a run in the 10th. However, Johnson's teammates finally came through, and a two-run rally had the double effect of raising Johnson's win total to 25 and hanging a defeat on the disliked Boston pitcher.

Washington's last road trip stopped first in St. Louis. George Sisler had already been converted to a first baseman and was having his first .300 season. He would have 14 more of them, including two which topped .400. However, on September 17 he hooked up in a pitching duel with Walter Johnson. Sisler had not pitched in two months, but he won the final game of his short pitching career, 1-0. It was Johnson's fourth 1-0 defeat. Branch Rickey was not a traditionalist like Bill Carrigan, Ruth's manager. George Sisler batted third, his regular spot in the batting order.

Johnson lost two more times by a single run. He lost in 13 innings in Cleveland, 3-2, and suffered his 20th loss of the season, 6-5, in Detroit. Ty Cobb applied the *coup de grâce* with a four-and-four day.

Cobb missed winning his 10th batting title in a row, finishing second to Tris Speaker, who was then with Cleveland.

Rather than have Johnson return to Washington to finish the season, Clark Griffith excused him, and Milan and McBride. Hazel and Walter Jr. had already reached Coffeyville and waited for him there.

This time there were two post-season games to be pitched for the folks back home. The Walter Johnson Day game had been canceled the year before, but the town now considered it a Coffeyville tradition. They booked the fast Parsons team to give their local pride a real tussle; Earl Hamilton of the St. Louis Browns was brought in to pitch. The stubby righthander owned a no-hitter, pitched in 1912 against Detroit, and for three years had been the Browns' top pitcher. It was a pitchers' battle all the way, and Walter Johnson went down, 1-0. Then Johnson's actual home town, Humbolt, Kansas, where he had been born, wanted him to uphold their local pride, too. Iola, up the road a piece and a bit larger than Humbolt, had their own local big leaguer, Ad Brennan. He had not done as well professionally as Johnson, but gave him a good tussle. The game went 10 innings. Johnson's two triples and a single helped more than his pitching, as Humbolt won local bragging rights, 4-3.

Pitching for a seventh-place team, Walter Johnson led the American League with 25 victories. He pitched the most complete games, 36, failing to finish only twice. Both times came early in the season. He pitched the most innings, 371, and as usual led in strikeouts with 228. He was third in ERA with 1.89. He dropped to three shutouts. Johnson was extensively used in relief, winning four, losing three, with one save. Anyone but Walter Johnson would have been hailed for what he had achieved with such limited support. However, critics chose to complain about the 20 losses rather than praise the league-leading 25 wins.

The 1916 elections brought mixed reactions to the Johnson's Coffeyville household. Congressman Roberts had been reelected, a Republican survivor of Democrat Wilson's landslide. Although Roberts had penned a parody of the 19th century music hall hit "Slide, Kelly, Slide" ridiculing Woodrow Wilson, it did not have an effect on the national election. For that matter, Walter Johnson might privately have voted for Washington's "good luck charm" himself.

18

A Man of Peace in a World at War

CLARK GRIFFITH moved the Senators' spring training site to Augusta, Georgia, to get ready for the 1917 season. It offered warmer weather than Charlottesville and a way to pay some of the costs of preparing the team. Griffith's team would barnstorm its way home, traveling with another team and playing exhibition games along the way. He hooked up with the pioneer of road trips, Frank Bancroft, general manager of the Cincinnati Reds.

The Reds had a new manager. Christy Mathewson had been traded by John McGraw of the Giants near the end of the 1916 season. Matty pitched and won a final game for the Reds, and then gave up his active career. However, for baseball fans along the waystop trail, just seeing the legendary Christy Mathewson, with the equally legendary Walter Johnson on the opposing team, was enough.

On the way from Kansas to Georgia, Walter Johnson dropped off Hazel and Walter Jr. with his in-laws in Washington. They would move to a place of their own for the summer after the team worked its way back from Augusta. Johnson checked into camp a few days late, and Paul W. Eaton, who was then writing for *The Sporting News*, observed, "The star twirler showed signs of strain and was below his pitching weight, which is about 200 pounds." Johnson's son, the year-old Walter Jr., had recovered from a threatening stomach condition before leaving Coffeyville, Eaton reported. He added that Walter Johnson would include a spitball in his repertoire for 1917, despite Clark Griffith's attempt to abolish "freak pitches."

Clark Griffith limited Johnson's spring training appearances to bring him into the season ready to reach his peak for Opening Day. Walter Johnson began the American League season in his usual style. He pitched a three-hit shutout, winning 3-0, and struck out 11. He did this, however, in Philadelphia and went to New York for his next start, where he lost, 2-1, despite allowing only two hits. An unearned run beat him.

The home season began on Friday, April 20. Clark Griffith did not start Walter Johnson. President Woodrow Wilson did not attend. He was busy at the White House with the concerns of State. The United States had formally declared war on Germany on April 7. Vice President Thomas Marshall substituted for Wilson, and with the Texan Bert Gallia substituting for Walter Johnson, the Senators lost to Philadelphia, 6-4, in 13 innings. A less than capacity crowd, but one filled with patriotic fervor, cheered as Assistant Secretary of Navy Franklin D. Roosevelt led a parade to hoist an immense national flag on the center-field flagpole.

Walter Johnson debuted before the home fans the next day. Griffith was able to pull him after six innings with a large enough lead for the team to coast to an 11-6 win. In the week that followed, the familiar pattern of Johnson losing well-pitched games took place. His team was shut out twice in a row, losing 2-0 and 1-0. The second of these was another close loss to Babe Ruth, who pitched a two-hitter. Johnson's record dropped to 2-5 as a western road trip began in Cleveland.

While the team was traveling from St. Louis to Chicago, the Senators stopped for an exhibition game in Bloomington, Illinois. The home folks welcomed Clark Griffith who, as a teenager, had left their town for a career in professional baseball. Griff had a new concern as a manager. A few days earlier, May 18, the Conscription Law was passed. The government began drafting able-bodied men for military service. Johnson, more able-bodied than most, had no immediate worry about being called. Single men would be drafted first.

When the Senators reeled home from a disastrous trip, it was evident they would repeat the previous season's dismal outcome. It would only differ in how far down in second division they would finish. Philadelphia, despite having two pitchers named Johnson and another Johnson in the outfield, was doomed to the bottom.

Walter Johnson lost 4-2 in 10 innings to the Browns, and his record dropped to 3-7. He began to seesaw his way back toward .500. Although he did not miss a turn in rotation and pitched low-scoring games, following a 1-0 shutout of Chicago, Paul W. Eaton observed about a previously unreported illness: "Walter Johnson showed he has entirely recovered from the case of ptomaine poisoning." When he relieved against Cleveland, Hazel had to keep dinner on the stove until the game was stopped by darkness after 16 innings. Johnson had kept the 2-2 tie going for six innings, giving up only one hit.

Washington suffered at shortstop now that George McBride could no longer cover the ground expected of him. A minor league flash, Sam "Red" Crane failed to hit well enough to hold the job. Bought from the hapless Philadelphia A's, he still had difficulty earning steady employment with the Senators. He hit only .179 in 32 games. Several years later, he killed his girlfriend, becoming a rare murderer in professional baseball's ranks—and finally found a steady job as shortstop for the Pennsylvania State Penitentiary team.

When the Senators again staggered home from a losing trip, Johnson's record was 7-13. However, when he opened with a 2-1 win over Cleveland, he began a run of victories. It continued with one of those overnight trips to play a Sunday game in Cleveland and resumed back in Washington with relief wins in two successive games against Detroit. He defeated Eddie Plank, now ending his career with St. Louis, 1-0 in 11 innings, and evened his record at 13-13 by shutting out Chicago and Red Faber, 4-0.

Johnson had been undefeated during the home stand and carried on his winning streak on the road. It was stopped at nine when Red Faber reversed the results, Chicago beating Johnson, 4-1. Babe Ruth had won eight in a row, starting with Opening Day. Johnson's nine straight was the season's high and brought him above the .500 mark. He built on that as Washington struggled toward first division.

Back home again, Walter Johnson shut out the Yankees, 6-0, edged the Red Sox, 4-3 on a two-hitter, and won his 20th game shutting out the hapless A's, 4-0. The winning pattern was interrupted only in Detroit where, on Military Day, Ty Cobb hit a three-run homer and Howard Ehmke pitched a shutout to beat Johnson, 4-0.

On September 26 Johnson, in relief, gained revenge on Red Faber in a 5-4 win by Washington. The White Sox had already wrapped up the 1917 pennant. This was virtually the same team that, in 1919, would throw the World Series. Joe Jackson sentimentalists, in particular, claim the Black Sox were the best team ever in baseball. No way. The 1917 team was much better. Not only did they try harder, they tried harder all the time.

There was another Ruth versus Johnson matchup waiting in Boston. Tim Murnane, a rare beloved sportswriter, had died on February 7 in Boston. He had been sports editor of the *Boston Globe* for 30 years. During that time he had also been president of one of the best-run minor leagues, the New England League. Murnane was a link with baseball's early history. He had played for Boston in the National League's first season, 1876. He was 66 when he dropped dead attending Victor Herbert's *Eileen* at the Shubert Theatre. Called "the Silver King" for his mane of white hair and large, silvery mustache, he had been widowed at 50 and left with two children. His second wife, Anne Dowling, raised the children, and Murnane's sudden death left them in need. The baseball fraternity, and the sports world in general, rallied to their aid.

A date was found when the Red Sox would be free to play a fundraising game, and that was Thursday, September 27. More than 17,000 people turned out in a festive mood. The Ziegfeld Follies was in town, and headliners Fannie Brice and Will Rogers appeared at the ball game. Show girls sold special programs. Rogers did his cowboy roping act and worked with the most popular of the All-Stars who came to play the Red Sox. Tris Speaker was a Texan and expert at rodeo stunts. Then he was still considered the greatest player in the team's history. He now ranks fifth-highest on the all-time list of career batting averages at .345. One point behind is Ted Williams, a later Boston icon and far, far less popular as a player than was Tris Speaker.

The All-Stars flanked Speaker in center with Ty Cobb and Joe Jackson. That outfield's lifetime averages is led by Cobb's .367, with Jackson third-best at .356, followed by Speaker's .345. The All-Stars were managed by Connie Mack. Diplomatically, he rotated the three great outfielders in center field. At first base he had Boston native Stuffy McInnis, who had been part of the A's $100,000 infield. Another local favorite, Rabbit Maranville, the key player of the 1914 Boston "Miracle Braves," was the shortstop. The only National Leaguer on the All-Stars rode a sleeper from Cincinnati to be there. Murnane had watched over his career since the Rabbit started in the New England League in 1911. Ray Chapman moved over to second base, and Buck Weaver played third base. Steve O'Neill, the Cleveland catcher, caught the game's first pitcher, Urban Shocker. Mack decided to close with Walter Johnson. Despite the holiday atmosphere, players of the caliber of the All-Stars were there to win.

Babe Ruth began by holding the All-Stars hitless through the first five innings. Shocker and Howard Ehmke, who replaced him in the fourth, had matched Ruth's zeros with goose eggs of their own. Rube Foster, who had been one of Boston's top pitchers, tried his lame arm one more time. He made the most of what was to be his final appearance as a major leaguer. He continued the shutout to the end.

Connie Mack waved Walter Johnson into the game in the bottom of the seventh. In the eighth inning the Red Sox finally scored. With two out, manager Jack Barry beat out a single and Dick Hoblitzel also singled. Duffy Lewis then nailed a Johnson fastball and drove it deep to center field, over Ty Cobb's head, for a triple. Years later, Gabby Street told an interviewer for a 1947 article in *The Sporting News*, "Duffy Lewis could hit Walter Johnson blindfolded. Duffy had the darnedest form, too. He wiggled his bat and everything else. He was the only one who could do anything with Walter."

Johnson had arrived a day early to pitch the Murnane game. Washington's season would end in Boston and provide one more Ruth and Johnson confrontation. This time it was Walter Johnson who pitched the shutout, his eighth of the season, to defeat Boston, 6-0. Washington never made it to the first division. In fact, although they came in fifth, the team's record was slightly worse than the previous season's seventh-place finish. They won two games fewer and lost two more than in 1916 for a 74-79 finish.

Walter Johnson's season stats were below expectation. He won 23 games and lost 16. His 2.30 ERA was higher than usual, although it was slightly askew due to a clerical error which still awaits correction in the encyclopedias. It has been recognized by the Baseball Hall of Fame after a SABR researcher, Neil Munro, reported it. He discovered from the original score sheet of Johnson's game of September 11 that several categories were transposed in posting the pitchers records for the 1917 official statistics. Johnson was charged with losing pitcher Dutch Leonard's runs allowed. It lowers his ERA from 2.30 to 2.21. Ed Cicotte of the White Sox had a career year. He led the league with 28 wins and a 1.53 ERA. He topped everyone in innings pitched with 347. Walter Johnson was second with 328. Johnson led only in strikeouts. His 188 topped runner-up Cicotte's 150. Ruth led everyone with complete games, 35, with Johnson next with 30. Both men were allowed to finish games others would not because of their ability to hit.

The Johnsons left Washington and returned to Coffeyville. The head of the family had drawn a high number in the wartime draft. With a wife and child, he was far down the list of the Coffeyville draft board. In fact, so many of Johnson's fellow townsmen had volunteered to serve that a draft quota was not needed. The "war to end all wars" got underway in earnest for America. The other war—the war on alcohol—neared victory for the "Drys" on the home front. Congressman Roberts fought a rear guard action on behalf of the men who were not home to vote for themselves. The annual Walter Johnson Day baseball game was a casualty of wartime concerns. However, at a community picnic fete, when a game between "the fats and skinnys" was played, Walter Johnson umpired. Otherwise, winter passed on the Coffeyville farm. The war in Europe was brought closer to home when casualty lists were printed in the Coffeyville *Daily Journal*.

19
1918
—"Work or Fight"

T HE UNITED STATES GOVERNMENT told America's athletes in 1918 to "work or fight." Jack Dempsey wore patent leather shoes to do his work in a shipyard, and the photograph shown to the public embarrassed the implausibly shod challenger of the heavyweight title. Baseball players, Joe Jackson prominent among them, took defense jobs. The major leagues downsized their schedule to 128 games. They would end play on Labor Day weekend, and the World Series would be over a month sooner than usual. The prime manpower represented on the ball field could then be put to more useful war work. Secretary of War Newton D. Baker laid down the law and baseball followed it.

The three-year contact for $12,500 a season which Walter Johnson had signed when Clark Griffith retrieved him from the Federal League had ended. This time he was willing to take a small cut because of the uncertainty that baseball would draw fans as it had; also the shorter schedule meant fewer games. Johnson had not wintered well. He had caught the mumps from his son. The common childhood disease is potentially disabling for an adult. During the year Johnson's second son, Edwin, would be added to the family, and over the years, four more children would follow. Walter Johnson had obviously been spared the impotency which mumps can cause in adult men.

Life during spring training in Augusta was touched by the Great War. There were only 22 players in camp, and part of their time was spent doing close order drill and marching in formation. Bats were shouldered to simulate rifles. Exhibition games were played at army camps, and Johnson's first spring appearance entertained the troops at Columbia, South Carolina. There was no report of Walter Johnson developing a spitball, but Clark Griffith ordered in a supply of paraffin and instructed his pitchers to work on the more sanitary shine ball.

It worked wonders for Eddie Cicotte and Johnson tried it. In a January 1921 article for *Baseball Magazine,* Johnson told how he had envied Cicotte's pitch and how one time he had used a ball Cicotte had left behind at the end of an inning. "I won't pretend to say that I controlled it as well as he could do. I pretty nearly hit Eddie Collins and Happy Felsch but Cicotte didn't like the way things were going and he stopped shining the ball."

A more pressing problem for Clark Griffith was the loss of players to the armed forces. Mike Menosky, a hard-hitting outfield prospect, was already sending postcards back from France. Sam Rice, the team's best player, thought he was safe. He had served a tour in the Navy as a teenager. In fact, that's where he began to play baseball. He expected his draft board to bypass him because he had already put in service time. They did not see it that way. The military said they needed experienced men, and Rice was sent on his way to a different kind of camp. He got into seven games while on furlough before he was shipped overseas. The time lost in 1918 kept Rice from reaching 3,000 hits. He was 13 short when he stopped playing in 1934.

Wartime duties again kept Woodrow Wilson away from the season's opener, which was played in Washington this time. Walter Johnson could have used President Wilson as a "good luck charm." He struggled to a 6-3 loss to the Yankees, not striking out anyone until the sixth inning and then only fanning two. He gave up 11 hits and walked five. It was hardly a typical Walter Johnson beginning.

Two days later, in an overtime game, he was charged with a loss in relief. He stopped the Yankees for three innings, but an unearned run in the 12th beat him. The Senators were hurting at shortstop. George McBride had slowed to a crawl the year before, and Griffith had traded Bert Gallia and $15,000 to the St. Louis Browns for Doc Lavan, a shortstop, and Burt Shotten, a leadoff type hitting outfielder. Shotten's time in baseball history would not arrive until Branch Rickey called him out of retirement in 1947 to manage the Brooklyn Dodgers in Jackie Robinson's epoch-making rookie year. Lavan covered more ground than McBride but made more errors on the balls he reached. He led the league's shortstops with 57 miscues even though he played in only 117 games.

Frank "Wildfire" Schulte, a longtime star of the Chicago Cubs who had played in four World Series for them, took Rice's place in the outfield. In his final season he turned in an adequate .288 performance. Griffith fashioned a four-man starting rotation keyed on Walter

Johnson. Grunting Jim Shaw, who threw noisily, Harry Harper, and Doc Ayers were competent starters who would collectively win 37 and lose 34 games.

Walter Johnson lost his third game in a row at home to Philadelphia but finally won his first game in New York, allowing two earned runs in a 9-4 contest. His first shutout came in Boston, but he lost again to the A's in relief before returning home. He pitched five innings and had two men out in the bottom of the 11th when the A's scored.

By using Johnson in relief in an extensive extra-inning game, Griffith could not pitch him the next day, May 5, when finally, Sunday baseball became legal in Washington, D.C. It took the argument that the games would be weekend recreation for the thousands of troops in nearby training camps to erase the restraining blue law. On Monday, Johnson began a modest winning streak which included a relief win in a game pitched by Babe Ruth. Two days earlier the Babe, playing the outfield, had hit a two-run homer to spoil a Johnson shutout. On May 9, Johnson and Ruth would face each other the final time as pitching rivals. Johnson entered the game with the score tied, 3-3, after nine innings. He blanked Boston in the 10th and the Senators scored with two out. It was Johnson's fourth win at Ruth's expense, but the Babe had won six of the 10 games they pitched to a decision against each other. Overall, each allowed 16 earned runs but Ruth had the better ERA, 1.44 to Johnson's 1.54. Johnson had 50 strikeouts and Ruth 40.

Next, Walter Johnson pitched successive shutouts that really added up to the equivalent of three. After beating Jim Bagby, 1-0 in Cleveland, he hooked up with Lefty Williams of the Chicago White Sox. He set another record, which is still on the books, for the longest shutout. Johnson and Willaims dueled 18 innings. Soon afterward, Lefty Williams departed for a war industries job. He joined his team-mate and closest friend, Joe Jackson, in a Delaware shipyard. They led their ball club to the championship of the Steel League, a circuit of war industry teams. The next year Williams led Jackson astray in the World Series...possibly. At least he split his $10,000 bribe money with his roomie.

After Johnson had pitched his first Sunday home game, a 4-0 shutout of Detroit, the team left on a road trip. A shutout loss, 3-0, to Boston stopped the abbreviated streak at five. Jim Bagby avenged his earlier 1-0 loss to Johnson by reversing the results, but he had to go 11 innings to do it. A pair of one-run margin victories, a save, and a shutout in Detroit brought Johnson's record to 10-6.

Moving on to St. Louis, Walter Johnson again became part of someone else's story. In 1988, *New York Times* columnist Ira Berkow tracked down former ballplayer Bob Berman in his New York City apartment, which contained many momentos of Berman's brief professional career as a catcher. Included was a photo of Walter Johnson, and Berman told how he had achieved the immortality of an entry in Macmillan's *Baseball Encyclopedia* with the barest of qualifications. He had never batted, but he caught one inning. On June 12, as a reserve catcher making his first—and only—road trip, he had been the only catcher available when Walter Johnson relieved in the ninth inning to protect a 6-4 lead. Berman had been used once as a pinch runner on June 6, but this was the first time he gotten behind the bat. He caught Johnson flawlessly, handling two strikeouts as the fastball pitcher saved the game; and Berman saved the memory to share with his grandchildren.

Two more one-run victories followed: a 13-inning, 3-2, win in New York followed by a shutout over the A's. Then Babe Ruth again beat Walter Johnson without pitching. On June 30, playing center field for Boston, he hit his 11th home run of the season, in the 10th inning, to defeat his former pitching rival, 3-1. Walter Johnson won a July 4 holiday game, 4-3. The Senators were in contention, although Boston and Cleveland set the pace. Johnson's record was 14-8.

The second half of the season was much like the first. Johnson continued to pitch in close games, trying to make the few runs his team scored stretch over nine innings. Often, he had to stretch them farther. He went 11 innings to beat Cleveland, 4-3, and then won a 15-inning, four hit, 1-0, game in St. Louis. George Sisler's triple was the only hit allowed in the first 11 innings.

In Chicago Johnson batted in the winning run to close another extra- inning game, a mere 10 innings before moving on to Detroit for yet another 18-inning marathon. It was a struggle all the way as the teams battled to a 7-6 Detroit victory. The Tigers scored with one out in the bottom of the 18th inning. Before the Senators got back to Washington, Johnson pitched his eighth shutout of the season and won his 20th game, in Philadelphia. Johnson's three-for-four day at bat included a home run.

The team still had a chance to win the pennant as they settled into a stretch run, conducted in the heat of August because of the shortened season. Another extra-long game with Detroit went 16 innings before Johnson lost on two unearned runs. Johnson had pitched the final seven innings in relief. Three days later Johnson pitched the entire 14 innings of a 3-2 win from the Browns. He won twice again and saved the final game of the season on Labor Day.

Washington came up short, finishing third with a 72-56 record, four games behind the pennant-winning Red Sox with Cleveland in between. Once again, Walter Johnson had to read about other teams meeting for the World Championship. Boston played the Chicago Cubs. Babe Ruth and Carl Mays each won two games as the Red Sox did something they have not been able to do since: win a World Series.

Walter Johnson had rebounded to the top of the stats. His 23 wins against 13 losses led the league, as did his 1.27 ERA. His eight shutouts were the most pitched, and he continued to win consecutive strikeout titles with 162. Despite the shortened season, he pitched 325 innings. Pitching in 15 extra-inning games made up for a lack of opportunities because of the shorter schedule. Impressively, he started 29 games and completed them all. His 10 relief appearances yielded 3 wins, 4 losses, and 3 saves.

The Johnsons traveled home to Kansas aboard trains carrying soldiers and sailors on furloughs. They took home one more child than had arrived with them in Washington at the beginning of the season. Walter Johnson now had two sons, the three-year-old toddler, Walter Jr., and the infant they named Edwin, after Hazel's father, and whom the family called Eddie.

The Walter Johnson Day baseball game was played with less local intensity than usual. Three weeks before the war-ending armistice, Johnson was on the mound as Coffeyville defeated the Bartlesville, Oklahoma, team, 3-0.

With the baseball season finished a month early, there was time for a longer fall harvest. Johnson's father-in-law decided against running for another congressional term. Instead, he ran for governor of Nevada, but he lost to Democrat Charles B. Henderson. Roberts could take some small satisfaction in finishing ahead of feminist Anne Martin, who had run as an Independent. Mr. and Mrs. Roberts moved to Reno where he opened a law office and in 1923 was elected to a four-year term as mayor. Mayor Roberts was reelected in 1927 and again in 1931. Hazel Johnson would no longer have her parents available as babysitters in Washington during the baseball season.

Coffeyville erupted in an old-fashioned celebration when the armistice ending the Great War was announced on November 11. The war was over and the ballplayers would be coming back to the big leagues and the local farm lads to the Kansas wheat fields.

20

The Dead Ball
Era Ends

When Congress proposed an 18th Amendment to the Constitution, prohibiting people from drinking alcohol, it made no difference to Walter Johnson. He didn't drink, but also said he had no argument with those who did. The proposal was viewed differently by his father-in-law who had fought the Prohibition forces in vain. However, Nevada's voters did not agree with their former Congressman and the state ratified the amendment, after it had already achieved the two-third acceptance needed for passage. The Johnsons had been spared from the influenza epidemic that killed over a half million people in the United States in 1918, but belatedly it caught up with Walter Johnson. He fought his way through two bouts of influenza and arrived in spring training camp underweight.

The third place finish in 1918 raised the expectations of the Senators' fans. After all, Sam Rice was back and the developing Mike Menosky would join him and Zeb Milan for a stronger outfield. The middle of the infield was strengthened by disposing of Doc Lavan and trading Eddie Ainsmith for Hal Janvrin of the Red Sox. It did not quite work out. Hank Shanks who could play anywhere passably well, became the shortstop. It is a position, however, where only excellence will do. Pennants may not always be won because of a superior shortstop, but they are often lost because of a lack of one.

Griffith started with the same four-man rotation anchored by Walter Johnson. Harry Harper would drop from 11-10 to 6-21. Jim Shaw grunted his way to a respectable 16-17, winning as many in 1919 as he had in 1918. Doc Ayers was traded during the season. He left with a 2-6 record and his replacement, Eric Erickson from Detroit, was not much better, winning five and losing 10.

Van Picinich replaced Ainsmith as Johnson's regular catcher and shared the work mostly with Sam Agnew. The catcher whose jaw once was broken by a Washington pitch and who wrestled George McBride in the melee at Fenway Park, was now a Senator.

The baseball season started with President Wilson in Europe where he was busy stitching together the League of Nations charter. It would be unraveled for him by a hostile Senate when he came home to explain it to a country already in an isolationist mood. General Peyton March, Army Chief of Staff, got the nod to throw out the first ball on opening day. Walter Johnson drew the starting role and he opened in mid-season form. Typically, he pitched a shutout and he had to carry the game into extra innings. Washington's batters also performed typically. They could not score runs for Johnson. Finally, in the bottom of the 13th, Sam Agnew lead off with a single. Johnson sacrificed him to second, Menosky ran for Agnew and scored on singles by Judge and Foster.

A review of the 20 seasons Walter Johnson pitched for Washington offers the challenge of knowing which was his best. At the very least, 191 is a prime example of Johnson's ability to win without a strong supporting team. On May 11, for example, the New York Yankees played their first-ever Sunday home game. No game could have been more frustrating for Johnson. He pitched a scoreless 12-inning tie. Washington filled the bases three times and could not score. They had 16 hits while Johnson gave the Yankees only two. He retired 28 consecutive batters in one stretch. In another example of frustration, the even-tempered Walter Johnson lost a game on August 5 to Detroit, 2-1. Val Picinich, his new catcher, had a mental lapse. He let a missed third strike roll to the backstop. Instead of chasing it, he asked the umpire for a new ball. In the confusion, the batter ended up on second base and scored the winning run on a two-out single.

On August 17 a Sunday crowd set a new attendance record of 31,000 in Detroit. They overflowed the field and fly balls became ground rule doubles. 10 of them were hit, two by Ty Cobb. The game went 11 innings before fortune, for once, favored Johnson. Joe Judge lofted a double into the encroaching crowd for a go-ahead run and Johnson closed out the Tigers in order.

The team went on to Chicago to play the still-unsullied White Sox. Washington was long out of contention but the series was important to Johnson. He liked to tackle the best teams on their own field. However, he missed the whole series. This time his disabling illness was diagnosed as malaria and he sweated it out in his hotel room. He did not start again until the team reached New York 11 days later.

The Yankees had just bought Carl Mays from the Red Sox. Boston owner, Harry Frazee, had begun to sell off his star players and had collected $40,000 for the surly underhand pitcher. Walter Johnson who could find something to like in everyone, found the least to like in Carl Mays. He would not retaliate in an exchange of dusters, but he bore down extra hard on every pitch when Mays was his opponent. But no matter how determined he was he did not always come out on top. On August 28 Walter Johnson battled Carl Mays until two were out in the 14th inning before losing, 5-4. Johnson gave up 19 hits and walked two. Yet, only two Yankee runs were earned. He pitched out of one tight spot after another until the last one. The game was also noteworthy for the arrival of a new infielder. Bucky Harris, who would solve the team's need at second base and, more importantly, as "The Boy Manager," lead the Senators to their first pennant five years later, made—his debut.

All that remained for Johnson's personal goals was to win 20 games. He needed two more victories as the Senators reeled into September. He won number 19 in the second game of a double header in Philadelphia, lost another when Washington was shut out, 2-0, and, pitching for a seventh-place team, he won his 20th victory on September 16 beating St. Louis, 5-3, despite George Sisler's three hits and three runs scored. Sisler circled the bases on one long hit but the scorer posted it as a triple. He ruled that unnecessarily slow fielding had let Sisler reach home. The scorer may not have known it, but had he given Sisler a home run it would have been the only one against Johnson that season. No other starting pitcher escaped getting tagged at least once. Babe Ruth, pitching while alternating in the outfield, gave up two home runs.

After the game, Clark Griffith announced, "Walter Johnson, having done a season's work, is allowed to go home and look after his farm." With two weeks remaining, Johnson took his family back to their Coffeyville home.

Walter Johnson's record was 20-14. His victories included five 1-0 games and he lost one game by that same narrow score. In all, eight of his 14 losses were by one run. Four more came in relief roles. For the eighth consecutive time, Walter Johnson led in strikeouts. It is still among the records he holds nearly 70 years after he retired from baseball. The best measurement of a pitcher for a second division team is his earned run average. Johnson's was the league's best, 1.49. The league average was 3.21.

There is one stunning statistic hidden in Johnson's lifetime ERA. 1919 ended baseball's dead ball era. Radical changes would take place for the coming 1920 season. A livelier baseball was used, more tightly wrapped with Australian wool and, just as important to batting averages, balls were thrown out of the game as soon as they were scuffed or stained. The split ball was outlawed except for a handful of established pitchers who were allowed to throw it until their careers ended. All doctored pitches were forbidden. Clark Griffith's investment in paraffin went down the drain. No shine balls, no spitters, no emery balls with scuffed surfaces would fool the batters.

From 1920 on, Walter Johnson's ERAs went up as did everyone else's. The people who enjoy programming their computers to compile lists of baseball players in various categories have generated a ranking of the top 25 career ERAs. Walter Johnson's 2.17 is seventh best of all time. Ahead of him are. Ed Walsh, 1.86; Addie Joss, 1.88; Three Fingers Brown, 2.06; Monty Ward, 2.10; Christy Mathewson, 2.13; and Rube Waddell, 2.16. In addition to all being in the Hall of Fame, all ended their careers before 1920. They all pitched exclusively during the dead ball era. Walter Johnson pitched extensively in that period, too. Except for the 19th century's Monty Ward, all ahead of Johnson were active when he broke in during the 1907 season. After Christy Mathewson's 4,781.2 innings pitched, Johnson's 4,089.2 dead ball era innings is next. Walsh, who leads the list, pitched 2,964.1 innings. Except for Three Fingers Brown who worked 3,172.1 innings, none of the others reached 3,000.

Let's have a list ranking pitchers of the dead ball era. The same names appear on it with the same ERAs. However, there's a new name on top of the list, Walter Johnson's. His ERA from 1907 through 1919 was 1.65! Ed Walsh's 1.82 is not even close.

When the ill-fated 1919 World Series between Chicago and Cincinnati began on October 1, Walter Johnson followed it from far away in Kansas. Coffeyville's Daily Journal carried wire service accounts of each game. A staunch American Leaguer, although with a special fondness for Frank Bancroft, Cincinnati's senior executive, Johnson would have been puzzled by Ed Cicotte's abysmal showing. How could Lefty Williams who matched him zero after zero for 18 innings the year before do so badly against the long shot Reds? In time Walter Johnson and the whole world would know about the 1919 Chicago Black Sox.

21
The Only No-Hitter
and Lone Sore Arm

I N 1920, three unimaginable things happened in baseball. It was learned that the 1919 World Series had been fixed by gamblers...Babe Ruth hit 54 home runs to break the old record of 29...and Walter Johnson developed a season-ending sore arm.

The 1920 season is a tidewater mark in baseball history. It marked a change in style of play. Not only were trick pitches forbidden and the balls made livelier and easier to hit, but batters changed their styles and fielders played deeper.

Johnson's arm trouble was a byproduct of the previous year's World Series. If the Cincinnati Reds had not unexpectedly become the World Champions, the idea of a triumphant spring training trip would not have occurred to the elder citizen of promotional tours, Frank Bancroft. As business manager of the new World Champions, he organized his final baseball odyssey. As Cincinnati lacked any of the era's "name players," the Reds needed an opponent with a box-office drawing card. Bancroft again contacted Clark Griffith, and the men agreed to a 14-game spring trip to start in Florida and wend its way north over 15 days.

While it was not promised that Walter Johnson would pitch in every town the teams visited, that was the fans' expectation. They might wish to see Cincinnati, the surprising World Champions, but Walter Johnson was the premier pitching attraction in baseball.

Walter Johnson had long ago earned the right to create his own spring training regimen. It would build on his year-round general physical conditioning. Johnson was never out of shape. Except for an indulgent fondness for ice cream, he ate carefully. He did not drink or smoke cigarettes, although he appeared in advertisements contentedly puffing on a pipe filled with Velvet Tobacco. His robust good health was maintained between seasons with hunting trips, hiking along rough trails with his dogs, and by doing hard farmyard chores.

Johnson would report to spring training each year ready to pitch, needing only to sharpen his control. He would begin with widely spaced three-inning appearances, then go the distance in several games without exertion. He was then ready for another stellar opening day appearance. However, his plans were skewed in 1920 by the expectations of the tour the Senators made with the Reds. At every stop he would at least warm up on the sidelines. He would occasionally cut loose a few fastballs in response to demands by the local fans who were seeing him for the only time in their lives. Along the tour route, he parceled out his appearances. Almost daily he would pitch two or three innings. He was never able to pace himself over a nine-inning game to get ready for the demands of the coming season.

The inevitable spring cold caught up with him and made matters worse. In previous seasons, when he came down with a bad cold or the flu, he would jump a town or two ahead of the team. He would hole up in a warm hotel room and wait for the others to arrive. In 1920 Johnson stayed with the team, riding in the troupe's private railroad cars. It was the World Champion Reds triumphal tour, and the 14-game string with the Senators wound up at Redlands Field. That was where Cincinnati had triumphed over the Chicago White Sox the previous fall, and no one knew yet how tainted the championship had been. The tiring train trip prompted Al Schacht, not yet the Clown Prince of Baseball, to say, "That's why they call it a *training* trip." This bad pun perhaps explains why Schacht made his comedy success as a pantomimist.

Years later, when asked to explain the only sore arm of his life, Johnson said he had caught a cold in his arm. He was reluctant to admit that even his fabulous arm could go lame from overwork. Yet, from the time the Senators checked into the Tampa Bay Hotel, their spring training center, there was pressure on him to make appearances. He was pulled off a World War One vintage biplane by an anxious Clark Griffith. It was to have flown Johnson to Jacksonville for a St. Patrick's Day exhibition game using the Senators second-string players.

Before hooking up with the Reds, there was a series of games with the Cuban stars. In Havana they played as a mixed array of both black and white players. But only those Cubans who could play in the segregated Florida ballparks made the trip. Even so, they won four of the seven games played. Walter Johnson's only appearance was for three scoreless innings in the next-to-last game. Washington signed one of the visitors, Ricardo Torres, a first baseman and catcher. His son, Gil Torres, was a wartime regular with the Senators in 1944 and 1945. After the set of games with the Cuban visitors, Washington began the trek north with Cincinnati. It did not get the team ready and it wasted the chances of Walter Johnson.

The 1920 season began with Washington on the road to open the season in Boston. The opener, already delayed a day because of the weather, was a somber occasion at Fenway Park. During the winter the team's great star, Babe Ruth, had been sold to the New York Yankees. However, the Red Sox did not need the Babe on Opening Day. Walter Johnson was knocked out of the box after two innings. It was painful for him to throw the ball, and it was painful for manager Clark Griffith to watch. He sent Johnson back to Washington to wait for the season's opener there. But, when the Red Sox came to Washington to reverse inaugural roles on April 22, Walter Johnson was still not ready to pitch.

The Washington ballpark, called Griffith Park, was completed for the 1920 season when the single-tier stands stretching down the foul lines past first and third base were double-decked to the foul poles. Clark Griffith was now the club president and starting his final season as a field manager. He would have liked to hand the opening day ball to Johnson but had to wait a bit longer. With Vice President Thomas Marshall substituting for Woodrow Wilson, who had suffered a stroke from which he never recovered, and with Grunting Jim Shaw in Walter Johnson's place, the Senators began the season with a loss.

All seemed well again three days later when Walter Johnson beat Boston with a shutout, defeating Joe Bush, 2-0. If Johnson was pitching in pain he wouldn't admit it, and four days later he beat the Yankees, outpitching John Quinn, 2-1. He held the Yankees to seven hits, four of them scratch singles. In the first meeting since Babe Ruth had become a full-time outfielder, the Bambino managed a single in four times at bat. He would not hit any of his season's 54 home runs off Johnson. Milan saved the game in the ninth inning with a spectacular catch after Val Picinich's seventh-inning home run had scored the only runs Johnson would need.

Washington settled in for a long home stand with Walter Johnson pitching erratically. The results in the box scores appeared better than his performances did to the eyes of reporters. Word was out that Walter Johnson was not quite right. He was throwing more change-ups and curve balls. He could strike out batters, but not at will as he

143

once did. The team was already deep in second division and Johnson's record was below .500 when the team took to the road.

Johnson was used in relief more than as a starter. He saved several games, but in one, a 16-inning game with Chicago in which Red Faber pitched the complete game, Johnson, in relief, gave up eight runs in the final inning. There were good appearances occasionally, such as a May 29 shutout against Philadelphia and a 2-1 win on June 3 from Boston. However, Johnson was struggling. It was thought that he might be back on track when he blanked Philadelphia on June 27 and headed for Boston.

On July 1 Walter Johnson almost missed what became his greatest game. He had stayed behind in Washington watching over his four-year-old son, Walter Jr., who was very ill. Johnson got to Fenway Park only an hour before game time. Sentimental accounts of the game have a sore-armed Johnson being coaxed along by Manager Griffith, asking for "just one more inning." Some accounts have his son cheering from a grandstand seat, and in others the boy is following the game from his sickroom. What gave Johnson the determination to keep plugging along can not be fathomed from the box score. What that starkly shows is that Johnson reached the ninth inning without giving up a base hit and only one batter had reached base. In the seventh inning a routine grounder went through Bucky Harris' legs but Johnson, as always, shrugged it off. A perfect game would not be possible, but victory would and a no-hitter a sign to send to his son at home. The batter who stood between him and success was Harry Hooper. Eventually elected to Baseball's Hall of Fame, Hooper was a career nemesis for Johnson. He was *the* batter, it seemed, that Johnson could never get out in a clutch situation. The tying run was on base, and Hooper could become the winning run if Johnson weakened.

Hooper hit a hot smash that knocked first baseman Joe Judge off his feet. He scrambled after the ball as Johnson raced to cover first base. An off-balance throw arrived just in time for Johnson to grab it barehanded as he stepped on the base. He beat Hooper by a half step. Walter Johnson had pitched his first and only no-hit game. No-hit games were rare then, unlike today when in many seasons they come in multiples. Johnson's was the only one between 1919 and 1922.

Cheered by Johnson's no-hitter, and assuming it signaled a full return to form, the fans expected him to pitch the opener of the July 4 doubleheader at Griffith Park. Over 20,000 people were there to salute his no-hit feat and see what he would do next. Johnson was to have been presented with a gold watch, but he left the ballpark early. He had pulled a tendon in his leg in the desperate rush to cover first base and retire Harry Hooper. The leg had tightened up during pre-game practice, and Johnson had to be sent home in a taxi.

The no-hitter evened Johnson's record at 8-8. He did it with a sore arm. It was to be the last game he would win in 1920. He lost his next two starts, 4-0 and 4-1. By mid-July Walter Johnson was finished for the season. When the Senators reached Cleveland on its next road trip, Walter Johnson departed for Rochester, New York, to see a specialist about his arm. Ballplayers called specialists who treated their limbs "bonesetters." Bonesetter Reese had been the ranking guru of chiropractors handling sore-armed pitchers. He had retired, but his practice had been taken over by Bonesetter Harry Knight. It was hoped he could help Johnson. He couldn't. He could give advice, though, and his advice to Johnson was to rest the arm until next season. Johnson rejoined the team in Cleveland, and when they moved on to St. Louis, Griffith told Walter Johnson to keep going west until he reached Coffeyville. The only pitching Johnson was expected to do for the rest of 1920 would be with a fork in a hayfield.

However, the restless pitcher returned to the team when it made its final western swing early in September. For a few weeks he took daily workouts and found he could throw without pain. Still, Griffith decided against putting him into a game, meaningless now with Washington deep in second division and the season almost over. He feared that Johnson would overexert himself in a close game. With two weeks left in the schedule, Walter Johnson again took a train back to Coffeyville. He would settle in for the winter with his wife, Hazel, and await the arrival of their next child. A daughter, Elinor Lee, was born in August, 1919. The baby girl was the only one of the children who did not survive early childhood.

Walter Johnson's 1920 season was over, but baseball's was reaching its climax. Other writers, the best among them Eliot Asinof who wrote *Eight Men Out*, have recounted the shock of discovery that the 1919 World Series had been thrown by White Sox players. Rumors had been heard all season, and the shoe was finally dropped in a Chicago courthouse with a week left in the season. At that point, Chicago was knotted in a tight pennant race finish. Cleveland saved baseball the embarrassment of having the remnants of the Chicago White Sox appear in the 1920 World Series. In the last days of the season, they edged out their decimated rivals, playing without Joe

Jackson, Buck Weaver, Happy Felsch, Swede Risberg, and their top pitchers, Eddie Cicotte and Lefty Williams. The reported ringleader of the group now called the Black Sox was former Washington first baseman Chick Gandil. He had not returned to play the 1920 season. Offsetting the scandal was the fortuitous outbreak of home runs hit by Babe Ruth. By mid-season he had passed his own record of 29, set the year before when he still doubled as a pitcher. His unprecedented slugging stunned the baseball world. Ruth hit more home runs than all the players on any other team did collectively. Before the 1920 season began, Babe Ruth was sold to New York where his former manager, Ed Barrow, now ruled the Yankees from the front office. He dictated that Babe Ruth was to give up pitching and concentrate on hitting those crowd-pleasing round-trippers. Largely because of the Babe, baseball survived the crisis year of 1920.

22

Judge Landis Takes Charge of Baseball

ORGANIZED BASEBALL feared it was in serious danger when 1921 began. The press was filled with editorials asserting that baseball had forfeited its claim to be the National Game. Advance ticket sales were slow, and the frightened owners had turned to an eccentric federal judge to be their savior. Kenesaw Mountain Landis, sitting in judgment in a Chicago courtroom, was a legal lightning rod who drew controversial cases. He had rocked the imaginations of Americans by fining the presumably untouchable Standard Oil cartel a staggering $29 million for flagrant monopolistic practices. Landis had been drawn into the maelstrom of the Federal League litigation when its case was assigned to him. He helped organized baseball by strategically delaying his decision for months until, finally, the Feds began making separate deals and their league dissolved. Landis personified an incorruptible bulwark against the forces of evil by meting out stern justice. He was known to be tough and to love the sport of baseball.

The owners of major league teams accepted the obvious reality that the men who ran baseball could not police themselves or their game. They made Kenesaw Mountain Landis their commissioner and gave him despotic powers, which he used gleefully. By the time the owners realized they had made a bad choice, Judge Landis, from their viewpoint, had become an inviolate institution. He could not be fired because the press and the public considered him the embodiment of integrity. Of all the possible choices, only Judge Landis was thought uniquely qualified to uphold the ideals of America's National Game.

On January 12, Kenesaw Mountain Landis began his new career without ending his present one. He saw nothing amiss in continuing to hear federal cases in his courtroom while making judgments for baseball in an office across town. His judiciary salary of $7,500 a year paled beside the $50,000 baseball offered him. However, he liked the perks that went with the bench and he preferred to be called "Judge." He made a decision to subtract his federal paycheck and take only $42,500 a year for the commissioner's job.

As Judge Landis began his reign, he might well have regarded Walter Johnson as an ideal ballplayer. The Big Train, as he was beginning to be called, like all players was inclined to make strong salary demands but was no trouble to management once he had signed a contract. If all baseball players were as honorable as Walter Johnson, baseball would not have needed a commissioner. Johnson had already signed for 1921, for terms not announced or even guessed at in the press. The Johnson-Griffith relationship had reached a stage of mutual accommodation that made the terms of any agreement a matter of formality. Both knew that if the tides of change lifted all of baseball's boats, Johnson's would float higher with them. The 1921 season was hard to predict, and Johnson was appreciative that Griffith had not only paid him his salary in full for 1920, but had excused him from working for it early.

In returning his signed contract, Walter Johnson told Griffith that he had not touched a baseball since the previous season had ended. There had been no pitching in post-season games, not even token efforts for local Kansas pride.

There was a new manager in charge when Walter Johnson reported for spring training in Tampa, Florida. Clark Griffith, the club president, had replaced himself in the dugout with George McBride, the shortstop who had been one of the few bright spots during the dark years of second-division finishes. It would always be Clark Griffith's team, and locally the team would be called, "the Griffs" or "the Griffmen" more than the Nationals or Senators. Griffith was the press contact, made the trades, and suggested lineup changes. The running of the team on the field was the manager's responsibility, but relationships with the fans and supporters was Griffith's.

McBride was given a squad that contained the nucleus of an eventual pennant winner. Of the players who would one day form a championship team for Washington, on hand were Joe Judge, Bucky Harris, Sam Rice, and, debuting late, Goose Goslin. Griffith set in place a trio of starters which included holdover Tom Zachary, the veteran George Mogridge just obtained in a trade and, of course, Walter Johnson. The trio would be the mainstays of the staff for the coming years.

To get the Philadelphia A's ready for the 1911 World Series with the New York Giants, the American League All-Stars played a series of tune-up games. L to R, Gabby Street, Frank "Home Run" Baker, Walter Johnson, Smokey Joe Wood. *Credit: Estate of Joe Wood (Bob Wood)*

Smokey Joe Wood and Walter Johnson shake hands before their 1912 duel when Johnson attempted to head off Wood's run of consecutive wins which was closing in on Johnson's 16 straight. *Credit: Estate of Joe Wood (Bob Wood)*

Walter Johnson in 1913 when he won 36 and lost 7, pitched 11 shutouts and led American League pitchers with 243 and the league with a 1.14 ERA. *Credit: Transcendental Graphics*

Walter Johnson was an outstanding batter. Seen in a 1913 action shot, he set an all-time batting record for pitchers when he hit .433 in 1925. *Credit: Transcendental Graphics*

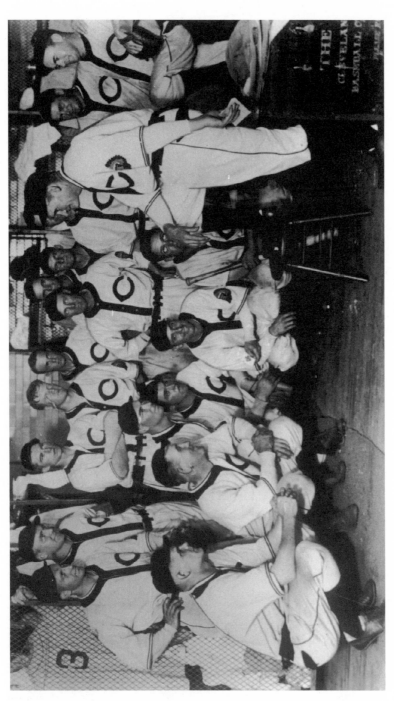

Walter Johnson took over a disgruntled Cleveland Indian team in 1933. At far right, behind Johnson's back, is Willie Kamm, the leading dissident. *Credit: Cleveland State University*

PRESIDENT COOLIDGE & THE WASHINGTON BASE BALL TEAM
ON VISIT TO THE WHITE HOUSE. SEPT. 2 1924

When the Senators headed for the 1924 pennant, their last road trip began with a send-off at the White House. President Calvin Coolidge and Walter Johnson are in the center of the team photo. Manager Bucky Harris stands beside the President and Clark Griffith flanks Johnson. *Credit: Transcendental Graphics*

Pitching greats whose careers touched Johnson's. L to R, Joe Wood, great rival during peak seasons, who coached Yale for 25 years, Cy Young, who pitched against Johnson at the start of The Big Train's career and Lefty Grove who took over Johnson's strike out role. *Credit: Estate of Joe Wood (Bob Wood)*

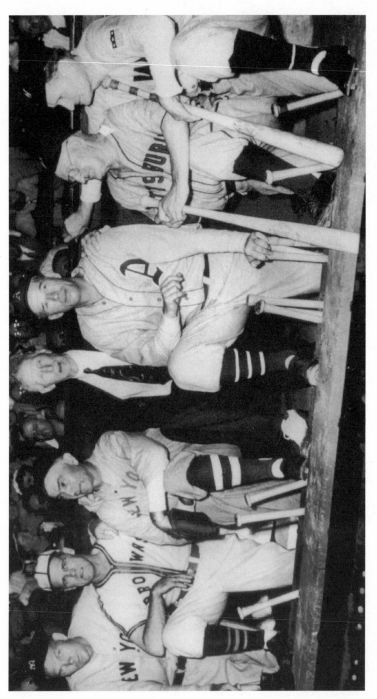

A gathering of superstars celebrates Connie Mack's 50th Anniversary as manager of the Philadelphia Athletics in August 1944. L to R, Bill Dickey, George Sisler, Home Run Baker, Connie Mack, Lefty Grove, Honus Wagner, Walter Johnson. *Credit: Transcendental Graphics*

Spring training followed more traditional lines. There was no grand tour. The man who had conceived it, Frank Bancroft, had been ill during the months that followed the discovery that his 1919 champions had not won their title on their own merits. Bancroft died on March 30, just before the season opened. He is only faintly remembered, but he is far more deserving of a plaque at Cooperstown than a number of nonplayers who are honored there.

Although Walter Johnson reported his arm was free of pain and seemed to throw with his usual effortless motion, he was not up to opening day form when the season began. There was a new U.S. president, Warren G. Harding, and he was probably at the ballpark early to throw out the first ball. Had America needed only a ceremonial figurehead as its chief executive, Harding would have outperformed the entire British monarchy. He was a handsome man, silver haired, ruddy cheeked, with a politician's memory for names and a gift for the friendly detail. He not only threw the first ball directly to Walter Johnson, but he had signed it in advance for Johnson's collection. He stayed for the whole game, kept a detailed scorecard and signed it, too. Harding presented it to Ban Johnson, the American League president, who had it framed and hung in his office. It quietly disappeared after Harding's death, perhaps blown away by the winds of scandal which followed.

The opening day ceremonies belonged to Harding, but an invalided Woodrow Wilson put in an enfeebled appearance and Vice President Calvin Coolidge watched carefully. Johnson's turn as a relief pitcher would come soon. Despite an assemblage of presidential boosters, he failed to finish an opening day game for the first time. He had not looked sharp in training games, but by now he was the automatic choice to start the season. He lasted four innings, giving up four earned runs on nine hits to the Red Sox. Washington lost, 6-3, and wondered about Walter Johnson.

He seemed to find himself the next time out. The press reported that Walter Johnson had passed Eddie Plank's existing American League record of 303 victories when he defeated Philadelphia, 3-1. Connie Mack described him as "the Johnson of old." The A's leader pointed out that when Whitey Witt opened the sixth inning with a triple, Johnson had kept the next three batters from hitting the ball back past him. Then, in the seventh, with two out and bases loaded, Johnson fanned Witt. Only a ninth-inning wild pitch cost Johnson a shutout.

Washington went to New York, and although Babe Ruth hit a first-inning home run, the game went to Johnson, 5-3. To make the victory sweeter, Carl Mays was the losing pitcher. On April 29 in Philadelphia, Johnson got caught up in one of those games which end up in a meaningless tie, the kind which use up a pitcher but give him nothing to show for his effort. The game, played in cold, damp weather with an intermittent drizzle, lasted 10 innings. It ended in a 3-3 tie, called because of darkness. Through April and May, at home and away, Johnson was not pitching up to expectations. By Memorial Day he was 2-5 and had been knocked out of the box twice. Although he lost three games by one run, they were not the usual low-scoring games of the past. He lost 6-5, 5-4, 4-3.

The 6-5 loss came on May 7 to the Yankees at Griffith Park. The Yankees scored three runs in the ninth inning to overtake Johnson's lead. The game's biggest blow was Babe Ruth's home run, which cleared the fence at 426 feet. The right-field fence was 48 feet high and the ball was estimated as landing not less than 500 feet away. It was the longest home run ever hit in Washington.

On June 1, Johnson staggered to an 8-7 win, largely because his mates rallied with five runs in the ninth. His buddy Zeb Milan pinch-hit for him and tripled to win the game. The next time out, however, Johnson did his own batting, going four-for-four and holding Chicago to five hits. Still, he could not get into a winning groove. By the end of June he had seesawed his way to a slightly improved 6-8 record. Johnson's record sagged further when he lost a game typical of the sort which plagued his career. Pat Gharrity, now catching Johnson regularly along with the rest of the staff, allowed a passed ball in the 10th inning, and Johnson lost, 2-1, to St. Louis. He split two decisions early in July and then, on July 8, personal tragedy struck. Walter Johnson received a telegram in Boston telling him his father had suddenly died.

Frank Johnson's heart had failed him. Myocarditis, an inflammation of the heart muscles, brought his death 15 hours after the attack. He was respected locally for his own worth, not simply for having sired a superstar baseball hero. The previous November he had been elected county commissioner for his local district. His son had helped distribute campaign flyers, although the two men joked that every time Walter spoke, the voters only wanted to hear about baseball. Frank Johnson and his son were great friends and relied on each other. Frank and Minnie had just moved into Walter and Hazel's Coffeyville farm home to spend the summer there. When the baseball season ended, they were to move back to their own residence. The Johnson farmhouse dealt with a shifting population. It was large and comfortable, and had a bed for any kin that needed a place to stay.

Walter Johnson rejoined his team in Detroit and lost another 2-1 game, again in 10 innings. Although he held the Tigers to six hits, Johnson, who had been absent for two weeks, lacked control and walked eight batters.

Finally, Walter Johnson hit his stride. He ended the Senators' road trip with a 14-6 romp over the Tigers and opened a home stand against them in another game without a decision, leaving the game tied 3-3 after eight innings. He beat Cleveland, 3-1, and had another lopsided win, beating St. Louis 16-5 on August 8. The lore of Walter Johnson's niceness often makes mention of him easing up in runaway games and letting a player in need of a hit swing at a fat pitch. It happened in the game of August 8. Luke Stuart is listed among players who hit a home run on their first time at bat in the major leagues. He hit it off Walter Johnson, to make the memory sweeter. Stuart had replaced Marty McManus at second base in the seventh inning of the lopsided game. When the Browns came to bat in the ninth inning, they trailed 16-3. Wally Gerber led off with a single, and Luke Stuart came to bat for his first time in the major leagues. Johnson smiled and laid in a soft pitch, which Stuart hit out of the ball park to make the final score 16-5. Luke Stuart's career batting average was .333. He was hitless in two more appearances. His home run was the only base hit he made in three partial games when he filled in late in games.

Johnson's record finally edged above .500 as the home stand ended, and he still had half of August and September to pull it up to Johnson standards. He needed nine more wins to reach 20, but he fell short by three. He had a short setback, missing a turn on the road when he caught another heavy cold. This time he had sat on deck admiring the stars during a summer night's crossing of Lake Erie from Detroit to Cleveland. The cold lake breezes chilled him, and he spent the Cleveland visit in bed in his hotel room. His record dropped back to .500 when he pitched again, this time being hard hit but going the route in an 8-1 loss in New York. In Philadelphia he lost in 10 innings, 4-3. Too late to raise his record to Johnson-like figures or help his fourth-place club move up in the standings, he won five of the remaining six games.

Among these games was a strange contest on September 14. Very questionable scoring gave the St. Louis Browns base hits on what most observers thought were errors. Walter Johnson only faced 27 batters. The three base runners were removed, two in a triple play, the other picked off first base. There were no walks or hit batters and no errors. An even more memorable game was played on the 24th. Walter Johnson was present, but not as a participant, for one of the most celebrated of Ty Cobb's fistfights. This one was with Johnson's frequent Boswell, umpire Billy Evans.

The line score reads as a relatively easy win for Walter Johnson, 5-1. That's not the way the hot-tempered Cobb saw it. He felt the umpires had cheated him out of steals which would have changed the outcome of the game. First, he was called out on an attempted steal of home by George Hildebrand. The next inning, Billy Evans thumbed Cobb out on a steal attempt of second base. Cobb fumed. When the game ended he went to the umpires' room and challenged Evans to meet him under the stands to settle matters man-to-man.

Billy Evans considered himself just as manly as the Georgia Peach. He was an all-around athlete, had boxed in college, and was tired of Cobb's belligerence. The men stripped to the waist and went at it. For 10 or more minutes they slugged it out, landing heavy body blows that staggered each other. Finally, the players stopped it. Hands were shaken and assurances of each other's gameness replaced the snarling cursing that started the fight. Cobb missed a few games, and Evans avoided the strain of home plate assignments for a week.

Walter Johnson closed the season with an easy win that brought his record to 17-14. He had not even led the staff in wins. The two left-handers, George Mogridge and Tom Zachary, each won 18. The only category in which Johnson led the American League was in strike-outs. He reclaimed his title, after losing it in the half season he pitched in 1920, with 143. He also broke Cy Young's career strikeout record...or maybe he only came close.

In August, the record watchers counted the strikeouts as Johnson neared what was understood to be Cy Young's final total of 2,771. This is what the record books of the time claimed. With a degree of fatalism, Young read in the newspapers that Johnson was closing in. On August 13, when he beat the Red Sox, Johnson was hailed as the new recordholder, and Cy Young sent a congratulatory telegram from his farm in Peoli, Ohio. However, Frank Williams' close examination of Johnson's actual records shows that he had registered numbers 2,771 and 2,772 in the previous game of August 8 against St. Louis.

Put that aside for the moment. The ninth edition of Macmillan's

Baseball Encyclopedia now lists Cy Young as having struck out 2,796 batters. That means Johnson did not catch and pass old Cy until the game of September 5, when he lost a 4-3 game in 11 innings with no one making a fuss about the new record. That is, unless you accept *Total Baseball* as your infallible source. They say Young struck out 2,800 batters in his career. That pushes the day of reckoning ahead to the game of September 10, back in Washington, with the Red Sox providing the final victims.

However, everyone might be wrong. The ranking figure filbert of the 1920s was Al Munro Elias. In 1923, *Baseball Magazine* published *This Baseball Dope Book* which contains Cy Young's lifetime record according to Elias. He claimed his count of the old records showed Cy Young had fanned 2,832. Walter Johnson's career strikeout total, according to Frank Williams' painstaking count of every K ever entered in an official score sheet, had only reached 2,831 by the end of the 1921 season. As they used to say in Brooklyn, "Wait'll next year." It would become an added touch to another opening day game. That is, if Al Munro Elias was right, and Macmillan and *Total Baseball* are wrong about Cy Young. Perhaps Frank Williams, or another SABR colleague, will peruse the official score sheets at Cooperstown someday so we can know definitely just how many strikeouts Cy Young actually registered. In that way, an asterisk can belatedly mark the game in which Walter Johnson broke the previous strikeout record.

The season-ending game was played on "Milan Day," and he responded with two hits. Although George McBride had managed a first-division finish and only missed third place by a half game, he would resign because of the after-effects of a mid-season injury. Milan would be given the manager's job for the coming season. McBride had suffered a severe injury when a ball thrown in infield practice struck him in the head. He had dizzy spells afterward and missed the last month of the season.

Coffeyville, Kansas, welcomed the Johnsons back home and on October 24 put on a benefit game for their favorite son. When he got back to the farm he learned Hazel had presented him with another boy, Robert. He now had three sons, Walter Jr., Eddie, and Bobby. There was also his fragile daughter, Elinor Lee. A few months later, just a week before Christmas, the baby girl passed away of an internal infection. She was buried in the Johnsons' family plot in Coffeyville. Walter and Hazel would have other daughters, but the three boys would be the only sons.

Baseball Magazine's February 1922 issue carried a first-person article written during the past winter under Walter Johnson's byline. He tipped off his self-image by entitling it "The Reflections Of An Old Timer." Just past his 33rd birthday, he is reminiscent and studying the prospects of retirement.

Johnson began by reflecting on the disappointing 1921 season. He admitted he began to pitch before he was really ready after the long layoff that had followed the previous year's mid-season end. Just as he was rounding into form, he wrote, "We moved on to Chicago where the temperature took a decided drop and I caught a severe cold, a kind of grippe cold. Ten years ago I wouldn't have bothered so much about such a cold. But I can't shake off ten years and things I could do easily once are not easy for me now."

Blaming that early-season cold and remembering the one caught crossing Lake Erie in August, Johnson predicted he would bounce back in the coming season. He said, "Personally, I believe I am good for three or four more fairly respectable seasons." He was more than prescient, he was overly modest in his projection, although he would have several more lesser seasons before reaching the heights again.

About his Coffeyville farm and its future, Johnson observed, "Generally, when a player is on the down grade, he begins to cast about for some other occupation. It is the other way around with me. I have had a good stock farm in Kansas for years. On that farm there are fifty head of registered cattle that cost me a lot of money, but I am seriously thinking of selling the farm. My father died last summer and there is no one else to look after the place for me." Johnson says he would be sorry to lose his cows, but he would still have his dogs. About his hunting he added, "I didn't go coon hunting so much last winter for that keeps you up nights and an old pitcher like myself must sleep to preserve his health." He described a new sport, coyote hunting with his pack of foxhounds. This was a daytime activity, with the hunters trailing the pack in automobiles. Driving across the rough prairie when the coyotes did not obligingly stick to the dirt roads was hard on the cars, but better than walking.

Among the photographs illustrating the piece, is one of Walter Johnson posed on the end of a diving board, wearing a two-piece swimsuit rented from the Miami Beach Baths. Another shows his sons Walter Jr. and Eddie in baseball uniforms with Eugenia Milan looking on. There is also a studio-posed photograph of the two boys, scrubbed and combed, wearing sailor suits. They are standing beside their little sister, Elinor Lee, seated on a table and wearing a baby bonnet. She is holding a rosary.

23

A Losing Season for Johnson

THE MID-JANUARY ANNOUNCEMENT that Clyde Milan would manage the Washington Senators in 1922 stirred a new interest in spring training in the Johnson household. With his closest friend as the manager, new arrangements would be necessary. Off the field their friendship could continue, but the new manager would no longer be Walter Johnson's roommate on the road. Other new factors were also considered. Mr. and Mrs. Roberts, Hazel's parents, no longer lived part of the year in Washington, D.C., so Hazel and the children could not stay with them while waiting for spring training to end.

Sitting in a Kansas farmhouse kitchen in mid-winter, it would seem a wonderful idea to have Hazel and the children go to Tampa first. The Milans, Zeb and Margaret and their young children, would be there. The wives and youngsters could go to the beach and swim in Tampa Bay while their husbands got ready for the season. Walter Jr. was six. It was time to start school, but that could wait until the family reached Washington, or until next year. Juggling school terms with Johnson's baseball job would always require difficult choices for the devoted couple. Later, it would mean that Johnson's family would remain in Coffeyville until the school year ended. When the team played in St. Louis on its first western swing, Johnson would start the first game. Then he would make a short visit home before rejoining the team for his next start.

All things considered, spring training of 1922 seemed a wonderful chance for a family vacation. However, all things had not been considered. Hazel became seriously ill soon after their arrival in Tampa. She complained of severe headaches. The diagnosis was that she had a major sinus problem. An operation was necessary.

Paul W. Eaton, who had covered Washington baseball for *The Sporting Life,* was now the correspondent for *The Sporting News.* He reported the Johnsons' ordeal in a dispatch headed "Washington Calls It a Rotten Break—Walter Johnson All Upset By Illness of His Wife —Griffith's Ace Just Recovering from Own Spell of Sickness When Misfortune Comes To Him."

Eaton told his readers, "The worst part of the misfortunes of the great pitcher is that they involve the quite serious illness of Mrs. Johnson with sinus trouble which is a particularly painful and dangerous ailment. An operation was performed but she is still suffering some pain, and it is feared that another incision may be necessary to relieve the gathering in the frontal sinus.

"Walter, who had already lost five or six days' practice and was in poor condition owing to a threatened attack of grippe, was completely upset by his wife's illness and came near suffering a nervous breakdown. He collapsed during the operation at which he was present because it was Mrs. Johnson's wish, and he had been too much worried about her condition to practice or give much attention to the game."

Clark Griffith took charge and ordered special accommodations aboard a northbound train as soon as Hazel Johnson could be transported. Mrs. Roberts was en route to Washington from Nevada and would take over the Johnson household. Although it was a long shot that Walter Johnson could be ready to pitch the opening game, Val Picinich, his catcher, and several surplus substitutes, were sent along. The idea was that Johnson could get his arm ready at Griffith Park while the squad worked its way north from Florida. It fell short of its objective. Walter Johnson's whole season was marred by the upset over Hazel's illness and the bout of grippe which cut into his strength. Because he seemed to effortlessly throw a steady stream of sidearm fastballs, he was viewed as a pitching machine. His even temperament concealed his emotions. "The Big Train" was a machine, but Walter Johnson, husband and father, was not.

Opening Day came, but Walter Johnson was not on the mound. He watched the panoply and hoopla of the occasion from the dugout. President Warren G. Harding arrived early for the game with the Yankees and had to compete with Babe Ruth for the crowd's attention. However, the Babe was not in the lineup. He was not even in uniform. Ruth had been suspended by Commissioner Judge Landis following the World Series. Landis had decreed that players who had already pocketed a sizable share of World Series profits could not then go barnstorming to pick up more money. Babe Ruth, a drawing card, ignored the Landis edict and was slapped down by the commissioner in a clash of roles. Ruth was not paid his $3,362.26 share of the World Series money. More devastating, particularly to his team and league, the commissioner banned him from playing until May 20, 1922. Judge Landis might have picked the issue purposely. It matched him, the embodiment of authority, against the most popular player. It also pitted him against Ban Johnson. The man who created the American League resented being outranked by an all-powerful commissioner. He openly criticized Judge Landis for suspending the biggest drawing card in his league. To show this, Ban Johnson deliberately seated himself with Babe Ruth.

Faced with being upstaged by the Home Run King, President Harding made the most of an unexpected photo opportunity. Walter Johnson, Jr., came to Harding's box and was lifted onto the presidential knee. The boy remained for several innings, then scampered off to find his father. Walter Johnson was back in the shadows of the dugout.

The Yankees without Ruth and the Senators without Johnson began the season. The Yankees would recover, but Washington would not. Ruth, playing only 110 games, would lose the home run crown but lead the league in slugging percentage. Johnson would lose the strikeout title and not lead the league in anything. Ruth was in the prime of his career, Walter Johnson seemed to have entered the twilight era of his.

On the eve of the season's opening, a welcoming banquet was given Clyde Milan at the Arlington Hotel. Although Clark Griffith's present had already been unwrapped in spring training, the team's new shortstop was introduced. The position had finally been filled by Roger Peckinpaugh. He was among the very best shortstops in the league. The Yankees had let him go after nine seasons to get one they considered even better, Everett Scott of the Boston Red Sox. Scott, midway through a consecutive game streak which would be the record until Lou Gehrig eventually broke it, and Peckinpaugh were part of a three-team swap. The Yankees were right about Scott, but they were wrong about Peckinpaugh, who had managed them earlier in his career. Working with Bucky Harris at second base, in 1922 he and the Senators would set a major league record for double plays. The next year they would set a new record. Optimism was high in Washington. Illness, injury, and a losing season by Walter Johnson would turn it to a disappointment.

A new attendance record, 24,673, was set on Opening Day, April

12, and George Mogridge edged out his former team, 6-5. Johnson made his first appearance six days later. It was a disaster. The final score was 17-2, with Philadelphia humiliating the great pitcher. He lasted five innings and was wild. He walked four and hit one batter. He was charged with six earned runs. It would be 22 days before Walter Johnson started another game.

Even without Walter Johnson's customary contributions, Washington was off to a promising start, winning seven of the first 11 games. When Johnson got into the starting rotation, the fans expected the team would climb to first place. It did not happen. Before he started again, Johnson made brief tune-up appearances in late-inning relief roles and looked as though he was rounding into form. He pitched hitless, scoreless innings in three games. When the St. Louis Browns, riding unexpectedly high at the top of the stand-ing, came to town with a seven-game win streak, Johnson stopped them. He pitched a complete game, winning 2-1. He won again, beating Cleveland 3-2 when Joe Judge hit a ninth-inning home run. Then he won a third game, 4-3. However, against the White Sox Johnson uncharacteristically walked eight batters, and only Judge's leaping stab of a line drive by Harry Hooper with the bases loaded in the ninth inning saved the game.

When the team went to New York, Walter Johnson managed a 5-3 victory. It was to be the only game that year that the Senators won at the Polo Grounds, where the Yankees were playing their last season before moving to their new home in the Yankee Stadium. Babe Ruth's suspension had ended, but he was very slow to regain his batting eye. Johnson made him the third out with bases loaded twice, the last time in the ninth inning. The crowd got on the Babe, and he petulantly resented it. The next day he threw dirt in the face of umpire George Hildebrand and went into the stands after a heckler. Ban Johnson sus-pended him before Judge Landis could. Walter Johnson raised his record to 5-1 with a 10-inning win over the Yankees back in Washington. Again, Joe Judge bailed him out, hitting a game-winning home run in the 10th. Johnson was pitching successfully, but not with the blazing speed of other years. By the end of May he had only 20 strikeouts and had pitched 56.1 innings.

A more momentous event for baseball also came at the end of May. The Federal League was still a specter. The Baltimore franchise had sued organized baseball for $240,000 in damages, citing violation of the Sherman Act and claiming an antitrust judgment. The case reached the Supreme Court, which decided organized baseball was exempt from compliance. The value to baseball's franchises since then is beyond calculation. It is still a fragile protection, but the hold on a player's services has been so altered that its importance is not what it once was.

June began with a typical Johnson loss, 2-1, at home to Boston, before Washington took off on a road trip to the western cities. It was to be Walter Johnson's best month of the season. He relieved in Cleveland and got the win in an 11-inning game, which brought Washington up to .500 and the first division. They never got higher, although Johnson was off to a scoreless-inning streak that reached 30. He shut out the White Sox and came home to blank the Athletics and Yankees. His 1-0 defeat of Waite Hoyt was hailed as his 97th shutout. Later removal of three shared shutouts made it number 94, but more were to come.

The pendulum of close games swung against Walter Johnson as July began with a 2-1 loss to the Red Sox. Then he lost 7-6, 2-0, and 1-0 before hitting a bad stretch where he was beaten 8-5 and gave up six runs, but he won a game when his team provided a rare 18-run backing. It still looked as though Johnson would salvage a representative season as August began. He won to reach an 11-8 record. From there on he alternated between winning and losing, including a 2-0 loss in 12 innings to a Cleveland rookie, Danny Boone. To make the memory of the event the biggest of his short and losing career, Boone batted in the winning run.

Walter Johnson won another 1-0 game, then lost, 3-1 and 1-0. On September 8, his record leveled off at 14-14 when he was beaten, 8-1. It was the game that sent the Yankees into first place ahead of the Browns, and they stayed there through a furious stretch drive. To make Johnson's drubbing even worse, the winning pitcher was Carl Mays.

Johnson's remaining games were pitched on the road. In Cleveland he lost a two-run lead when the Indians scored three in the ninth. In St. Louis he figured in the hectic pennant race. He opened the series with a 4-3 win which dropped the Browns $2\frac{1}{2}$ games behind the Yankees. Even worse for their chances, George Sisler, playing with a wrenched shoulder which limited him to swinging the bat with one hand, had his consecutive game hitting streak stopped at 41 the day before. It topped Ty Cobb's 40-game streak of 1911 and lasted as the American League record until Joe DiMaggio broke it in 1941. Sisler pinch-hit against Walter Johnson, but he was an easy out. With his season record balanced at 15-15, Johnson pitched poorly against the

White Sox, losing 8-3, on September 23, and concluded his year's work with a losing record.

24

Milestones of the Past and More Ahead

T HE FARM IN COFFEYVILLE was becoming more of a retreat for the Johnsons than the hub of existence. Minnie Johnson sat at the head of the table now that her husband, Frank, was gone. Hired help did most of the work, and the farm and its buildings were a playground for the three active boys. There had been no annual Walter Johnson Day game, probably because Johnson had not hurried home soon enough after the season ended. There was now a large home on Irving Street in Washington, D.C., where the Johnsons lived half the year. They had close friends in both places. The day was coming when they would have to choose one over the other. Johnson's pitching career would probably decide that. It was coming to an end, he judged.

The idea of using spring training as a family vacation did not arise in 1923. Zeb Milan had been replaced as manager. Too easygoing, people believed. Yet they would argue for the even more placid Walter Johnson to lead the team soon in the future. Donie Bush, a longtime teammate of Ty Cobb in Detroit and also a strong personality, had his playing career wane to an end with Washington. He took over as manager. He could have been ordered from a stock catalog of managers, all with roughly the same specifications, interchangeable with the George McBrides, Kid Elberfelds, and other "brainy" players.

During the season, Bush was to develop an animosity toward Sam Rice which foreshadowed a future split with another Hall of Fame outfielder. In 1927, when Bush bobbed up to lead Pittsburgh into a devastating World Series rout by Ruth, Gehrig, and the Murderers' Row Yankees, he limited his team's chances by benching Hazen "KiKi" Cuyler over a dispute as to whether the hard-hitting star should learn to hit and run and bat second. In 1923 Bush pushed Washington higher in the standings to a fourth-place finish. He added six wins to the team totals of the year before, thanks specifically to Walter Johnson, who lost four fewer games and won two more in 1923 than in 1922.

Walter Johnson's importance to his team was eulogized in an editorial in *The Sporting News*. In the May 10 issue, J.G. Taylor Spink wrote a tribute, headed "What Walter Johnson Means." Spink keyed his editorial on the co-event of May 2 when Everett Scott played his 1,000th consecutive game and Walter Johnson pitched his 100th shutout. He pointed out that whether Scott had missed a few games along the way would not have mattered to the fortunes of the Red Sox or Yankees. However, he said, "Without Walter Johnson and his shutouts there might even be no Washington in the American League; but for the work of Johnson in winning ball games for the team that represents the capital city and for the hold he has on the public of the capital, the team that represents Washington might be labeled Toronto or Milwaukee, possibly Baltimore—we are not joking."

Pitching the first game of the season was an almost annual act for Walter Johnson. He was ready this year but had to open on the road in Philadelphia. Ban Johnson was still blindly passing up a now standing offer, particularly with Warren G. Harding in the White House, to start the season off with the nation's official blessing. Johnson had a new catcher. In one of his best trades ever, Clark Griffith had landed Herold "Muddy" Ruel in a swap with the Red Sox. He sent Val Picinich, Johnson's catcher, to Boston along with all-purpose player Hank Shanks and a young outfield prospect, Ed Goebel. Along with Ruel came Allan Russell, a spitballer still allowed to throw the wet pitch, who was an effective reliever. In 1923 he would lead the league with nine wins and nine saves while working in relief. As with Roger Peckinpaugh's arrival in 1922, Griffith had filled a glaring need. Ruel hit .316 for his new team and was rock-steady behind the plate. He was an exceptional person in baseball. A lawyer who was admitted to practice before the U.S. Supreme Court, he later was Detroit's general manager, managed the St. Louis Browns, and was Commissioner Happy Chandler's administrative assistant. On April 18, he caught Walter Johnson for the first time. And, for the third straight time, Johnson lost an opening day game. This time, the loss was largely due to Slim Harriss' mastery over the Senators. The elongated Philadelphia righthander had won only nine games the year before but beat Washington four times. Harriss had lost 20 games, but none to the Senators. Jimmy Dykes' two-run homer made the difference in a 3-1 opening day loss for Walter Johnson.

President Harding was not easily discouraged. When the Senators went next to New York, the president showed up. He was in the city for some ceremonial presidential purpose and decided to take in a game at the new Yankee Stadium. Johnson had already pitched his turn. He defeated the champions, 4-3, in the first Sunday game in the new park, played before 60,000 people. When he turned up two days later, the president sought out Johnson and told him, "Walter, I came out to root for Washington." The incident was recounted in Johnson's memoirs when he wrote: "I distinctly remember the last game President Harding witnessed. He was in New York and showed up at Yankee Stadium unannounced." Harding rooted for the Senators in vain. Babe Ruth homered and Sad Sam Jones pitched the first shutout in the brief history of the new stadium, 4-0. It was the first ballpark to be called a stadium, and it prompted Clark Griffith to rename his own field Griffith Stadium.

Warren G. Harding did not live out the 1923 season. He died August 2, under circumstances which some, especially those who sense a conspiracy plot whenever a prominent officeholder dies suddenly, believe were contrived to cover up scandals in the White House. The day the president died was the 16th anniversary of Walter Johnson's debut as a big league pitcher. Unlike many times in the past, including the previous season, Johnson was not scheduled to pitch the anniversary game. Once, the fans had presented him a trophy filled with money. Either the fans were growing blasé, or Donie Bush was still more of a Detroit Tiger at heart than a Washington sentimentalist.

Walter Johnson made his first home start and pitched what was deemed to be his 100th shutout. The calculations were off, even according to the records which included the three partial shutouts which were later dropped from the total. However, you can't undo a good promotion and there was extra press coverage of the game because it was Everett Scott's 1,000th in a row. He eventually played 307 more, leaving the record for Gehrig to shatter. Now, with the durable Cal Ripken, Jr. having bettered Gehrig's iron-man stunt, Scott is no longer even the runner-up.

Johnson watchers in the press box noted that he was weakening in the late innings. Griffith's acquisition of reliever Russell was proving wise. He had saved Johnson a defeat in a game on April 27. Johnson bowed out after Philadelphia had scored seven runs in 4.1 innings, but Russell held the game to a 12-inning 10-10 tie. Johnson's era of completing almost all of his starts was over. In 1923 he would start 34 games but finish only 18 of them. Allan Russell's relief work made the difference in Johnson's final won-lost mark. On June 18, however, Johnson needed no help, winning a 13-inning complete game which lifted Washington from the cellar. Johnson's leg cramped with a charley horse on June 30 and he limped off the field. His road roomie, Joe Judge, also left with a leg injury. Russell came in and maintained a 1-1 tie until the Senators scored in the 10th.

When the team went on to New York, Walter Johnson stayed behind. His family might have hoped to spend the Fourth of July with a limping father at home, but he rejoined the team for a holiday doubleheader at Yankee Stadium. There were fireworks, but of the wrong kind. Johnson did not last through the second inning, yielding six runs of an eventual 12-2 Washington defeat. As the team swung west, Johnson's record dropped back toward .500. He hit three batters while losing to the White Sox. Charlie Robertson, who had pitched a rare perfect game the year before, was the winning pitcher. Johnson lost in Cleveland and was past the mid-season mark with a record of 8-8. Four days later he won from the Indians, and the press hailed his 3,000th strikeout. Johnson breezed, 15-3, in Boston and came home to win 1-0 from Detroit. August fell into a similar Johnson pattern of one-run games. He won 2-1 and lost 3-2.

When the Senators went on their final western road trip, Johnson had no decisions in two games he started but did not finish. He was forced out of a game in Detroit on August 25 with another leg injury. Johnson had coasted into second base on a hit, and when the outfielder bobbled the ball, started up again. He popped a tendon and hobbled on to third base. He left with Washington in the lead, but the Tigers rallied in the ninth to win. Johnson was sent back to Washington the next day but rejoined the team in Boston for a Labor Day doubleheader. He gave up the winning hit to the one batter he faced, but the loss went to the pitcher he had relieved. Once, the defeat would have been charged to Johnson. That same sort of situation had ended his 16-game consecutive win streak in 1912, as it did Rube Marquard's 19-game string. However, the old scoring rule had been changed. It became the same as it is today; the pitcher who puts the winning run on base gets the loss.

Fred Marberry, a hulk of a man, made his major league debut by starting the second game. He was relieved by the team's reigning stopper, Allan Russell. The next year, Marberry became famous himself as a reliever, perhaps the best there ever was.

The Senators finished the season at home. The long stretches of games at Griffith Stadium offered a lifestyle Walter Johnson relished. *The Literary Digest*, a very popular monthly for a readership with general interests, reprinted an affectionately written article from Henry Ford's *Dearborn Magazine*. The writer, who used the byline "A Neighbor," described Johnson's comfortable home life, although he also wrote about the pitcher's life in baseball. The account of his early years in California, how he broke into baseball and was recruited by the Senators, was familiar to sports page readers. The general public, though, was learning it for the first time.

An apparently mellowing Walter Johnson confided to his Washington friend about his sense of well being. He is described as sitting in an oversized armchair, wearing slippers, and playing with a favorite dog, an Airedale. Hazel tolerated a few chewed bones on the living-room rug so that her three boys had a dog available. She was busy with the fourth member of the family, the newly arrived infant daughter, Carolyn.

Another neighbor, living next door, was a minister, the pastor of one of the most fashionable churches in Washington according to the author of the article. The author observed, "When I was about to move into the neighborhood, I had a talk with him. 'It's a very select situation,' he told me. 'One of your neighbors will be Walter Johnson—a great man.' I was somewhat surprised at the minister's evident admiration for the baseball star.

"But later I learned the reason, for I came to know Walter Johnson in his home and the minister was right."

Walter Johnson, starting the month at 12-10, rolled through September. He won five times and lost twice to post a final 17-12 record for the year. He won twice in a doubleheader with the St. Louis Browns. He relieved in the first game with the score tied and got the win when Washington scored in the 10th inning. He started the second game and won a lopsided 12-2 victory with the game called because of darkness after seven innings. Johnson pitched his third shutout of the season, another 1-0 classic, against the White Sox to close the home stand against western clubs. Before the season ended the next week, Walter Johnson lost at Philadelphia, 4-3 in 11 innings. He closed out the 1923 campaign with his highest strikeout total of the year, fanning a dozen Red Sox and winning, 4-2. It was one of the few times ever that he set out to strike out as many batters as he could. In the closing days of the season he was in a battle with Joe Bush and Bob Shawkey of the Yankees for the strikeout title. Johnson, after leading the American League eight straight times, had lost the title in 1922. He was out to get it back. Johnson's final surge carried him to a six strikeout margin over both Bush and Shawkey. In this game, Johnson hit a ball into the stands, a home run distance by any measure. However, new center-field stands were being built and a ground rule limited a ball hit into them to a double. The added seats brought Griffith Stadium's capacity to 33,000.

On the final day of the season, Washington managed to slip into first division by a half game. The Senators won their last three games while Ty Cobb's Detroit Tigers knocked off the St. Louis Browns in their final three-game set. Still, it was not good enough for Clark Griffith. He believed he had assembled a team that could win the pennant. He decided that Donie Bush was not the man to lead the way to a championship. On October 23, Bush joined Milan and McBride as only a short-term surrogate for Griffith. Eddie Collins was rumored to be coming to Washington in a trade with a lot of Griffith's dollars added to the pot. Collins wanted to manage. Cobb and Speaker led their teams. George Sisler, out all of 1923 with sinusitis, expected to return as manager of the Browns. Collins was their peer. However, the deal fell through. The "usual suspects," unemployed ex-managers or managers in shaky situations were constantly rumored to be the next Washington field leader. George Stallings, who had led the 1914 "Miracle Braves" to immortality, reportedly refused to give up a comfortable berth as owner-manager of Rochester in the International League. Roger Peckinpaugh, who had been a "boy manager" with New York when he was 24, might have been a good choice. When Clark Griffith finally acted, he named a "boy manager" of his own. The job went to Stanley "Bucky" Harris, the 27-year-old second baseman. He was as surprised as anyone. Asked to explain why Griffith had chosen him, he offered that perhaps it was his willingness to move to third base and make room for Eddie Collins should he come to the Senators that had impressed Griffith. It certified Harris as a team-oriented player. For whatever reason, a calculated judgment or a hunch, picking Bucky Harris proved to be an inspired choice.

25

"The Boy Manager" —Harris Leads Way to Pennant

Aｌｔｈｏｕｇｈ Sｔａｎｌｅｙ Rａｙｍｏｎｄ Hａｒｒｉｓ was the youngest manager in the major leagues, he was ready to lead a big league team. Harris had scrabbled his way through lower-class leagues in the anthracite coal cities of Pennsylvania. Always a good glove man, he became a better hitter as he moved upward toward the major leagues. Several of his fielding records still stand, and teamed with Roger Peckinpaugh, he broke all double-play records made until his time.

A bachelor when he arrived in Washington, he moved in better social circles as manager, and when he married a few years later, President Calvin Coolidge attended the ceremony.

There was an informal gathering of some of the veteran players at Hot Springs, Arkansas, before they headed to Tampa for the regular spring training session. Harris led the way, and Walter Johnson, who had only visited the spa in earlier years for the pickup baseball games he could find there, now made good use of the mineral springs. He soaked away his winter stiffness with Joe Judge, Roger Peckinpaugh, Tom Zachary, and a few others. The idea that Washington could win the pennant took hold, and when they assembled again in Florida, the cadre was set. This could be the year that Walter Johnson finally pitched in a World Series.

The team was virtually unchanged from the year before. There was a new pitching coach, Jack Chesbro. Johnson's rival from 1908 took over the pitchers from Nick Altrock, leaving him to coach bases and work on comedy routines with Al Schacht. Ossie Bluege at third base had rounded out the infield last season. With Peckinpaugh, Harris, and Judge, he formed as solid a defensive unit as has ever played together. Goslin, who had missed part of the previous season, and Sam Rice flanked Nemo Leibold. During the season Griffith bought right-handed hitting Earl McNeely from Sacramento of the Pacific Coast League. He alternated with left-handed hitting Leibold. Muddy Ruel resumed his role as a master handler of pitchers. The staff was primarily the same, except that Fred Marberry would be on hand from the start of the season.

In addition to Walter Johnson's resurgence, Marberry made the primary difference in the two seasons. Jack Dempsey had knocked out Luis Firpo, billed as the Wild Man of the Pampas the year before. Dempsey won, but first the Argentinean slugger sent the heavyweight champ flying out of the ring in a sensational two-round brawl. When someone noticed that Marberry resembled the colorful South American, he became known as "Firpo" Marberry. Whether they were look-alikes or not, both intimidated their opponents. Marberry became a fourth starter behind Walter Johnson and the lefties, Tom Zachary and George Mogridge, and also joined Allan Russell as a reliever. Marberry made a league-leading 50 appearances in both roles and saved 15 games.

Walter Johnson got ready for 1924 in his usual way, with three-inning stints against major league teams. Griffith scheduled his training games against National League teams. Johnson went three innings, allowing one run, against the Giants and repeated the pattern against the Dodgers. The Senators raised the hopes of the fans back home, winning five of six games from the Braves.

When the 1924 season began, it was like old times. Walter Johnson had not won an opener since 1919. This time he not only won, he shut out the Philadelphia Athletics, 4-0. He gave up only four hits, one, a single, to a rookie making his first big league appearance. Al Simmons was to add 2,925 more hits, just failing to reach 3,000 for his career. Johnson won four of his first five decisions, but only two came in complete games. Simmons knocked him out of a game in Philadelphia with a three-run homer, and Marberry saved two 3-2 victories over the Yankees and the A's.

Despite Johnson's winning stats, the Senators were off slowly, and the New York Yankees, looking for a fourth straight pennant, led the league. Washington was sixth. On May 23, Walter Johnson pitched one of his greatest games. At home against the Chicago White Sox, Johnson allowed only one hit, a fourth-inning single off the bat of his longtime nemesis, Harry Hooper. In this game Johnson struck out 14 batters. The win sent a strong signal to the rest of the league that the Big Train was back on track and running at full throttle. Boston overtook New York, but Washington was moving up, too. The fans began to stir in anticipation. When the Senators won 10-straight in one stretch of their first western trip, and Walter Johnson won four times on the road, the national capital buzzed with excitement.

On June 26, President Calvin Coolidge took his family to the welcome-back game. With his wife, Grace, keeping a scorecard, and his sons, John and Calvin Jr., leading the cheers, the president saw Walter Johnson pitch his fourth shutout of the season, 5-0. The Senators were now in first place. Boston and Detroit stayed close, but closest of all to the new front-runners were the New York Yankees. They defeated the Senators twice in a July 4 doubleheader and beat Johnson the next day, 2-0.

The Yankees and everyone in Griffith Stadium had a major scare in the fifth inning. Babe Ruth, in hot pursuit of a foul ball curving away from him in right field, raced full speed after it. He smashed into a concrete abutment in front of the right-field stands and crumbled to the ground. Doc Painter, the Yankee trainer, grabbed the water bucket and his first-aid kit and raced the police to the scene. Ruth, stretched out on the ground, could not move. The players hovering over him saw he was conscious. He just could not move. Ruth had taken as hard a blow in the solar plexus as any ever thrown in the ring by Jack Dempsey. The effects gradually wore off, and Ruth insisted on staying in the game. He managed to get a single with a restrained swing later but had to sit out the next several games.

On July 10, New York and Washington were tied for first place. From that point on it was ding-dong all the way; neither team could open a lead on the other. The Detroit Tigers were in the thick of the race, too. On August 10 they got to the front only to have the Yankees regain the lead on August 13.

The Senators got a tremendous boost when a player who had burned up the Pacific Coast League, Earl McNeely, joined the team in Chicago. When his new player reported with a sore shoulder, Griffith first thought the Sacramento Sacs had sold him damaged goods and wanted to cancel the deal. He protested to Judge Landis, who luckily said the matter was not in his jurisdiction. Harris used McNeely only against left-handed pitchers and the right-handed batter wore them out, hitting .330 the rest of the season.

Walter Johnson came within a cloudburst of pitching his second no-hitter against St. Louis. A deluge after the seventh inning stopped the game with Washington ahead, 2-0. George Sisler, manager of the hitless Browns, was quoted by the wire services as saying, "The Browns all regretted that the game could not go nine innings as there seemed little doubt that Walter Johnson would pitch a no-hitter." That night Walter and Hazel Johnson went to B.F. Keith's Theatre. Frank Crummit and Julia Sanderson, a theatrical husband and wife singing duo, headlined the bill. "America's Singing Sweethearts" were to their profession's matrimonial standards what the Johnsons were to baseball's.

Walter Johnson was urged to his feet by a tumultuous ovation, and the couple on stage tossed large bouquets of roses across the footlights. The men in the audience threw their straw hats in the air. It was almost Labor Day and time to discard the summer skimmers. Usually they were disposed of at the ballpark. Sailing straw hats onto the ball field was more fun than throwing seat cushions, and fans didn't forfeit a deposit. It was a Labor Day tradition for men to discard their straw hats at the ballpark, usually at the end of the holiday twin bills. This long-forgotten impromptu ceremony ceased about the time of the Great Depression when disposable hard straw hats went out of fashion.

Getting Johnson to take a bow was never easy. Will Rogers once spotted Walter Johnson in a rear orchestra row at a performance of the Ziegfeld Follies. He slipped around to the back of the house and lassoed the pitcher. Securely roped, the shy pitcher was led to a better seat by the wisecracking cowboy entertainer.

The seven-inning no-hitter was Johnson's seventh straight victory. He would not lose again until his last appearance, when he was literally knocked out of the box. A line drive hit his left elbow when he was trailing 2-0 late in a game. In another game he hurt his pitching hand on a hot line drive back at the box. He was not as mobile as he had been. Age was slowing his reflexes.

Although almost three weeks of the pennant race remained, the results of the 1924 Most Valuable Player contest were announced on September 12. The trophy went to Walter Johnson. An automobile no longer went with it. However, local fans would make up for that. Johnson might end up with a fleet of personal cars the way he was pitching. The MVP achievement so excited the only woman in Congress, Mae E. Nolan of California, that she promised to introduce a bill making Walter Johnson's birthday a legal holiday in the District of Columbia.

On August 28 Washington beat New York at Yankee Stadium and edged to the front again. It is only of passing sartorial interest, but on

September 2 the umpires appeared in olive drab uniforms. Babe Ruth was on his way to the only batting title he would ever win. He was hitting .389. Ty Cobb was fourth at .342. He was driving the Tigers with an undiminished determination. At 37, in his 21st season, Cobb played in every game in 1924. He hit .338, had 211 hits, and led the league in fielding at .986. Tris Speaker hit .344 and Eddie Collins .349. If the old guard was passing, it was going out in a blaze of glory.

A few days after his abbreviated no-hitter, Walter Johnson coasted to an easy victory, turning over a nine-run lead to Allan Russell after seven innings. Waite Hoyt lost a game for the Yankees and the lead was two games. It seemed safe to invite the ball club to the White House for a final pat of encouragement and approval. On September 5, photographers posed Calvin Coolidge with Walter Johnson's huge hand covering the president's as he held a baseball. Johnson showed the chief executive how to throw a fastball. In exchange, Coolidge showed how he used to bend a nickel curve as a teenager.

The purpose of the visit was to send the Washington Senators off on a final road trip with not only the city's blessings but the nation's, too. The country was enthralled with the battle the longtime doormats of baseball were putting on. Of course, Walter Johnson was the focus of national affection. Strangely, the schedule put both Washington and New York on the road for the rest of the season. They would make a final swing to the western cities. When they came back east, Washington would finish with a series in Boston, and New York a series in Philadelphia.

A quandary arose for the Johnsons. It would show confidence to wait for the team to clinch the pennant on the road and come back to play the World Series. However, a school term was beginning in Coffeyville and the two oldest boys were expected. If Washington won and played the World Series, there would be time for Hazel and her sons to get back. If the worst happened, Walter Johnson could quietly close down the house and join his family in Kansas. On September 7 the Yankees closed their home season with a 2-1 loss, and Washington also bid adieu on a losing note. What straw hats remained among local baseball fans were sent sailing across a ball field that the fans prayed had not been used for the last time in 1924.

Johnson started the trip off with his 20th victory, an 8-4 win over Philadelphia. When they went west to meet the still-contending Detroit Tigers, he beat them, too, with some late-inning help from Firpo Marberry. Neither Washington nor New York could pull away from the other. Detroit was only close enough to be a spoiler in the final drive. However, if the smart money was backing the New Yorkers because of their experience, they did not figure the race the way Bucky Harris did. Arriving in Cleveland, where his team had been beaten six out of seven games early in the season, Harris said during a press conference, "We have two great qualities a pennant contender must have—fine pitching and a winning spirit. Certainly none of the New York pitchers is as good as Walter Johnson, and we are much better fortified with reserve pitching. We also have another incentive—to win a pennant for the sake of Walter Johnson. We want him to close his major league career on a championship team."

The sentiments of the country were behind Walter Johnson's quest to finish with the glory of a World Championship. Will Rogers added his thoughts in his syndicated Sunday column. Headed "Everybody Is Pulling For Walter," the homespun humorist with the Populist's viewpoint wrote, "It is certainly a wonderful tribute that everybody is pulling for Walter. I don't suppose that ever in the history of any sporting event has sentiment played so big a part as it is playing in the case of this one man this year."

Rogers admired Walter Johnson for all the reasons everyone did, for both his personal values and his professional achievements. Rogers also took this view: "Johnson has never grumbled because he was with a team at the bottom of the list. He could have sulked and demanded to be traded and been with a pennant winner almost every year and made heaps of money. But not with this old Country Boy. That is why he stands in public estimation today where he does. He is known as a wonderful man, and today the entire baseball world is not just pulling for Johnson the Pitcher; they are pulling for Johnson the Man."

For the next two weeks, New York stuck doggedly on Washington's heels, and the teams again tied for first place on September 17. Johnson won his 12th straight, and Sam Rice hit in his 24th consecutive game. However, that day the Yankees took a pair to close the half-game gap. A few days later the American League president, Ban Johnson, announced the teams would meet in a three-game playoff if the season ended in a tie.

Ty Cobb's Tigers swept three games from the Yankees to help the Senators gain a two-game lead. A brawny newcomer to the Yankees, Lou Gehrig, singled as a pinch hitter. He rashly tried to stretch the hit to a double, and Ty Cobb gunned him down. Cobb jeered the rookie, and Everett Scott, the Yankee captain, challenged him. Gehrig needed no help. He yammered back at Cobb and the teams surged onto the field. When things were quieted down, Scott and Gehrig had been banished, but Cobb remained.

The Yankees were in trouble. Their pitchers were overworked. Hoyt, Pennock, Bush, and Shawkey started and relieved. Babe Ruth was in a slump. He was held to two singles in the Detroit series. The home run he hit on September 13, his 46th, was the last he would hit for the season.

Back in Washington, workmen hurriedly built stands in center field and fronted those in left and right field with rows of planks, rising in low tiers, to expand Griffith Stadium's capacity to 37,000. The city was spellbound by the possibility of their team winning the pennant. When rain delayed the start of a game in St. Louis, it was almost dark back east when it began. The departing government workers stopped on their way home to watch the illuminated scoreboards that tracked the game. There were three, one outside each of the daily newspapers. As darkness came to the capital, 20,000 people watched, cheering every turn of the game until Washington won, 6-4, in a game called after seven innings because darkness had also fallen in Missouri.

"The city is tense with excitement," reported the *New York Times*. They also carried the alarming news that President Coolidge might miss the opening World Series game even if Washington won. He had agreed to dedicate a memorial to the veterans of the Great War on the same afternoon the World Series was to begin. Not to worry, remember to "Keep Cool With Coolidge"; America did not win the war only to lose its sense of values. The dedication ceremony and its parade were rescheduled to start in the morning. All the Senators had to do was win the pennant and the president could go to the ball game in the afternoon. Meanwhile, in optimistic anticipation that God would not deny Walter Johnson his belated World Series appearance, a parade to welcome back the assumed conquering heroes was set for the day after the season ended. It might take until the final game for the Senators to shake off the persistent Yankees.

The embattled teams returned to the East, but not to their home ballparks. The Yankees opened their final set of three games in Shibe Park with the Philadelphia Athletics, and Herb Pennock won easily, 7-1. Walter Johnson, at Fenway Park, lost another of those 2-1 games that had plagued him throughout his career. The 12,000 Boston fans had rooted for Johnson, but in vain. The lead was one game.

Washington went two games ahead again the next day when a little-used rookie, Wade Lefler, pinch-hit a double with the bases loaded. Mogridge had been knocked out in the first inning, but Firpo Marberry, Allan Russell, and Tom Zachary took turns holding off the Red Sox. In Philadelphia, Joe Bush wild-pitched the winning run home to lose, 4-3, after driving in all three Yankee runs.

There was still no Sunday baseball in Boston or Philadelphia. Matters would have to wait until after the Sabbath. Walter Johnson, Bucky Harris, and Roger Peckinpaugh went for a Sunday drive in the New England countryside. Washington led by two games with two to play. They could end the suspense the next day by winning. Even if the Yankees took their remaining games from Philadelphia, they could not catch the Senators unless Washington lost.

On Monday, September 29, 1924, the event for which Walter Johnson had waited happened. It was not his turn to pitch, so he sat on the edge of his seat in the dugout and watched Tom Zachary work three shaky innings. Washington scored three early runs but led only 3-2 when Firpo Marberry came to the rescue. He blanked Boston the rest of the way for a 4-2 win. Back in Washington, the city erupted with a celebration that rivaled the one in 1918 hailing the Armistice.

In the White House, Grace Coolidge had listened to the game on the radio. The telegraphed account was read off the ticker in the studio and broadcast to the local listeners. The First Lady quickly spread the news throughout the White House. Outside the revelry began up and down Pennsylvania Avenue. It was raining, but that dampened no one's enthusiasm. Men who were strangers shook hands in wonderment that the day had finally come, girls kissed men they had never met before, and Democrats joyfully clapped Republicans on the back. The city was rejoicing that it had finally happened—Walter Johnson would pitch in a World Series.

It was raining in Philadelphia, too. The Yankees had not been able to play the A's, but it did not matter. Washington had won the game it needed to cinch its first pennant ever. Both teams had a day remaining on the schedule. Before they could come home to celebrate, the Senators frolicked through a meaningless finale. Nick Altrock clowned through a few innings on the mound and the substitutes had a chance to play. The Yankees did not even have that. It kept raining in Philadelphia and washed out the doubleheader that had been scheduled. Only the remote chance that Babe Ruth might win a Triple Crown might have drawn the fans. The 1924 season was as close as

175

he ever came. The Babe had widened his lead for the batting title to a 19-point advantage, and his 46 home runs topped that department. However, Goose Goslin took the RBI title, 129 to 121. Could Ruth have caught him? Maybe. With two meaningless games to play, the Bambino might have had a great afternoon. But, we'll never know— it rained in Philadelphia. It was raining in Washington, too, but to the fans, the world had never looked brighter.

26

Washington Wild
on Eve of Series

E VEN BEFORE THE SENATORS finally clinched the pennant, Walter Johnson sent a two-word telegram from Boston to Coffeyville. "Come on!" he wired Hazel on Sunday, and she packed up the two youngest children, Bobby and Carolyn, and with Minnie Johnson at her side, headed for Washington. Walter Jr. and Eddie wailed at being left behind with Aunt Effie.

It had taken 18 years for Walter Johnson to reach the World Series, and 10 for Hazel to see her husband achieve his goal. With the pennant won, on the eve of the World Series, Walter Johnson announced he planned to retire. The wire services carried his statement:

> I realize that I cannot go much further. My arm is still good but I know I haven't the stuff I used to have. When the season started I had fully made up my mind to retire at the end of this year. Now it all depends on what comes up this winter.
>
> If I can get located in baseball somewhere in the West, that would suit me perfectly. I want to get settled. I have four little children and I want to get out of baseball before I get useless. If I can help Washington to win a world pennant this fall, that certainly would be the time to quit.

A vanguard of Senators reached Washington early Tuesday morning. Walter Johnson, Clark Griffith, Bucky Harris, and Sam Rice arrived on the 7:30 A.M. Federal Express. The others remained behind to play Tuesday's now meaningless final game with the Red Sox.

On Wednesday afternoon all the players, riding in open touring cars, were led down Pennsylvania Avenue by a mounted United States cavalry band. The boulevard, where Washington paraded its presidents to their inaugurations and welcomed its military heroes back from wars, was lined 10-deep with cheering, laughing, and excited citizens.

The elite red-jacketed Washington Riding and Hunt Club cantered by, their mounts prancing to the band's music. They were followed by limousines carrying politicians and business leaders. Then came the players, riding three to an open car. Bucky Harris was in the lead car, but the cheers were loudest when Walter Johnson, in the next car, waved to the crowds. The route ended at The Ellipse, where President Coolidge, accompanied by every officeholder who could find space on the reviewing stand, welcomed the team. Seats had been found for Hazel Johnson and Minnie Johnson, and they watched as the president presented a trophy to Bucky Harris. Clark Griffith and Harris thanked the president; they thanked the fans, they thanked the players, and, most of all, they thanked God for Walter Johnson.

Radio broadcasting and baseball were forming a symbiotic relationship in 1924. During the season WCAP kept listeners pressed against their earphones or loudspeakers to hear Stuart Hayes give the scores and highlights of Washington's games. The day after the welcoming parade, Hayes broadcast studio interviews with Walter Johnson, Clark Griffith, Bucky Harris, and Nick Altrock. Sales of radios boomed with the word that Graham McNamee would broadcast the World Series games live from the Polo Grounds and Griffith Stadium. Station WEAF in New York and WCAP would combine their fledgling facilities. McNamee, who would become the first "big name" sports broadcaster, despite a flimsy knowledge of games, had become famous for broadcasting the 1924 Democratic and Republican national conventions.

Walter Johnson was busy rounding up opening game tickets for visitors from Coffeyville. He had promised his neighbors, "If we win and you get here, I'll make sure you get to see the game." He worried more about this obligation, perhaps, than pitching the opening game. The commissioner's office had control of tickets and a familiar pattern emerged. Staunch fans of the home team, those who had supported them through the dark years, discovered large blocks of tickets had been set aside for out-of-towners. The best seats were assigned to the "connected"—in politics, business, or sports.

When he was not distracted trying to round up tickets, Walter Johnson was variously reported to be relaxed and confident or nervously worrying he might let his supporters down. Friendly legend has it that he was cool and unconcerned. Joe Engel, a neighbor of

Johnson's, who was a former pitcher and was a scout for the Senators in 1924, recalled that they had played cassino in the clubhouse until it was time for his friend Barney to go out and pitch the opening game. "We talked about everything 'cept baseball," Engel said. "He asked me if I thought 'Bob,' one of the hunting hounds out at his farm, would 'run tonight.' We were intending to work the dogs after the game."

Engel became a minor league equivalent of Bill Veeck, featuring bizarre promotions as owner of the Chattanooga Lookouts. Perhaps the account of Art Nehf, the New York Giants starting pitcher, is more reliable. In a February 1947 *Baseball Magazine* story, Frank Graham reported Nehf telling him, "The photographers got Walter and me together to take our pictures shaking hands and I could see what a strain he was under. Here he was, about to start his first World Series game after all the years of waiting and he knew what was expected of him. He also must have known that, all over the country, literally millions of people were hoping, wishing, even praying for him to win. He was so nervous that his hand trembled as I grasped it and I felt very sorry for him. But I didn't feel sorry for him when the game began. Much as I admired him, I never knew what a really great pitcher he was until that day."

Take your choice as to how Walter Johnson felt. The record shows how he pitched. The pregame ceremonies began with the presentation of a dark green Lincoln limousine, valued at $8,000, to Walter Johnson, bought by donations from the fans. It did not matter that winning the Most Valuable Player title no longer brought a Chalmers car with it; Johnson's admirers topped it with a superior one. A silver plate mounted on the hood proclaimed the love and admiration of the thousands of donors who had chipped in to buy the Lincoln limo. The Automobile Club of America gave Johnson a lifetime membership, Metropolitan Life insured the car for as long as it ran, and the District of Columbia issued a special license plate, number 100,000.

Proudest of all were Hazel and Minnie Johnson, the wife and mother of the man at the emotional center of attention. It was the first baseball game Walter's mother had ever seen. She knew nothing of the game's rules but took a mother's pride in the obvious high regard in which everyone held her son. The ladies were escorted by Rev. Brewster Adams, the pastor of the Baptist Church in Reno; Hazel's father could not attend, his mayoral duties keeping him in Reno, Nevada. The pastor was a hearty, athletic "man's man" who was close to the Roberts and Johnson families. He was the perfect escort and had been sent as Reno's emissary.

179

The Senators were truly called "America's Team," particularly outside of New York City. Walter Johnson was America's most heroic figure. The country had rooted for Washington over the New York Yankees and now wanted them to defeat the New York Giants. Most people across the country did not care much for New Yorkers, their city, or their baseball teams. The Yankees and Giants had monopolized the World Series since 1921, reducing the games to intramural contests played at the Polo Grounds, until the previous year when Yankee Stadium became an even bigger Gotham showcase.

John McGraw's Giants were slightly favored by the oddsmakers when the World Series started on Saturday. The same smart money that had backed the Yankees to win and Washington to fold, was now wagered on the National League Champions. It was the Giants fourth appearance in a row. After meeting Babe Ruth and the Yankees for the past three years, Bucky Harris' Senators looked easy. Walter Johnson might win a game, even two, reckoned McGraw, but he believed he had an even better staff. Yes, Washington had a smooth infield, but he had a better one which hit with more power. The Giants had George Kelly at first when he wasn't playing second base or the outfield, Frankie Frisch and Travis Jackson in the middle, and a teenager, Freddie Lindstrom, at third base. Heinie Groh, the regular at third, was out of the series with a damaged knee. Lindstrom was an impressive recruit, headed, as were the others, for the Baseball Hall of Fame. An undue influence later on the selections of the Veterans Committee by the persuasive Frank Frisch might have had more to do with so many of the 1924 Giants ending up in Cooperstown than their records supported, but Frisch swung the portal for his infield mates and Ross Youngs, too. Hack Wilson and Bill Terry, prominent alternates on the team, made the Hall of Fame without a push from Frisch.

The Giants' pitching was formidable, although lacking in immortals. Art Nehf, at his best in World Series competition, led the staff. Virgil Barnes, Jack Bentley, and Hugh McQuillan were the other starters. McGraw had spent $50,000 to bring McQuillan from the Braves and twice that, it was reported, to pry Bentley loose from Baltimore. The International League could withhold its players from the majors and Jack Dunn built a dynasty on the Chesapeake as a result. Bentley had been a protégé of Johnson's when he was a young pitcher on the Washington staff. McGraw was never sure whether he should pitch him or get his bat in the lineup as a regular. Such ambivalence, plus spending his best career years as a minor league superstar, kept Bentley from gaining the honors he should have achieved. McQuillan, called "Handsome Hugh," was a puzzle of unrealized promise, too. Both pitchers figured significantly later in Johnson's career.

Before the curtain could rise on the 1924 World Series, another scandal broke. The New York Giants had barely struggled to a fourth pennant. The National League race was even more tightly contested than the battle the Yankees and Senators had waged. There were three teams switching first place among themselves until the final days. Brooklyn and Pittsburgh were in contention until the Giants managed to win by a game and a half over the Dodgers and were three ahead of the Pirates at the end. The specter of New York gamblers, who had bet the Giants would win the pennant by at least two games, arose to haunt organized baseball and its czar, Judge Landis.

Heinie Sand, a player for the futile Phillies, the Giants' final opponent, was approached with a bribe offered by Jimmy O'Connell, a young New York outfielder. The two knew each other from the Pacific Coast League, and McGraw's coach, Cozy Dolan, suggested to O'Connell that he try to get the Philadelphia team to ease up in the game of September 27. Sand turned in his supposed buddy, reporting the bribe offer of $500 to Art Fletcher, his manager, who called Landis. Alerted on the eve of the World Series, the commissioner held a hearing with National League president John Heydler sitting in. O'Connell did not deny he had made an offer, but he claimed he was used by Dolan, with the knowledge of Giant stars Frisch, Kelly, and Youngs. Landis dismissed O'Connell's charge against his teammates, except for Dolan. On October 1, on the eve of the World Series, Commissioner Landis announced that Jimmy O'Connell and Cozy Dolan were forever banished from baseball.

Ban Johnson, believing he should have shared in the hearings with Landis and Heydler as a third member of the ruling triumvirate, was outraged. He argued that the whole World Series should be called off, lest any remaining suspicion of crookedness carry over. His protests were ignored, and he refused to attend the games.

Judge Landis was concerned about the image of baseball. The Black Sox scandal still stained the game. To add to his concerns, the umpires were talking of striking to get better terms for working the World Series. The honor was not enough, said veteran arbiters Bill Klem and Tommy Connolly. Bill Dinneen and Ernie Quigley concurred. The umpires shook hands in agreement among themselves

181

that unless the World Series paid the men who ran the game shares of the gate receipts equivalent to that paid to the players, they would strike before the next year's event. However, the discontent and betrayals that had surfaced were matters of off-field administration. What the fans cared about would take place in the ballpark.

The presidential party arrived only five minutes before the 2:00 P.M. start. Babe Ruth brushed past the Secret Service men and shook the president's hand. The players formed in ranks before the first base dugout, and a military band from nearby Fort Myer broke into the first strains of "The Star Spangled Banner." The crowd stood with bared heads while the flag rose to the top of the flagpole behind the center-field bleachers. It waved in the gentle breeze of the Indian summer afternoon.

President Coolidge was photographed throwing out the first ball. Umpire Connolly waited to make the catch, but the high arcing toss which cleared the cameramen in front of the presidential box was far off the mark. Coolidge was trying for distance, not accuracy. However, Tommy Connolly sprinted after it and made a leaping, one-handed catch, saving Coolidge an error and making one of the best plays of the day. Having the World Series open in Washington was wonderful theater for a man running to be *elected* president. Calvin Coolidge was finishing out Harding's term and wanted to be elected to one of his own. A few days before the World Series, it was announced that Walter Johnson would vote for Coolidge. This did not surprise anyone as Johnson's conservatism was well known. Future "politically correct" adherents might be startled to learn that "Mother" Jones, memorialized now as her era's ranking feminist labor agitator, visited the White House and was photographed assuring Calvin Coolidge of her vote. To present an image of impartiality, Coolidge kept his cool during the early innings, only gradually thawing until he became as involved a home team partisan as his wife Grace, the First Lady of Fans.

There was no public-address system but the one-arm megaphone announcer. E. Lawrence Phillips, after receiving the information from umpire Tommy Connolly, hollered to the crowd and press, "The batteries for New York, Nehf and Gowdy; for Washington, Johnson and Ruel." Connolly had umpired the first game played in the American League in 1901 and the first World Series in 1903. He never hesitated to name the 1924 championship series as the best he ever worked. Sports historians broaden this to identify the 1924 meeting between the Senators and the Giants as the most emotionally intense World Series ever played.

The stage was set. President and Mrs. Coolidge watched from their field box. Grantland Rice, covering for the *New York Herald*, and Bill Corum, writing for the *New York Times*, whose views would be syndicated nationally, were at their typewriters in the press box, as were ghostwriters for Babe Ruth, Ty Cobb, and George Sisler. Behind home plate, holding a hand mike and peering through chicken-wire screening, Graham McNamee cleared his throat. Then Tommy Connolly yelled, "Play Ball," and Freddie Lindstrom, an 18-year-old boy, stepped into the batter's box. On the mound, a 36-year-old veteran didn't wait for Muddy Ruel's sign. Lindstrom knew what was coming. Everyone in the ballpark knew Walter Johnson's first pitch would be a fastball, as hard as he could still throw it. The most thrilling World Series ever played had begun.

27
Johnson Fails
in Series Opener

UMPIRE CONNOLLY watched Walter Johnson's first pitch closely. It thudded into Muddy Ruel's mitt. A bit outside, he decided. Ball one. On a two and one count, Freddie Lindstrom lifted a soft fly ball to center field. Frankie Frisch attempted to bunt for
a single, but Ossie Bluege's one-handed pickup and throw nailed the
Fordham Flash at first. Johnson brought the count to three and two on
Ross Youngs, and got the call for his first strikeout. Youngs argued
and threw his bat away in protest.

Washington went out in order and quickly the Giants were at bat
again. Long George Kelly lifted a lazy fly ball to left field. Goose
Goslin drifted back and tumbled over the low railing fronting the temporary bleachers. Goslin fell into the first row of spectators. Several
rows farther back someone in the jerry-built seats caught Kelly's
home run. The Giants had scored the first run. Artie Nehf continued
to cut the Washington batters down. He gave up two walks but pitched
hitless ball until the fourth inning. In the top of the fourth, Johnson
fanned the side but not in order. After two were out, Bill Terry hit an
off-field home run into those temporary stands in left field. The extra
seats they provided put more money in the till, but so far, only the
Giants had put baseballs into the seats. In the bottom half of the
fourth, Joe Judge broke the ice with a sharp single, but there were two
out and Bluege made the third.

Walter Johnson picked up where he left off, striking out Travis
Jackson. Gowdy singled, was forced at second, and a fly out ended the
inning. The Senators went out quickly in the fifth, as did the Giants in
the top of the sixth. Only the two cheap home runs kept the game from
being a scoreless duel. Then Washington got its first run. McNeely
doubled down the left-field foul line and scored on two ground outs.
Goslin beat out an infield single that Nehf deflected to Frisch, hurting

his pitching hand. After a delay, Goslin tried to steal second but was cut down.

The Giants threatened in the seventh inning. Hack Wilson singled, but Washington's lightning-fast double play—Bluege to Harris to Judge—cleared the bases. Gowdy claimed a Johnson pitch nicked his finger, but Umpire Connolly disagreed. Gowdy still got to first base on a walk. Artie Nehf singled Gowdy to second, and both advanced on a Walter Johnson wild pitch. Lindstrom grounded to Peckinpaugh for the third out.

President Coolidge abandoned impartiality in the home half of the seventh. He stood up with Grace and the hometown fans. "Silent Cal" nodded his approval when, with two out, Peckinpaugh singled and stole second. Muddy Ruel drew a pass, and it was up to Walter Johnson to even the score. He hit a line drive over second that Frankie Frisch snared with a leaping catch. The Giant captain happily loped off the field, tossing the ball in the air.

It was getting late. The Giants threatened again in the eighth but, on a double steal attempt, Ruel faked a throw to second and nailed Ross Youngs at third. In the bottom of the eighth Nehf set the Senators down in order. It was getting later.

The Giants almost scored again in the ninth. Hack Wilson led off with a single and Travis Jackson sacrificed him to second. Johnson bore down and fanned Hank Gowdy with a wide curve that he missed by a foot. Artie Nehf, a good hitting pitcher who had hit five home runs in 1924, singled sharply to right field, but the squat Wilson, chugging around third, was out at the plate on Rice's rifle-sharp throw to Ruel. It was still a 2-1 game, and Washington had one last chance.

It started badly: Judge was called out on strikes. Then Bluege singled off the tip of Jackson's glove. When Roger Peckinpaugh drove a double off the left-field wall, Bluege scored the tying run and the crowd went wild. All kinds of wearing apparel and disposable debris came from the stands. Gloves, hats, programs, seat cushions, a tardy straw boater, were flung in abandon. The police had to rush to right field to keep the spectators from jumping down to the field. Pandemonium reigned, then subsided. Washington had only tied the score. The excitement built again when Ruel grounded out to Jackson and Peckinpaugh moved to third base. We'll never know what excesses of emotion waited in check. With the winning run 90 feet from home plate, the game was in Walter Johnson's hands. Alas, he hit a high fly to George Kelly in center field, and the crowd settled down for extra innings. The Secret Service men whispered about leaving, but Mrs. Coolidge told the president that if he left now, he would go home without her.

Walter Johnson started into overtime as though the game had just begun. He struck out Lindstrom, his 10th victim. Frisch singled and, after another out, stole second with one of his head-first dives. Johnson then poured in fastballs to fan the dangerous George Kelly.

Tommy Connolly, an American League umpire, kept a wary eye on Artie Nehf, who was known to doctor a ball. With one out in the bottom of the 10th, the arbiter took a discolored ball away from the Giants' crafty southpaw and gave him a nice clean one in its place. Bucky Harris knocked it past Lindstrom. Sam Rice singled Harris to second and Washington's fans rose in mass anticipation. Goslin just missed a game-winning hit when his drive down the right-field foul stripe was inches on the wrong side of the line. He then flew out. It was Joe Judge's turn to be frustrated next as his long drive into the right-field stands curved foul at the last moment. Then he drove the ball to Ross Youngs in deep right-center to make the third out.

McNeely, far from a sure-handed outfielder, was also not very sure footed, slipping while chasing Terry's fly ball to open the 11th. But, he turned it into a circus catch. Walter Johnson, pitching with his seemingly tireless sidearm motion, made Wilson his 12th strikeout victim, and Jackson grounded out.

Once more President Coolidge stood up with the crowd and clapped his hands to urge the Senators to rally. Again, Connolly warned Nehf, who had discolored another ball; the sun was setting and the shadows made a darkened ball harder to see. Washington went out in order. The game moved into the 12th inning.

Would Johnson tire first? He seemed to weaken when he hit Hank Gowdy with a pitch that would have been ball four. Then Artie Nehf got his third hit of the game and the Senators unraveled. McNeely threw wildly to second trying to force the slow-footed Gowdy on Nehf's hit, but the ball went wide and ended up bouncing against the stands behind first base. Muddy Ruel chased it down, but Gowdy was on third and Nehf on second with no one out. Jack Bentley pinch-hit and Johnson, working around him, loaded the bases. Billy Southworth ran for Bentley. Frisch hit a ground ball to Harris, who forced Gowdy at the plate. Then on a short fly to center, Earl McNeely pulled up and the ball fell in for a Texas League single. It was a ball McNeely should have caught, or missed only after diving for it. Nehf scored to go-ahead run. Then Kelly scored Southworth with a deep fly. Terry loaded the bases again with a single, but Goslin tracked down Wilson's fly ball in left field. The Giants led by two runs. Could the Senators rally?

The Giants rearranged their defense. Kelly moved to second base, Frisch to third, and Southworth to center. Walter Johnson was due to lead off, but Harris sent the left-handed Mule Shirley in to pinch-hit. Whether it was bad strategy to replace the right-handed hitting Johnson against lefty-throwing Aft Nehf did not matter. Shirley's high fly was dropped by Jackson for a two-base error. McNeely flied to Southworth, then Bucky Harris singled to score Shirley and close to within one run of a tie. Sam Rice singled to center sending Harris to third but was out trying to stretch his hit into a double. On the next play the versatile Kelly, now at second base, made a great barehanded play on Goslin's slow roller and caught him by a step at first for the third and final out.

Walter Johnson had come close to victory, but the day belonged to Artie Nehf and the Giants. The fans slowly filed out of the ballpark. A flying squadron of Secret Service agents bundled the presidential party into cars pulled up in front of their box seats. President Coolidge murmured his condolences to several Washington players and promised he would be back and see them win. The presidential party drove to the Potomac Basin where the presidential yacht, The Mayflower, waited to take them on an evening cruise.

The press crowded into the clubhouses for assessments by the rival managers. John J. McGraw was gracious in victory, but condescending in judgment. "We got a break in the 12th inning," he acknowledged, "by Rice trying to stretch his single into two bases. If he had stayed on first there would have been only one out when Goslin hit to Kelly and Harris would have scored the tying run. As it was, Goslin's tap made the third out and gave us the game."

That was not the way Bucky Harris saw it. "We might have played it safe in the 12th and earned a tie, but we were willing to take the chance of winning when Rice tried to reach second on his single. If he was safe we would have tied the score anyway when Goslin bounced to Kelly, and we would have had a man in scoring position. It was the right play to make and I'm not blaming Rice or Altrock, who was coaching at first base, for telling him to go on."

McGraw's praise was mostly for his own pitcher, Art Nehf. He pitched a wonderful game, boasted the Giants manager, adding, "As did Walter Johnson."

Bucky Harris poured out his admiration for his veteran: "Johnson pitched a wonderful game. With men on bases he was almost invincible and those home runs would have been caught on a larger field."

In a corner of the clubhouse sat Walter Johnson. He had labored so long and so energetically through 12 innings that he drooped with fatigue. His eyes glistened and his voice trembled as he said, "It was hard to lose. I would have given anything to have won that game for Washington and the people who have expected so much of me. But I gave them everything I had and it wasn't good enough. I'm tired— you bet I'm tired—but I'll be all right again and I'm ready to go back in there anytime Bucky wants me."

Forty thousand people had watched the titanic struggle inside Griffith Stadium. Hundreds of thousands more had followed the game away from the ballpark. In Washington and New York City huge throngs gathered wherever the game was reported on scoreboards. They clustered on sidewalks outside radio stores or anywhere Graham McNamee's voice could be heard. It was estimated that 100,000 people in the metropolitan area had listened to the game being "radiated," as broadcasting was called. As many as a million listeners were estimated in the full coverage range of the improvised network.

The next day the pattern would be repeated, except that, since it was Sunday, WEAF would be replaced by WNYC. Graham McNamee's station had religious programs scheduled but allowed him to work on the Sabbath for the other station.

Before going into the locker room, Walter Johnson had signaled the Reverend Mr. Adams to get the ladies to the safety of the corridor under the stands leading to the clubhouse. Hazel was saddened, and Minnie was puzzled but aware that something unwanted had happened to her son. Eventually, they all got back to the shelter and gloom of the Johnsons' house. Walter had fallen short of his goal and his fans' expectations. He had carried the quest 12 innings. There would be another game, maybe two, he assured the others. The house was filled with flowers, plants, and gift baskets which well-wishers had sent. Now, instead of a joyful display, the tokens seemed funereal. In the morning, Walter solved that problem. He and the Reverend loaded everything into the new Lincoln limo and, with Hazel and Minnie, drove to Walter Reed Army Hospital, where the Big Train found time to visit with the military patients.

28

Baseball's Most
Dramatic World Series

JONATHAN THOMPSON WALTON ZACHARY, called "Tom" for brevity, was Bucky Harris' choice for the second game of the 1924 World Series. A rangy lefthander from the mountains of North Carolina, Zachary was seasoned and had been sharp in his late-season assignments. All games are crucial in a seven-game series, but the second game, when you have lost the first and must play the next three in the other team's park, is doubly critical. Another 40,000 people packed Griffith Stadium, knowing that unless the Senators won that day, it would likely be the last baseball game they would see that year. Missing were the political figures and men of position. These dignitaries are always on hand for festive openings, but they never come to the second game. Mrs. Coolidge would have to settle for listening to Graham McNamee's account on radio aboard The Mayflower. The presidential yacht went for a Sunday sail on Chesapeake Bay and off the breezy Virginia capes. Coolidge was running for election, and there were blocks of Baptist voters and strongholds where Puritan values held that playing baseball on the Lord's Day was sinful. Walter Johnson had taken his family to an early church service, then hurried to the ballpark. He could help in some way, he hoped, although he would not pitch again until the series shifted to New York.

The fans, some of whom had paid ticket speculators as much as $75, found their seats, consoling each other, "We'll never see another game like the one Walter lost yesterday." They almost did. In a short series every break, bobble, and blunder is decisive. Game Two had them all.

The Giants started fast on successive singles by Lindstrom and Frisch. Ross Youngs popped up his sacrifice bunt try to Zachary. Then Bucky Harris, who missed a base-line tag of Frisch after scooping up Kelly's grounder, threw high to Peckinpaugh trying for a force-out and the bases were full. An early rout? No. The slick Senators infield reeled off a Bluege-to-Harris-to-Judge double play and the home team fans breathed easy.

They let out a sudden roar in the bottom of the inning when, after two were out, Rice singled and Goose Goslin, after Rice had stolen second, lined a line drive into the temporary right-field bleachers. Ross Youngs fell into the stands trying to reach the ball, as Goslin himself had done the day before. However, tables turn, and the Goose was on his way to a Ruthian World Series. He had led the league in RBIs but, in the unusually spacious Griffith Stadium, had been limited to 16 home runs, tops on the team. Judge beat out a slow roller down the first base line, but Bluege hit into a force play. The Senators had an early lead, and the teams settled down into a tense series of scoreless innings.

Neither team threatened until the bottom of the fifth, when Bucky Harris lashed a line drive into the inviting left-field bleachers to give Tom Zachary a three-run lead with the game more than half over. Washington's relief specialist, Allan Russell, was available, and the super-stopper, Fred Marberry, was also sitting in the bull pen. Harris wanted to save him to start the third game, and it wasn't until the seventh inning anyone had to warm up. Even so, although the Giants scored a run after two singles, another lightning-fast twin killing, from Bluege to Harris to Judge, snuffed out the threat. A run scored, but the third out came on a fly ball and the pitchers in the bull pen sat down. Both teams were hitless in the eighth and, with a 3-1 lead, many fans began to edge toward the exits. Sunday dinner waited at home. However, the exodus stopped short when the Giants came to life in the top of the ninth.

Zachary, who had been pitching like a machine, walked Frisch on four straight balls. Ross Youngs, after just missing a game-tying homer on a long foul ball down the right-field line, popped up to Peckinpaugh. After a disputed call on a pitch Ruel and Zachary thought was a third strike, Kelly singled to right, and Frisch, running as though he was the tying run, scored on a very close play at the plate. This time Klem stirred the Washington bench and fans with a call that seemed to them to be motivated by his National League allegiance. From the stands Frisch looked to have been tagged out, but Klem, closer up, decided his feet touched the plate before Ruel touched him. Despite the play at the plate, Kelly remained at first. He moved to second when Bucky Harris made a sensational, glove-hand pickup of a hard ground ball and threw out Irish Meusel. Washington was one out away from the win that would tie the series. It was a long time coming. Hack Wilson singled and Kelly scored in a tangle of bodies. Rice's throw bounced low, and when Ruel dug it out of the dirt, Long George Kelly dove over the catcher to reach home plate. Ruel lost the ball and Wilson moved to second as the go-ahead run. It was time to stop the Giants rally. Bucky Harris thanked Tom Zachary for a job well done and beckoned big Fred Marberry in from the bull pen. He could not have been more efficient. He blew three straight strikes past Travis Jackson.

Would the teams play another extra-inning game? Would Marberry be used up stemming Giant rallies inning after inning and not be able to pitch the opening game in New York? It did not take long to find out. Judge walked and Bluege sacrificed the winning run to second. Too bad, thought the Senators, that first base was open with the hot-hitting Roger Peckinpaugh coming to bat. Surely the Giants would walk him; his run did not count, anyway. The logical choice was to try for a double play with the slow-running catcher Muddy Ruel due up. Surely, a manager as smart and experienced as John J. McGraw would order an intentional walk. He did not. Instead, he instructed Jack Bentley to pitch to Peckinpaugh. The count went to two and one and then Peckinpaugh smashed a double past Lindstrom and Judge raced home with the winning run. It did not quite equal the dramatic finish of the previous day's 12-inning game, but it had the greater benefit of evening the World Series as the teams moved to the Polo Grounds for the third game.

Game Three had the same crowd-involving dramatics as the first two games, but was viewed disdainfully by those who expect higher standards in World Series play. The 6-4 Giants win was viewed as a downright shoddy contest, except for Frankie Frisch's heroics. He flashed all over the ballpark to snare looping fly balls and snap up sizzling grounders. Both teams used four pitchers, with only the Giants veteran Mule Watson earning press-box approval for his game-saving relief stint.

Roger Peckinpaugh, the hero of Game Two, had strained a tendon running out his ninth-inning, game-winning hit. He packed his leg in ice for hours before the game and limped to his shortstop position. He could only hurt the team, Harris decided, and shifted Bluege to short and put Ralph Miller at third base.

Fred Marberry was ineffective as a starter, not the sharp ace he had been in relief the day before. By the fourth inning he was gone with Washington trailing, 4-2. The Giants' starter, Hugh McQuillan, also failed to last the fourth inning. Rosy Ryan replaced him and not only held the Senators in check but became the first National League pitcher to homer in World Series play. The Giants widened the lead to 5-2 with a run in the sixth. Washington got it back in the eighth, but New York scored again in their half of the inning and took a three-run lead into the final frame. With a surprising number of the Polo Ground patrons loudly rooting for a Washington rally, the gods of mischance stirred themselves once more.

Bucky Harris blooped a ball safely into center field but Rice popped up to third. Goslin—whose Texas League bids earlier in the game provided the tough chances that Frisch, running out from under his hat, had grabbed—crossed up everyone by bunting. Ryan fielded the ball but could make no play. Harris went to second. Then Joe Judge lined a single to right field and the bases were loaded.

Claude Jonnard, McGraw's first call out of the bull pen in tight situations, replaced Ryan. For added security, Billy Southworth took over center field from Long George Kelly. Ossie Bluege drew a walk, forcing in Harris. McGraw made another change. In strolled Mule Watson, ambling slowly to let the pressure build up. With the bases loaded and the game on the line, Watson reckoned the more he fussed before throwing the ball, the more it would string out Ralph Miller, the batter. He was right. Miller fouled to Lindstrom. When Muddy Ruel's ground ball to third base was gobbled up by young Freddie Lindstrom, the teenager who made all the put-outs in the inning, stepped on third base, and the Giants were the winners.

Game Four became Goose Goslin's game. He had four hits and knocked in five runs. His hard hitting, including a three-run homer in the third inning, opened so much distance on the Giants that George Mogridge had little difficulty in keeping the Giants at bay. Bucky Harris turned in two more scintillating plays to cut off New York rallies. When New York loaded the bases in the ninth inning, trailing 7-4 with the potential tying run and George Kelly at bat, Fred Marberry responded as he had in the second game. Kelly, whose 21 home runs helped him to win the National League RBI title, had the power to tie the game. Marberry struck him out on three straight pitches.

Game Five was supposed to be Walter Johnson's revenge. Maybe Harris asked too much of a 36-year-old veteran who had worked 12 very hard innings and was pitching on three days' rest. With the series tied again at two apiece, Harris did not want to risk falling behind. With a Johnson victory at the Polo Grounds, the Senators would need to win only one of two remaining games, both possibly at home. The site of a seventh game was not decided until after the fifth game raised the possibility that it would be needed. Then a toss of the coin would determine whether the final game would require a return to the Polo Grounds or if the teams would stay in Washington and play it there. Anyway, Walter Johnson was a legend. He had pitched three shutouts in four days in New York City once before. But that had been in 1908, when Johnson was 20 years old. However, optimism was high as the Senators took early practice.

Walter Johnson was such a nice man that he kept signing autographs and posing for snapshots near the stands when he should have been loosening his pitching arm. The *New York Times* observed he had signed 66 programs and posed for a half-dozen photographs, including one photo with a very elderly man who had to be half-supported by the pitcher while a friend snapped the picture. In a modern era, when even the World Series is reported with 30-second sound-bite journalism, it is surprising to review the coverage given by the *Times*. Granted, the New York Giants were a local team, but still, every game, home and away, was reported with a front-page story which was continued to the sports section for extended coverage. More viewpoints and sidebar pieces half filled the next page.

From the pregame observations we know that a weakened Christy Mathewson, bundled in an overcoat, watched from an upper-tier seat. Babe Ruth and Ty Cobb sat side by side signing programs and ticket stubs next to the Senators' dugout for a half-hour before the game. Casey Stengel was there, reliving the two home runs he had hit for the Giants the previous fall before being traded away.

There is comment that the Giants' brand-new World Series uniforms were already showing wear from the headlong dives of Frankie Frisch and sliding catches of Ross Youngs.

It was apparent from the start that Walter Johnson was not the pitcher of yore. In fact, he wasn't even half the pitcher he had been in Game One. A bare report of the game, inning by inning, makes it appear that Johnson was hooked up in a pitcher's duel with the Giants' starter, Jack Bentley. Walter Johnson received a great hand from the crowd when he walked to the mound to start the game.

Lindstrom immediately singled. Frisch hit a high foul pop-up caught near the Washington dugout, and Youngs hit a deep fly ball which Earl McNeely raced back and caught in center field. Lindstrom ended the inning by trying to steal second base. It went that way throughout the opening innings. Seasoned observers kept expecting the Giants to overcome their eagerness to take a cut at a fastball that was no longer traveling at express speed. The Big Train was lumbering like a freight train on an upgrade. The Giants did more to put themselves out than Johnson did.

Walter Johnson's aged arm might be tired, but his bat was still quick. He slammed a drive off the left-field wall. However, he rounded first base too far, stumbled trying to get back, and was tagged out by Bill Terry when Hack Wilson's throw beat him back to the bag. Nick Altrock, the first base coach, was at fault, Harris decided, and replaced him with Nemo Leibold. NcNeely beat out a bunt to third base and Harris had an infield hit. The bases would have been loaded. Instead, Bentley got out of the inning on a pop-up and ground out.

In the third inning, Jackson beat out a slow roller to short, and Johnson got his first strikeout with Hank Gowdy looking at a 3-2 pitch. Jack Bentley did not wait. He singled on the first pitch and Jackson went to third. He scored when Lindstrom out-legged another slow roller. Frisch grounded to Bluege, playing shortstop in place of the still sidelined Roger Peckinpaugh. Bluege threw to third baseman Miller, who missed the tag on Lindstrom. The bases were filled. Next, Ross Youngs hit a line drive to Sam Rice. Bentley got confused. He had to go back and tag up, and Rice's throw, relayed by Johnson, nailed him at the plate. Johnson had escaped, trailing only 1-0.

Washington tied the game in the fourth on Judge's leadoff single, a sacrifice, an infield out, and a single by Miller. He tried to stretch this to a double but Ross Youngs threw him out. A run scored but another opportunity was wasted.

Johnson again evaded trouble in the Giants' fourth. He got another 3-2 third-strike call, this time George Kelly watched the pitch go by. Then Bill Terry hit a monstrously high drive into right-center and reached third. Only Sam Rice's great throw pinned him there. When Hack Wilson lined the ball back to the box, Johnson's glove saved him. He speared the ball and trapped Terry off third. Jackson hit a high fly ball to Bucky Harris. Walter Johnson was getting by, but on luck, the Giants overeagerness, and his innate, all-around ability.

The Senators went out one, two, three to start the fifth inning, and

Johnson was back at work with hardly time to catch his breath. Gowdy greeted him with a single to right, and Jack Bentley showed why McGraw was torn between using him as a hitter or as a pitcher. He hit a towering drive into the upper right-field grandstand. Lindstrom popped up and Frisch had a wind-blown double fall out of McNeely's reach. A low pitch caught Ross Youngs on the ankle and he limped to first base. On the brink of absolute ruin, the inner defense pulled off an inning-ending double play, Bluege to Harris to Judge. It could have been worse. It would be. The sixth and seventh innings were scoreless. The Giants helped Johnson survive with dumb base running.

In the eighth the Senators closed to within a run of the lead. Goslin hit a line drive to the upper tier of the right-field grandstand. His third homer of the series tied Babe Ruth's record set the year before, and once again a series game seemed headed for a final-inning showdown.

Bucky Harris was determined to go all the way with Walter Johnson. In retrospect, Johnson had not done too badly. The Giants had six hits and three runs. Hindsight, and the absence of sentimentality, says it was the spot for Fred Marberry or Allan Russell. They were not even warming up.

Kelly opened up with a sharp single and Terry walked. Hack Wilson bunted the ball, and Walter Johnson, who had not made an error all season, booted the ball. Everyone was safe, the bases were loaded, and no one was out. In the old days, Walter Johnson might have hitched up his belt and fanned the side. These were not the old days—only Walter Johnson was old. Jackson's long fly to Rice scored Kelly. Gowdy's ground ball was too slow to turn into a double play and Terry moved to third base. Hugh McQuillan, who had replaced Bentley in the top of the inning, stayed in to hit for himself. Even he was fearless against Johnson's diminished fastball. A weak batter, he bailed out, taking a wide sweeping cut at the ball. It looped into short left field for a single that scored Terry. It was not over yet. Freddie Lindstrom stroked his fourth hit of the game and Gowdy scored the third run of the inning. Before Frankie Frisch hit into a force play to end the inning, a fight nearly started in the press box. Some cynic shouted at the battered Johnson, "Take him out." This enraged Billy Evans, Johnson's admirer, who was covering the game as a reporter. He climbed over two rows of seats and typewriters to get at the loudmouth. He explained later, after being subdued, "It hurt to have someone shout that old line at a great player like Walter Johnson. I realize it was unprofessional of me to step out and assert myself, but it seemed a shame to razz a man like Walter who was in there giving all he had."

Trailing 6-2, the Senators went out meekly. Yet, even as they trooped into the clubhouse, a spirit of almost unjustified optimism began to be felt. Everyone was saddened that Barney had not pitched the way America had hoped and prayed he would. But the Senators, down three games to two, insisted the glass was really half full. When Bucky Harris brought the news that Clark Griffith had won the toss to decide where the seventh game would be played, they assumed that a seventh game would be necessary. The Senators took it almost for granted that Tom Zachary would win the sixth game. Once they were at home, the team believed they were better than the Giants. And, Bucky Harris was already plotting a strategy to pull on McGraw in Game Seven. When the team boarded the early evening train for Washington at Pennsylvania Station it was hard to tell who were the winners. In Washington, 5,000 die-hard fans waited for the team to arrive. Walter Johnson, carrying his youngest son on his shoulder, cleared the way for Hazel, who was carrying Carolyn, and his mother. He heard shouts of sympathy, but the loudest voices insisted the Senators were far from beaten.

29

Johnson's Greatest Triumph

G RIFFITH STADIUM was again packed to its newly expanded capacity. The Senators believed this would be the penultimate game of the 1924 World Series. A team of destiny, which is how Bucky Harris viewed his crew, fulfills its mission in whatever way it must. If the scenario lacked victories pitched by Walter Johnson, a team triumph would be all the more impressive. Tom Zachary, George Mogridge, and Fred Marberry had pitched well. Now it was up to Zachary to pitch even better than he had in his first start. He would be up against the Giants' ace, Artie Nehf, winner over Walter Johnson in the opening game, in a duel of lefthanders.

President Coolidge surprised people by accompanying Mrs. Coolidge to the game. She, the die-hard fan, had been expected; he had not. Their party arrived only a few minutes before game time. As they began to descend the steps behind home plate toward their box seats, the army band began playing "The Star Spangled Banner" too soon. The crowd arose and the president removed his hat and stood at attention in the aisle. There was no throwing out of a first ball or extra formalities. The Coolidges, like thousands of other couples and fans, were there to see a ball game.

Roger Peckinpaugh was back at shortstop. His movements were tentative as though he dared not risk sudden starts and stops. With the left-handed Zachary on the mound, John McGraw started his right-handed lineup. Mostly this meant George Kelly would open at first base and the dangerous young Bill Terry would wait on the bench. The versatile Kelly could play the outfield or second base whenever Terry played against a right-handed starter. Artie Nehf's left hand had healed since he injured it in the opening game, and he was well rested. The rotation of the four umpires put the National League's Bill Klem behind the plate.

Freddie Lindstrom pushed a bunt toward Ossie Bluege, back at third base, and was out by a half step. Frankie Frisch doubled down the right-field foul line, but when Ross Youngs hit back to Zachary, Frisch was caught off second base and tagged out in a rundown. A former broken field runner at Fordham, Frisch jockeyed on the base path long enough for Youngs to move to second base. The first run scored on Kelly's single. Zachary survived a shaky start when Sam Rice chased down a long fly by Irish Meusel. From then on Zachary was in full control of the Giants batters. The opening inning run was all he yielded through the rest of the game. Except for one lapse, Artie Nehf matched Zachary's string of runless innings with a row of zeros of his own. He faltered only in the fifth inning.

The inspired Roger Peckinpaugh lashed a clean single into left field, and Muddy Ruel moved him into scoring position with a sacrifice bunt. Zachary's roller to Kelly got Peckinpaugh to third base, but now there were two out. Nehf walked McNeely on four straight pitches. McNeely then stole second base with the gimpy-legged Peckinpaugh only feinting a double-steal break to the plate. McGraw had to choose. He could pass Bucky Harris, his rival manager who was a hot batter, and have Nehf pitch to the left-handed hitting Sam Rice, the Senators' best batter. The righthanders Rosy Ryan and Mule Watson were working in the bull pen, but first McGraw had to chose whether to pitch to Harris. He made the wrong choice.

With a full count, Harris hit an outside pitch into right field and both runners scored. Youngs' throw was too late to catch the sliding Earl McNeely. Washington was ahead and the crowd went wild. Harris had moved to second on the play at the plate, but Rice was called out on strikes and Tom Zachary was asked to maintain the slim, one-run lead. It was a razor-thin margin on which to rest a season's hopes, but it held up due as much to splendid fielding as to Zachary's finesse and control. Except for a single when Rice just failed to make a shoestring catch on a Wilson short fly, no Giant reached base. Not until the ninth inning.

After Ross Youngs popped up to Bluege, George Kelly singled to right field and Billy Southworth ran for him. Irish Meusel, after first hitting a long foul ball over the top of the left-field stands, hit a ground ball over second base. Peckinpaugh barely got to the ball. He tried to stop and had to flip the ball backhanded to Harris, who grabbed it barehanded for the force play on Southworth. Peckinpaugh's leg buckled again and he crumbled to the ground.

Once more, Peckinpaugh had to be helped from the field. The standing fans cheered him as, refusing to be carried, he hopped to the bench, with his arms around the shoulders of two teammates. Bluege again moved to shortstop and Tommy Taylor took over at third base. Tom Zachary then ended the game by striking out Hack Wilson.

There was a degree of restraint in the postgame celebration. There had been drama but no surprise. It was as though the sixth game was played—its outcome a foregone conclusion—only to make the seventh and final game possible. The teams had played each other to a standstill, but tomorrow, one would have to give way.

Thousands of fans left the ballpark and got on line to buy tickets for the next day's game, willing to wait through the night until the box-office windows opened at 10 A.M. Due to planning a schedule and ticket distribution for six games instead of the potential of seven, the arrangements provided only a coupon to be exchanged for admission if a seventh game became necessary. Because the home-team choice was left for a coin toss after the fifth game, seventh-game tickets were difficult to obtain. Although the bleacher seats and general-admissions stands filled early, stretches of seats went unoccupied, and scalpers had to take face value for most of their ducats.

The game to decide the World Championship became one of the most written about in baseball history. Bill Corum's account, written without a byline for the *New York Times*, is among the selections in Charles Einstein's *The Fireside Book of Baseball Stories,* and Grantland Rice was given an award by the Baseball Writer's Association for the best news account of the year for his coverage in the *New York Herald Tribune*. Rice's lead was: "Destiny, waiting for the final curtain, stepped from the wings today and handed the king his crown."

In preparing for the game, Bucky Harris had one strategy move to make. He wanted to nullify the left-handed hitting Bill Terry. The ploy was an old one: pretend you are going to start a righthander and then switch to a lefty once you have Terry in the starting lineup. That would force McGraw to replace him with a right-handed batter by moving George Kelly to first base and using one of his right-handed hitting outfielders, Hack Wilson or Irish Meusel. Ross Youngs was a fixture regardless of who pitched. The Senators showcased Curly Ogden, right-handed and a spot starter during the season. However, to keep McGraw guessing, George Mogridge, the lefty, and Firpo Marberry, the righty, warmed up down in the bull pen. Zachary was finished and there were no plans for Walter Johnson.

McGraw took the bait. He guessed that Ogden was a ruse and named Bill Terry as his first baseman. Youngs, Kelly, and Meusel formed the outfield. Heinie Groh was still unable to play, so Freddie Lindstrom, who had been a rookie revelation at third, again started in his place. Once again, Hank Gowdy was behind the bat. Now in his 14th season, having missed 1918 for World War I service, he had caught less than half of the Giants' games. Pancho Snyder, who caught more often, was among McGraw's "walking wounded" and able only to pinch-hit.

McGraw gave the starting assignment to Virgil Barnes even though he had not been effective in the third game. He had everyone else ready to help out, even Artie Nehf, the previous day's tough-luck starter.

Curly Ogden was supposed to face one batter as he was required to do when he had been announced. But when he blew Freddie Lindstrom away on three pitches, Harris let him continue. But when Frankie Frisch walked, Harris summoned his lefthander, George Mogridge. He kept Marberry in readiness. Mogridge fanned Ross Youngs and got Kelly on an easy ground out.

Barnes set the Senators down in order, and the game moved though its opening innings quickly and without either team threatening. Bill Terry was easy for Mogridge, grounding out and striking out. The ice-breaker came in the fourth inning when Bucky Harris drove a ball over the left-field wall. Hack Wilson ran back as far as the temporary bleachers and fell over the low railing. However, the ball carried out of the ballpark, a full-size homer at any time.

New York took the lead in the top of the sixth inning. Ross Youngs walked and raced to third on Kelly's single past short. Now McGraw replaced Terry, sending Meusel in to bat for him. And Harris countered by bringing in Firpo Marberry. Meusel's sacrifice fly to right brought home Youngs with the tying run. Then Washington's defense cracked. After Wilson singled, sending Kelly to third, Joe Judge fumbled a ground ball. Kelly scored and Wilson reached third on the error. Next Gowdy hit a double-play ball to Bluege, but it went through him for another error and Wilson scored. Marberry got the pitcher, Barnes, on a short fly to right and struck out Lindstrom. The Giants had a 3-1 lead. Maybe they would have had more had McGraw pinch-hit for Barnes or squeezed Jackson home. However, except for the Harris homer, Barnes had pitched a great game. He continued his mastery for another inning, but in the eighth he weakened and McGraw was slow to relieve him.

With one out, veteran Nemo Leibold pinch-hit a double and Muddy Ruel got his first hit of the series, a hard drive off George Kelly's first baseman's mitt. Bennie Tate, a rookie backup catcher, who had a .500 average as a pinch hitter during the season, hit for Marberry and walked to load the bases. Mule Shirley ran for Tate, but all the runners held their bases when McNeely's fly was too short for Leibold to risk trying to score. It left matters to manager Bucky Harris. Two out, bases loaded, an inning to play: a perfect scenario for the Boy Wonder, and he played his role with a lot of help from Fate. His ground ball to third base took a high bound over Lindstrom's head for a two-base hit which scored Leibold and Ruel, who came thundering home. The score was tied and the fans went into a frenzy. McGraw lifted Barnes and called on Artie Nehf to pitch to Sam Rice. All he wanted from Nehf was one-third of an inning, and he got it. Rice grounded out to first base.

The fans were on their feet in anticipation of Bucky Harris' next move. There was only one pitcher warming up in the bull pen. He had been throwing since Tate batted for Marberry. It was Walter Johnson. Harris pointed to him and Bill Klem summoned him. The waves of applause, the shouts of encouragement echoed through Griffith Stadium. Walter Johnson seemed to shed the years as he walked with his unmistakable ploughboy stride to the pitcher's mound. He was back again to claim his title, King of the Hill. His warm-up pitches whistled to the plate. Ruel asked to see the curve and it broke sharply, dropping to an outside corner. Walter Johnson was ready to hold the Giants at bay until the Senators could score again.

Today he was not an old-timer trying to get by on the memory of a fastball. People who could compare the warrior on the mound to the one of legend swore he was the Johnson of old. He faced a Herculean challenge and would be tested inning by inning until he completed his tasks or was defeated by them. No one was warming up to come to Johnson's rescue. Bucky Harris explained later, "You go with your best."

Lindstrom popped to third, but Frankie Frisch boomed a triple to deep center field. There was task number one: Keep the Fordham Flash at third base. Harris and Johnson had sized up Ross Youngs and George Kelly. Of the two, Johnson was confident he had Kelly's number. An intentional walk to Youngs put Johnson's judgment on the line. He struck out George Kelly on three pitches. On the third strike Ross Youngs stole second, Ruel not wanting to risk a throw with

201

Frisch on third. Irish Meusel grounded to third base where Miller was now playing and was thrown out at first.

It seemed the fates favored the Senators when with one out Joe Judge singled to center. Bluege hit to Kelly but Travis Jackson dropped the ball trying for a double play. Judge went to third base on the error. The Washington fans smelled victory. However, McGraw brought in Hugh McQuillan to pitch to Ralph Miller. A .133 hitter in only nine regular-season games, Miller was overmatched. However, with Peckinpaugh injured and Taylor out of the game, Harris hoped for the best. He got the worst: a 6-4-3 double play, and Walter Johnson went back to work to hold New York for another inning.

Wilson walked, but Travis Jackson was called out on strikes and Hank Gowdy hit the ball back to Johnson, who whirled and pegged it to Bluege, who relayed it to Judge for an inning-ending double play.

It appeared for a moment that the scenario would call for Johnson himself to provide the ultimate highlight, a game-winning home run. He drove a fly to deep left-center field, but Hack Wilson had enough room to haul it in just short of the fence. After McNeely struck out, Johnson had to take the mound for his 11th-inning challenge.

McGraw sent Heinie Groh, out of the series with a leg injury, to pinch-hit for McQuillan, and he used his famous "bottle bat" to poke a single into right field. He gave way to a pinch runner, Billy Southworth. Lindstrom sacrificed and the dangerous Frankie Frisch stepped into the batter's box. Last time up against Johnson, Frisch had boomed a triple. This time he went down swinging. Would it be Ross Youngs or George Kelly for the third out? For the fourth time in the game, Youngs was walked. Kelly again proved easy for Johnson, who struck him out, leaving the runner stranded.

Jack Bentley took up McGraw's cause from the mound in the 11th inning. He had lost Game Two and won Game Five. Washington threatened when, with two out, Goslin dropped a Texas League double into left-center. McGraw's managerial wheels were spinning. He walked Joe Judge to set up a force play at second. In the event of a single to the outfield, he wanted the best throwing arm where the ball was most likely to go. Youngs, the better thrower, moved to left and Meusel to right field. Bluege hit a ground ball to Jackson, who flipped it to Frisch for the force-out.

Hercules had been confronted with 12 difficult labors; Johnson faced his fourth inning's challenge determined to perform as many tasks as it took until his team could score. He would outdo Hercules if he had to. Irish Meusel singled to left, but Wilson fanned. It was Johnson's fifth strikeout. Jackson forced Meusel at second and Gowdy flied to left.

The afternoon sun was dropping fast toward the horizon. Hercules had no time limit set on performing his labors; Johnson had to finish his tasks before darkness came and forced another game to be played. It was time for other gods to stir themselves.

Youngs and Meusel returned to their original outfield posts. After Miller grounded out, Muddy Ruel lifted a pop foul behind the plate. Veteran Hank Gowdy had caught a thousand of these. But he had never tried it with his mask tangled around his foot. As he pivoted to line up the ball, Gowdy stepped on the mask he had dropped near the plate. He tried to kick it loose, stumbled, and dropped the ball. An error. The gods watching from afar howled in glee. Given another chance, Ruel hit a double. Now came Walter Johnson. A solid single would win the game. Again the gods snickered. A mere mortal, Johnson hit a ground ball to shortstop. The ball was fumbled by Travis Jackson; Ruel held second while Johnson hurried to first base. Another error. Fate had one last trick up its sleeve. Remember the ground ball Harris had hit in the eighth inning? The one that took a high hop over Lindstrom's head? It was déjà vu time. Earl McNeely's routine ground ball skidded along the ground toward Freddie Lindstrom. It, too, hit a pebble—or something—that caused it to leap high over the third baseman while the runners raced around the bases. Muddy Ruel, running on any batted ball, rounded third base while the ball bounded toward left fielder Meusel. Ruel was slow. A hard charge on the ball and a strong throw might have cut down the winning run. Meusel reached the ball, looked at the distance Ruel still had to cover, and decided the throw would be wasted. He stuck the ball in his pocket and raced for the safety of the clubhouse.

Down on the field thousands of delirious fans erupted from the stands. They pummeled McNeely almost senseless in a frenzy of joy. The players who had been on the field, Johnson in particular, needed to be rescued. Police pushed, players pulled, and Johnson inched his way to the dugout. He kept gasping out his happiness, a wondrous acceptance of the way fate had finally broken for him.

If he had looked toward the presidential box, he would have seen a rare sight. Calvin Coolidge was publicly performing like an average fan. Ford Frick, who would one day be commissioner of baseball, was a reporter covering the game. He wrote in his autobiography that

Coolidge had danced on the dugout roof. More believably, it was Grace Coolidge, disheveled and ecstatic, who reportedly hopped onto the dugout roof. Maybe the Coolidges did the Charleston. Everyone was going mad. A celebration broke out across the District of Columbia, and the partying went on endlessly. A wall of noise began inside Griffith Stadium and traveled like a sonic boom across the city. Guns were fired, whistles blown, horns tooted, voices were made hoarse with endless shouts. No baseball celebration since has equaled it. The fans had it their way. No mounted police had galloped onto the field to stem a tide of enthusiasts. No public-address system appealed to an assumption of good sportsmanship among the masses asking that they please refrain from entering the playing area. No warnings of impending arrests were made. The police focused on getting the players and officials to safe havens. The fans in their wild demonstrations did not set fire to cars, burn buildings, or loot stores. By today's standards it might seem tame. At the time, it was enough to hit an emotional high and sustain it by exclaiming over the wonderful luck to live in the same city as Walter Johnson.

Clark Griffith summarized the outcome, saying, "That mask up and bit Gowdy. He was going to catch that pop foul and it grabbed him away from it. Had to be that God was on our side today. Else, how did those pebbles get in front of Lindstrom not once but twice?"

The clangor and joyful noisemaking was long in dying down. Fred Lieb, in his wonderful baseball memoir *Baseball As I have Known It*, tells how the victory celebration affected Judge Landis. He explains he was alone with the commissioner on a little balcony outside his room in the Raleigh Hotel. Below, along Pennsylvania Avenue, snake-danced a joy-maddened crowd. They beat drums, some beat washtubs with large spoons, some blew horns. Anything that could make a noise was used in this joyous paean of victory.

Lieb concluded, "Landis put his hand on my shoulder and looked directly in my eyes as he said, 'Freddy, what we are looking at now—could this be the highest point of what we affectionately call our national sport? Greece had its sports and its Olympics; they must have reached a zenith and then waned. The same for the sports of ancient Rome: there must have been a year at which they were at their peak. I repeat, Freddy, are we looking at the zenith of baseball?' "

Looking back, Lieb concluded that Washington's affection for its 1924 team was baseball's finest moment up to that point. Then he added that even Landis had lived to see other demonstrations as big and delirious. In one sense, Landis' perception that he was witnessing a zenith was correct. The moment of triumph had lifted Walter Johnson to the peak of achievement. He had fulfilled himself, with his wife and mother watching. No husband or son could offer more to those he loved most.

Everything that followed would be anticlimactic. Eventually, his time as the supreme idol of the fans would pass. There are many people who boast of themselves as great baseball fans, who have never heard his name, let alone know of his feats. In his remaining lifetime, great tragedy lay ahead. Disappointments and failures, too. It is good that he savored the moment and sensed it was time to step down from the pedestal. Remember, even before the dramatic World Series and his eventual triumph, he had told reporters of his wish to end his big league career at that point. With the World Series behind him, Walter Johnson set out to find a new destiny.

30
A Hometown Hero's Welcome

WALTER AND HAZEL celebrated the final triumph of the World Series victory at a favorite restaurant on Vermont Avenue. They were given a table with some privacy, but messengers tracked down the Big Train and poured hundreds of congratulatory telegrams on the table. Hazel swept them into a bag to be answered later. It was the Johnsons' policy to answer everyone who wrote to them. The winters were a time to catch up on the mail. However, that lifestyle was changing. In several years the Johnsons would sell the Coffeyville farm. They now wintered in Nevada, in a house near Hazel's parents. The ex-congressman was now the mayor of Reno.

The Johnsons had a goal. He wanted to stay in baseball, but not as the King of the Mound. He was ready to abdicate to a lesser realm. He wanted to own a team. A good minor league city would suit him. In his plan he would manage, pitch as often as practical, and profit directly from his own baseball labors. Clark Griffith, Charles Comiskey, and Connie Mack had done it at the major league level. Christy Mathewson was president of the Boston Braves. Ty Cobb owned part of the Augusta franchise, Eddie Collins was part-owner in Baltimore, George Stallings was comfortable as an owner-manager in Rochester. Perhaps Johnson had asked Stallings' advice when he pitched there for a barnstorming team *the day after winning the World Series.*

As incongruous as it seems, along with Joe Judge, George Mogridge, and coaches Nick Altrock and Al Schacht, Johnson left a city of revelers on Friday night for the upstate New York city. Among his barnstorming teammates was the young Yankee first baseman, Lou Gehrig. Johnson pitched the two opening innings against a team rounded up locally. He would play only a few games of the tour, then turn his role over to Tom Zachary.

The incongruity of Walter Johnson leaving Washington before the cheering had stopped to pick up a fee for an exhibition appearance was lost on the editors of the Ken Burns documentary *Baseball,* a Public Broadcasting Service epic. They warped the events of this historic moment by stating that the next day Walter Johnson headed a victory parade in Washington. The film was eye-catching. There were the mounted elite cantering past, the open touring cars, the sidewalks deep with cheering spectators. *Of course, it was the parade which had celebrated winning the American League pennant a week earlier.*

Meanwhile, there were other matters to occupy Johnson. His family had motored back to Coffeyville in the new Lincoln sedan. There were plans afoot to make this the biggest Walter Johnson Day the town had ever celebrated. However, he first had to confer with George Weiss, his partner-to-be in the plan to buy a West Coast team. Oakland was for sale, he had heard, and that suited him ideally. It was close enough to Reno to make the Nevada city his year-round home.

This year's return to Coffeyville was probably his last appearance as a hometown hero. He could not announce that he and his family were permanently leaving, it was too uncertain. Yet Walter Johnson had separated himself from farm life in the rural backwater. He let the herd run down and rented out his fields to others. Johnson slipped into town unannounced a few days before Walter Johnson Day, which had been rescheduled several times. He attended Sunday afternoon services at the First Methodist Episcopal Church, entering as the congregation was singing, and soon he joined in. "That Old Time Religion" rang out, and the minister, Rev. Gordon B. Thompson, interpolated, "It was good for Walter Johnson and it's good enough for me." In an informal talk, Reverend Thompson praised Walter Johnson for setting the example of clean living and gentlemanly conduct during his 18 years of national prominence. He explained there was a family reunion in progress at the Johnson home and that it had been a great sacrifice for Walter to attend the church service, even for a few minutes. He added that because of Johnson's natural modesty, he would not ask him to talk. "Have him stand for a moment, anyhow," urged several members of the congregation.

Walter Johnson slowly rose to his feet and, after a great ovation died down, began to speak in a slow, drawling voice. "I want you men to know that you have been a great help to me, and that I appreciate your kindly interest," he said. "It was a great inspiration to receive the telegram just before the World's Series started, with so many old familiar names signed to it. I was thinking of you all the time during the game."

He told how his first two losses had not discouraged him. Still, he added, "I believe I was the happiest man in the world when they called on me in the last game. I tried to forget about my two defeats and think of you boys back home." Once started, Johnson kept talking. He spoke directly to the boys who were present about the importance of good healthy habits and came down hard on cigarette smoking.

Coffeyville turned October 20 into a town holiday. It was Monday, but schools and businesses closed and everyone turned out for the special parade. At 1:30 P.M. whistles and sirens gave the signal and, with Walter Johnson and his family riding in the new Lincoln limousine he had been given by his fans in Washington, the parade was on. More than 3,000 school children passed by flag-bedecked buildings. With delegations and floats from fraternal organizations and businesses, with the Coffeyville Boys Band and the Coffeyville City Band playing, Walter Johnson's connections to the community marched past.

The parade ended at Forest Park, where crowds estimated from 6,000 to 15,000 packed the city's ball field. They ebbed out of the stands, formed an oval across the outfield, and cheered when the first player appeared. He was Gabby Street, recruited from nearby Joplin, Missouri, where Johnson's first battery mate was managing the team in the Western Association. The game was between nearby Caney's town nine and Coffeyville. Walter Johnson, of course, pitched and alternately blazed strikeouts or lobbed up fat pitches. The score did not matter to Johnson; he was happy to be on a ball field surrounded by hometown friends.

Walter Johnson Day ended with a banquet. He did respond when asked to talk and assured everyone he would be back to Coffeyville, although he and his family were off to California in the morning. The next day, Walter and Hazel, Walter Jr., Edwin, Robert, and Carolyn left on the Missouri Pacific's "Rainbow Special." The boys would go to Reno schools, and their father would try to buy the Oakland ball club. There would still be Johnsons in Coffeyville—his brothers, his married sister, and Minnie Johnson, his mother—for years to come.

Walter Johnson deposited Hazel and the children with Mr. and Mrs. Roberts and began a concentrated series of exhibition games. Always a big gate attraction anywhere, especially in California between seasons, Johnson capitalized on his current status as baseball's number one hero. On October 26 he pitched for a pickup team of semipros, losing to Vernon of the Pacific Coast League, 5-1. The next day, 16,000 people saw him throw seven shutout innings in a charity game for the benefit of the House of the Good Shepherd, a home for unwed mothers. On October 31, a highly publicized game was played, with Babe Ruth pitching against Johnson. It was the first time the two superstars had met since Ruth had given up pitching in favor of hitting home runs. Johnson pitched for the Elks and Babe for his All-Stars. The lineups had California-based major leaguers and minor league stars. Donie Bush and Sam Crawford had emerged from retirement, Bush to back up Johnson and Wahoo Sam to play first base for Babe Ruth. It was a triumph for the Babe. Johnson pitched the first five innings and gave up eight runs, including two homers by Ruth and one by Crawford. The Babe had a no-hitter with two out in the bottom of the ninth inning. Bob Meusel, Ruth's Yankee teammate, was the final batter. You can invent a scenario to suit your sense of drama. Meusel homered.

Two days later George Weiss arrived, and he and Walter Johnson met with Cal Ewing, the wealthy owner of the Oakland Oaks. It's probable that Ewing never was serious in offering to sell. However, he accepted a $5,000 down payment, with the balance of the $50,000 purchase price due in 30 days. Even if Ewing was not serious, Clark Griffith was very seriously concerned. He had known of Johnson's ambitions and they had discussed them. As Johnson's friend, Griffith wanted to see him achieve his goal. As Johnson's owner, he regarded with horror the idea of losing the league's Most Valuable Player, the superstar pitcher, the crowd-pleasing attraction who filled ballparks. An agreement was reached. Unless Johnson made his deal by the end of December, he would commit to returning to the Senators for 1925.

It was time for Johnson's eastern backers to put up, and they let him down. What might have sounded like an enjoyable way to invest profits taken from the sky-high stock market, lost its appeal when the team they would own played on the opposite side of the continent. Besides, who was this George Weiss fellow? The future general manager of the New York Yankees and Hall of Fame member, was known only as a small-time New Haven baseball entrepreneur. Walter Johnson had to withdraw his offer. The Oakland directors returned the $5,000 down payment and Johnson, briefly, looked elsewhere. Some weak franchises thrust themselves at him, but nothing offered the arrangement he thought he had found with Oakland. Resigned, he abandoned his plan and turned his thoughts to pitching the Washington Senators to a repeat World Championship.

Clark Griffith had been busy insuring himself against the loss of Walter Johnson. Although, surely, a large amount of cash must have gone to Cleveland for Stan Coveleski, it was reported as a trade. Griffith obtained the veteran right-handed spitballer in exchange for two prospects, Byron Speece and Carr Smith. Coveleski had been 15-16 for the Indians and might have been thought washed up. Still, he had led the American League in ERA two years earlier. His 1925 performance for Washington cemented his claim on the Baseball Hall of Fame. He even out-performed Walter Johnson, giving the Senators a glamorous one-two punch.

In mid-winter Walter Johnson's fans were treated to two autobiographies which ran in syndication in national newspapers. One, a concoction spun from clips dug up from a newspaper's morgue, previously published interviews, and invented philosophical observations, was offered as "My Twenty Years On The Mound," by Walter Johnson *as related to Lillian Barker*. The blurb introducing the series claimed she was a writer who knew a great deal about baseball. The material ran in a 12-part series, marketed by the Thompson Syndicate. It repeated almost all of the warped stories of Johnson's early life. The highlights of his career were retold: his debut against Ty Cobb and the Tigers, his three shutouts in four days, the 16-game win streak, the deliberate dusting of Frank Baker, the no-hitter, and other staples which are still inherent in any account of Walter Johnson.

Johnson had been working on a definitive account of his life with the Christy Walsh Syndicate. The actual writing was done by Hazel Johnson. When the Barker series got the jump, Johnson was as outraged as his usually tolerant nature allowed. His series, published in the *Washington Times*, began on January 5, 1925. It ran three times a week, with 61 installments in all. The first chapter carried the following "Warning To Readers":

> Unfortunately I find it necessary to assure the reading public that this is my own personal story. There has been a story appearing in certain newspapers alleging to express my opinions on my life in baseball. The unauthorized story is being published without my permission, without my assistance, in spite of my protests and contains many statements attributed to me which I never said. Disputes have always been distasteful to me but I feel my many friends are entitled to know that this is my own story and accurate. The other is not.

With that said, Johnson provided a wonderfully detailed account of his life before baseball and away from the diamond. He opened with the recent 1924 World Series. He was as moved and thrilled by the ultimate triumph as the most emotional fan. Over the span of 20 weeks, readers were offered observations and evaluations of other players, fitness tips, and observations about key career achievements (his 56 consecutive scoreless innings thrilled him the most). He defined himself at the pinnacle as a man with five home towns: Humboldt, where he was born; Olinda, where he was a teenager; Weiser, where he entered professional baseball; Coffeyville, where he lived during his prime years; and Washington, where he pitched. Now, Reno, Nevada, had a claim on him. He said that he presently owned a home in Washington, D.C., a farm in Coffeyville, Kansas, and a home in Reno, Nevada.

In an attempt to stifle the unauthorized biography by Lillian Barker, presumably the Kitty Kelly of her era, Johnson sued the *Brooklyn Eagle*, which carried the series, for $50,000. He asked the New York Supreme Court to issue an injunction to prevent the Thompson Syndicate from expanding its sales. Johnson lost his first decision of 1925. On February 2, Justice O'Malley denied the application, pointing out the 12-part series had already run. The court permitted Johnson to renew his complaint if there were any more articles from the pen of Lillian Barker.

Although there were rewards left in his life—a second daughter, another pennant and World Series appearance, a managerial career—with the climax win of the seventh game of the World Series, Walter Johnson had reached the peak of his life and career. All else was to be epilogue.

31
Another Pennant but No Miracle

THE CITY OF TAMPA billed itself as the Spring Training Home of the new World Champion Washington Senators. When the 1925 squad assembled the city fathers rolled out the red carpet. It would have been better if they had rolled the cinder track circling the ballpark. The first day, Walter Johnson stepped into a hole and severely sprained his ankle. The mishap put him 10 days behind his schedule and slowed his progress toward opening day readiness.

In all other respects it was a very successful preparation for a team some baseball historians, obsessed with power-hitting factors, downgrade among world championship teams. In most respects, the 1925 team can be rated even better than the 1924 stalwarts. In addition to Stan Coveleski, Clark Griffith had added two other veterans to the staff. One, Dutch Ruether, had led the National League in winning percentage in 1919 in Cincinnati's pennant-winning season and later was also a winner with Brooklyn. He had one thing in common with Walter Johnson. Ruether had been the best hitting pitcher in the National League and, in 1925, would battle Johnson for similar honors. Vean Gregg, the American League's dominant lefthander of a decade earlier, was brought back from the minor leagues. Although past 40, he had been rejuvenated in the Pacific Coast League and had pitched Seattle to a championship.

Ban Johnson found another sour note to sound, notifying all American League teams they were not to play exhibition games with the National League Champions. The Giants and Senators had been meeting in pre-season games and traveling north from Florida together for several years. What would be more natural than for the two World Series rivals to continue the arrangement? Ban Johnson's petulant edict was ignored, and he modified it to begin the next year. A New York and Washington 13-game series was arranged to culminate with weekend games in Washington and New York on the eve of the 1925 season.

A 15-year-old redheaded Florida high school boy, enrolled at Sanford High School, saw the teams play when a sports-minded principal gave the students the afternoon off so they could watch Walter Johnson and the others. Red Barber, baseball's finest broadcaster, shared the memory with his retirement-era Public Broadcast audience. Johnson did not pitch, the Old Redhead recalled, but was introduced and took a bow. Barber titled his piece "My Idol Was Walter Johnson," giving as his reason not just the pitching ability of his hero but the style of life he led. Barber held family values in high esteem in boyhood and all his life.

Before starting the series with the Giants, the Senators were awarded their 1924 World Series medals (rings were not yet the customary jewelry). They were distributed by Judge Landis before a game with the Boston Braves on March 14. Tim McNamara, who remembers the day well, pitched for the Braves although Johnson was still too hobbled to even work out, let alone pitch. When the Giants won five of the first six games, the jaunty McGraw could not restrain himself. He boasted, "I have always insisted the Giants were stronger than the Senators last year but were out-lucked in the World Series." The Senators squelched McGraw's bragging by winning five of the remaining six games, including the final game at the Polo Grounds on April 11. One game was rained out. Johnson, nearing his best form, pitched scoreless ball for the final three innings at the Polo Grounds.

Before that, Johnson had methodically rounded into shape, not rushing to catch up after his delayed beginning. An interesting exploitation of the World Series rivalry took place, with Artie Nehf and Walter Johnson billed as opposing pitchers in a game in Tampa on March 28. The day before, Nehf, while pitching batting practice, had been hit in the face by a line drive and knocked unconscious. His severely cut lip was stitched together, and a man with a less determined manager than John McGraw would have been sidelined. Seeming more like a fight manager than a baseball manager, with a "they can't hurt us" attitude, McGraw started the battle-scarred Nehf. He held the Senators to two runs in five innings, which was enough to defeat Walter Johnson, who was making his first start of the spring. Johnson gave up four hits and three runs in the three opening innings he pitched.

Johnson pitched three-inning stints, as was his custom, as the teams worked their way north interspersing their tour games with separate games against Southern Association teams. The recent World Series rivals did not make the biggest news coming from teams traveling north. On April 5, a story datelined Chattanooga told of Babe Ruth shaking off an illness to hit two home runs for his fans. Two days later the headlines read: "Ruth Collapses in South—Stricken as He Reaches Asheville." These precursory news bulletins warned baseball fans that the Bambino had to be burped. The world's greatest stomachache nearly ended the Babe's career, and his life with it. He missed two months of playing time, never returned to his King of Swat form, and dragged the Yankees down from being the Senators' most formidable challenger, as they had been in 1924, to a seventh-place finish. Nothing Clark Griffith did to strengthen his team weighed as much in the balance as Ruth's absence from the Yankee lineup and his subpar playing when he was in it. Connie Mack was several seasons short of fielding his last dynastic champions, winners in 1929-31. The Yankees, once again led by the Babe, rebounded with great teams in 1926, '27, and '28. But the field was virtually left to the Senators in 1925. They played superbly and, although the A's made a race of it until late summer, eventually coasted home.

Walter Johnson said he was not ready to pitch by Opening Day, tradition or not. Anyway, Ban Johnson was still snubbing the president, whoever he might be. Calvin Coolidge was on call for all Washington openings, but Johnson decreed it was the Yankees turn to host the league's opener. Washington was named as their opponent. Bucky Harris started George Mogridge and lost. He lost the next day with Tom Zachary pitching. Then his newly added veteran starters showed how smart the Senators had been to add them to the staff. Stan Coveleski won 7-4 and Dutch Ruether won 4-1. The next day in Philadelphia, Walter Johnson pitched his first game of 1925. He lost to a familiar nemesis, Slim Harriss, 3-0, going nine innings for the first time. Had he been on schedule he would have done nine innings before the season opened. This game actually completed his standard regime to reach form. Now he was ready to do his season's work.

It began with Washington's own season opener, April 22, with the Ruth-less Yankees in town. President Coolidge, with his wife Grace attentively scoring the game for the presidential party, may have warmed up under the grandstand. With the photographer's bulbs popping, he whipped the ceremonial first pitch directly into Walter Johnson's glove. The Big Train got underway with an easy 10-1 win. He was on his way to what would be his final 20-victory season.

Interesting events occurred as Johnson reeled off a successful season, never losing two decisions in a row. In addition to pitching consistent winning ball, Walter Johnson was engaged in the most prodigious season any pitcher has ever had as a batter. His season's average was .433, with 42 hits in 97 times at bat. With the American League persisting in warping the true play of baseball with a bastard rule permitting a "designated hitter" to bat for the pitcher and the likelihood the National League will succumb to the seductive promises that more hitting will excite its easily stimulated baseball followers, Johnson's never-excelled 1925 feat may become permanent by default.

Johnson's lifetime batting average, prior to his flare-out season, was .226. Good, but not spectacular. He had always demonstrated power. He had hit 16 home runs in the dead ball era, more than any other pitcher, although Ruth had hit 13 in half as many games. Johnson finished with 24, with only six pitchers who batted exclusively in the post-1920 live ball era ahead of him. In 1925 Johnson had a number of special days at the plate. He pinch-hit a double to drive in two ninth-inning runs to defeat Herb Pennock of the Yankees, 2-1, on April 23. On May 19 he beat the Indians with a ninth-inning pinch-hit homer that won the game, 4-3. It was the first ball to ever clear the right-field wall hit by a right-handed batter. Even when he lost to Bullet Joe Bush's one-hitter on August 27, it was Johnson who got the hit, a sixth-inning double. He raised his average far above .400 in September, with a pair of three-for-four days against the A's on September 1 and 7. His new teammate, Dutch Ruether, hovered around the .400 mark himself but slipped back to .333.

Against Johnson's personal achievements, one opponent's feat is noteworthy. Slim Harriss, who could beat Washington almost at will and outpitched Johnson himself several times, not only demonstrated his pitching mastery on May 28, when Philadelphia beat Washington 9-4, but Harriss also homered. The sight of the ball leaving the ballpark off the usually futile bat of Harriss broke up Johnson. He laughed almost uncontrollably at the incongruity. Harriss, a 6-foot-6 string bean, had a career batting average of .145. In 565 times at bat, he managed only one home run. When Johnson saw it sail over the fence, he was nearly helpless with laughter. It was not Johnson's day, but he was good-humored about it. He left after four innings, having given up four runs. The ioss was only his second of the season, against seven wins. He won his next start, beating the Yankees at the Stadium, on June 1. The game marked Babe Ruth's return to the Yankee line-up. He had been in New York City's St. Vincent Hospital for two months regaining the health he had wasted. Although hitless against

Johnson, Ruth made a great running catch on a Joe Judge drive before bowing out of the game.

On May 27 at Philadelphia, Walter Johnson had already gone to the showers—hit hard in less than five innings and giving up seven earned runs—before the newest phenom, Bob Groves, entered the game. Johnson would have heard of the misanthropic fireballer from Lonaconing, Maryland. Alternately known as Groves or Grove, it took time to find out the true spelling as he never signed autographs. Later, when he began using a rubber stamp to expedite the process, it was taken as evidence that the lefthander was illiterate. Not so. He was taciturn, surly, ill at ease with all but a few teammates, but he could write his name. When he finally was signed by Connie Mack, after five scintillating seasons at Baltimore, it was as Robert Grove, mostly called "Lefty" and mellowing in late years to "Mose."

At Baltimore, where Jack Dunn refused to sell his stars, he had pitched in five pennant winners, winning 109 games for a .751 average. He was the heir apparent to Johnson's strikeout crown, and they hooked up for the first time at Philadelphia on June 26. It was not a strikeout duel, Johnson not fanning anyone. Goose Goslin's three-run homer made the difference in a 5-3 win for the Senators over the A's, who led the league at that point. Grove was alarmingly wild and bullet fast, a combination which would enable him to take the strikeout crown from Johnson in this, his rookie season. Just as Walter Johnson had reigned for a string of seasons, so did Lefty Grove. He won seven consecutive strikeout titles before guile was needed to replace sheer speed.

Walter Johnson's penchant for disabling illness hit again, this time in mid-season. On June 30 at Philadelphia, a Johnson two-hit shutout vaulted Washington into the league lead for the first time. Before he could take his next turn, he was in bed with influenza contracted in Boston over the July 4 holiday. Johnson was sent back to Washington to be nursed back to health by his wife, Hazel. He missed almost a month in mid-season, but returned on July 28 against the Chicago White Sox. Johnson was off form and wild. When he hit Johnny Mostil in the head, knocking him cold for five minutes, Walter unraveled as he always did when an errant pitch damaged an opponent. Although Mostil revived and stayed in the game, Johnson was gone before the sixth inning, the loser of a 10-5 game. Mostil was the fifth batter to be inadvertently beaned by Johnson. He was the last.

Johnson quickly recovered his poise, looking sharp while winning in relief the next day. He hit peak form his next start, on August 2, with a two-hitter, one unearned run depriving him of a shutout. He had no decision, pitching the first nine innings of a 12-inning game, on August 9. August 13 was dog-day hot in humid Washington, and Barney—as he was now called even by his longtime chronicler, Paul A. Eaton—had to leave too early for a decision. He was two-for-two at the plate and had scored from first base on a double in the second inning. In the fourth inning he raced from first to third on a single. It was too much for the 38-year-old pitcher, and he ran out of gas pitching the fifth inning. Vean Gregg replaced him with two out and the score tied, 3-3. Gregg got the win when Washington rallied for a 5-4 victory.

Bucky Harris was easing Johnson toward a 20-win season and preserving him for the World Series which lay ahead. He had a chance to lift his star early at Detroit on August 22. Johnson, who had homered and driven in three runs early, was able to leave in the sixth inning with the team rolling to a 20-5 win. It was Johnson's 17th victory against only five losses.

September opened with an easy win at home from the A's as Washington drew clear of the pack and the fans began to plan on a repeat triumph in the World Series. They glanced at the standings in the National League to see who would oppose the Senators. Pittsburgh and New York were neck and neck. The fans knew about the Giants, and the knowledgeable among them were also aware how potent Pittsburgh's bats were. Like the Giants, they lacked an individual pitcher of the stature of Walter Johnson or Stan Coveleski but, like the McGraw men, they had a solid rotation of experienced pitchers.

Johnson's 19th win came when he again beat Lefty Grove, although fanning only one batter. Maybe he didn't want to give away any strikeout secrets to the upstart as he scattered nine hits for a 2-1 win on September 7. Four days later, pitching in turn, he edged out the Boston Red Sox, 5-4, winning his 20th game and getting his 100th strikeout for the season.

Unlike 1924, this season the schedule provided the Senators with a home stand that lasted almost the entire month of September. Johnson began pointing for the coming World Series, satisfied with a 20-win season. When the Most Valuable Player award was announced, Johnson, the previous year's winner, received no votes. His teammate, the veteran shortstop Roger Peckinpaugh, had a career year and was given the award. Johnson could not even be regarded as the top pitcher on the Washington staff. Coveleski's stats were better. Both won 20

217

games, but the spitballer lost two fewer. Still, Walter Johnson's admirers could relish a 20-victory season, begun late and with a month taken out in mid-season because of illness.

On September 20, in a game with the A's, Johnson pulled up with a charley horse while sliding into third base. Bucky Harris played it safe. The pennant was as good as won, and his job was to get his team ready for the World Series. Having Walter Johnson in top form, rested and ready for the opening game, was the first priority. It was time to give the regulars a rest, work future prospects into the lineup, and plan for Pittsburgh. The Bucs had pulled away at the end, finishing eight games on top as the Giants collapsed. Washington's margin over the A's was a half-game better, being eight and a half games ahead at the end. The Pirates would come into the World Series with momentum and the Senators with a rested, well-balanced ball club.

32

Johnson's Most
Terrible Defeat

THE 1925 WORLD SERIES became virtually a mirror image of the 1924 event. Both series went the full seven games. Both sent hometown fans into spasms of ecstasy and sent jubilant throngs reveling through downtown streets. However, this time it would be Washington and Walter Johnson gazing darkly into the looking glass. Once again, jerry-built stands encroached on the normal playing areas of both ballparks and altered the outcome of games. Walter Johnson, saved from ignominy by the quirks of fate in the final game of 1924, was humbled by uncaring gods in the final home-team inning a year later.

Washington fielded much the same team as had narrowly defeated the Giants the year before. Earl McNeely alternated with Nemo Leibold in center field the full season. The most potent addition was Joe Harris, obtained from Boston early in the season. He brought power to the lineup but was less than an adroit fielder. He had played 100 games, two-thirds of them at first base and the rest in the outfield. To get his bat into the lineup, Sam Rice was shifted to center field and Joe Harris played right field.

In 1924 the Senators were the new challengers taking the battle to the World Series–tested Giants. This time the Senators were the experienced team and the Pirates the upstart newcomers. Pittsburgh had not been in a World Series since 1909, when the Cobb-Wagner confrontation had taken place. One member of those winning Pirates, Babe Adams, remained. Now 43 years old, Adams, whose nickname "Babe" came from his boyish appearance as he won three games from Detroit in the 1909 World Series, was still useful in relief.

Except for the seasoned superstar Max Carey, the other Pirates were emerging talents. Pie Traynor ranks as baseball's most effective third baseman. Spare those who saw him play with comparisons to the vacuum-gloved Brooks Robinson. Traynor was superlative in a time of hand-sized gloves and dirt infields; look at his hitting records, particularly runs batted in. Glenn Wright was the best in his brief time at shortstop until an arm injury curtailed his career. He exceeded everything expected of a middle infielder and had a powerful bat as well. The only regular that failed to hit over .300 was the pepper-pot second baseman, Eddie Moore, who fell short by two points. First base offered a problem the Pirates solved by platooning the still-slick fielding veteran of Connie Mack's $100,000 infield, Stuffy McInnis, with George "Boots" Grantham. His nickname did not derive from his fascination with footwear, it arose from his lack of success with ground balls. Grantham hit .326 with extra-base power. At that, in 59 games McInnis clubbed .368.

Max Carey was joined in the outfield by KiKi Cuyler (mystifyingly called "Kee Kee" by some moderns when his nickname obviously stemmed from "CUYler") and Clyde Barnhart, a solid performer. He batted .325 to go with Carey's .343 and Cuyler's .357. During the World Series it was announced that Pittsburgh had bought Paul Waner from San Francisco, for 1926 delivery, to replace Barnhart. Earl "Oil" Smith, whose years as a backstop for the Giants had found the Texan called, in the patois of New Yorkers, "Oil" for Earl, hit .313. The team's .307 batting average was nine points better than the next highest team.

As had the 1924 Giants, the Bucs' staff lacked a dominant starter but could rotate among four established pitchers: Vic Aldrich, 15-7; Remy Kremer, 17-8; Lee Meadows, 19-10; and Johnny Morrison, 17-14. Adams had been 6-5 and with Red Oldham, another veteran, was a spot starter and reliever. Oldham was to play a decisive part as manager Bill McKechnie's trump card. McKechnie himself is a presence in the Baseball Hall of Fame for his field managerial skills. In 1925 he won the first of four pennants; he would then lead the 1928 St. Louis Cardinals and later the 1939 and 1940 Cincinnati Reds to pennants.

Unlike the 1924 World Series, when the experience of the Giants drew the backing of professional bettors, the 1925 event was not heavily bet and the favorite's odds were narrowly set according to where the wagering was done; in Washington, the Senators were favored and in Pittsburgh, the Pirates were. In New York City and other places where sporting money was laid on the line, it was 6-5 and take your choice. The odds for the opening game, with Walter Johnson the obvious pitching choice, favored the Senators everywhere.

Each city served as a metaphor for a lifestyle. Pittsburgh was a blue-collar community, called "the Smokey City." Towering brick smokestacks billowed clouds of anthracite soot and gave the area an almost permanent pall of gloomy, sun-hiding smoke. Although Forbes Field was set in an upscale suburb, seemingly always upwind from the billows of factory smoke, with the greenery of spacious Schenley Park as a background, Pittsburgh conjured up a soot-covered image.

Washington meant cherry trees blossoming in springtime and the sparkling waters of Chesapeake Bay. The nation's capital had been systematically laid out with boulevards converging on the centers of power: the White House, Congress, and the Supreme Court. The Washington Monument reached toward permanently blue skies. Its memorials hailed historic giants tracing back to the American Revolution. Pittsburgh's monuments celebrated icons of the industrial revolution. These metaphors of light and dark would apply to the shifting tides of success during the World Series. A virtually unmoving low-pressure system hovered over the eastern half of the United States. An occasional day of intermittent sunshine brightened communities alternately, but the rain returned and seemed to prevail wherever a baseball game was attempted. Pittsburgh had played its final game the Sunday before the series opened in the rain, and Washington's final contest had been called off after four wet innings.

The Senators arrived in Pittsburgh aboard a special train the evening of October 5. Manager Bucky Harris was given a six-foot long "Key to the City," and the team stayed at the fashionable Morrow Field Apartments located in the suburban splendors of elegant Squirrel Hill. The Senators got in a morning practice at Forbes Field on the 6th while workmen finished nailing together 6,500 temporary bleacher seats. They would go on sale for $1.50 each the day of the game. The added seats brought Forbes Field's capacity to 45,000. In addition to those who could find a place inside the ballpark, radio would again bring the games to millions of listeners. Harold Arlin of Pittsburgh's KDKA had broadcast the first regular-season game in 1921. He was not called on for the Pirates appearance in the World Series, however. Graham McNamee, of New York City's WEAF, arrived from the east and Quinn Ryan, of WGN in Chicago, from the west to handle broadcasts arranged by the American Telephone and Telegraph Company. Both pioneer baseball broadcasters described the game to listeners along relay lines, McNamee handling the feed going east. There was an extra person to

221

help McNamee with the broadcast of the opening game. At the start of the Pirates' ninth inning, Honus Wagner was introduced and promised the home fans a rally. He gave his opinion of the abilities of the Pirates as they were coming to bat. It can be claimed that Honus was the first "color man" in World Series broadcasting.

Although Washington had gone through a workout, the Pirates were rained out of their practice session in the afternoon. The morning headlines of October 7th's newspapers threatened: "Rain May Prevent Series Start Today."

It turned out to be a darkly overcast day, perfect for Walter Johnson's fastball. He had all his old-time speed and control and the poise of a seasoned veteran. In the fifth inning Pie Traynor arched an off-field home run into the temporary seats fronting the right-field stands. It was Pittsburgh's only score, although Johnson teetered a bit though the bottom of the final inning. He nicked Carey with an errant pitch for the second time in the game but fanned Cuyler on a called strike. Then, after Barnhart singled to bring the momentary hope of the tying run to bat, Johnson's sidearm pitches were too much for Pie Traynor who flied to center and Glenn Wright who popped up to Joe Judge at first base. It was a comfortable 4-1 win for the King of the Mound. He had struck out 10, walked only one, and scattered five hits. It was the kind of performance the public expected from Walter Johnson. In the game's statistics only one negative speck appeared. The league's MVP and the team's leader, Roger Peckinpaugh, had made the game's only error. It was of no consequence. Unfortunately, most of the next seven he made in the series were disastrous.

The night after the opening game was played, Christy Mathewson died at Saranac Lake, New York, where he had hoped to regain his health. Gassed in the World War, he had sought to repair his damaged lungs at a sanitarium in the Adirondack Mountains. Early reports had been optimistic, and his death shocked the baseball world. Walter Johnson would have his own memories of the great Matty as he donned a uniform with a hastily sewn black armband for the next day's game.

Stan Coveleski's experience was expected to prevail the next day. He pitched a good game, giving up only two earned runs. It was an unearned one that beat him, 3-2, as Vic Aldrich topped the veteran spitballer. In the eighth inning of a 1-1 contest, Eddie Moore's routine leadoff ground ball ran up Roger Peckinpaugh's arm for the first error of the game. Moore scampered to second as Max Carey was out at first on a chopper to Bucky Harris. Then KiKi Cuyler hit a wrong-field home run into the temporary right-field bleachers. The ball would have been easily caught if the field was its normal depth. In fact, four of the first five home runs hit in this series landed in the temporary seats. The Senators got one run back in the top of the ninth but fell one unearned run short. The teams headed for Washington, even at a game apiece.

The Washington fans were confidently expectant. Series tickets were at a premium, even those in the restored temporary bleachers ringing the outfield. The section in center field was reserved for the team's colored fans. Ironically, the city where Abraham Lincoln had signed the Emancipation Proclamation enforced the Jim Crow restrictions of the South. Rain, which fell indiscriminately on all fans, washed out Sunday's game.

Although it meant an extra day's rest for Johnson and Coveleski before they would pitch again, it only delayed the tough choice Bucky Harris faced in naming a third-game starter. The Pittsburgh lineup was loaded with right-handed batters. Max Carey was a switch hitter, as was Johnny Gooch, the alternate catcher. Stuffy McInnis, a righty, would replace Grantham if Harris started either of his seasoned lefties, George Mogridge or Tom Zachary. Harris and Clark Griffith had planned ahead. Late in the season they obtained Alex Ferguson. He had lost in double figures for three seasons but had been doomed to pitch for the decimated Boston Red Sox. Most importantly, he threw right-handed and won five of six starts with the Senators in the closing weeks of the season. He kept right on winning in the World Series. Ferguson battled Remy Kremer for seven innings before giving way to a pinch hitter. He held the Bucs to two earned runs plus one contributed by another Peckinpaugh error. Washington scored twice in the seventh to take a 4-3 lead, and Fred Marberry was called on to protect it. He did so with the help of a catch by Sam Rice that became one of the most disputed of all time. Rice had raced back to the temporary seats in right-center field chasing a long, towering drive by Earl Smith. He leaped high, caught the ball in his glove, and fell into the stands. Umpire Cy Rigler had raced out to get a close look. There was a delay, then when Rice climbed back over the low railing triumphantly brandishing the ball in his glove, the National League umpire called the batter out.

The Pirates argued that some fan must have put the ball back into Rice's glove. Later, there were eyewitnesses who swore the ball had bounced out of Rice's grasp and landed several sections away. Different Pirate fans produced baseballs they claimed had ricocheted off Rice's glove. Rice later tired of both the dispute and answering the question. On July 26, 1965, he wrote a letter to Paul S. Kerr, president of the National Baseball Hall of Fame and Museum. It was his statement of what had occurred, and he instructed *that it was not to be opened until after his death*. This, Rice believed, would gain authenticity as either a form of deathbed confession if he had been lying since 1925 or an irrefutable statement if it sustained his claim.

When Sam Rice died on October 13, 1974, Paul Kerr opened Sam's envelope. This is the handwritten statement Sam left behind:

> It was a cold and windy day—the right field bleachers were crowded with people in overcoats and wrapped in blankets, the ball was a line drive headed for the bleachers toward right center. I turned slightly to my right and had the ball in view all the way, going at top speed and about 15 feet from the bleachers jumped as high as I could and back handed [it] and the ball hit the center of pocket in glove (I had a death grip on it). I hit the ground about five feet from a barrier about four feet high in front of the bleachers with all the brakes on but couldn't stop so I tried to jump it to land in the crowd but my feet hit the barrier about a foot from top and I toppled over on my stomach into first row of bleachers. I hit my Adam's apple on something which sort of knocked me out for a few seconds but McNeely arrived about that time and grabbed me by the shirt and pulled me out. I remember trotting back towards the infield still carrying the ball for about halfway and then tossed it towards the pitcher's mound. (How I have wished many times I had kept it.)
>
> At no time did I lose possession of the ball.
>
> [signed] "Sam" Rice

On November 10, 1974, a letter was written to Paul Kerr by Norman E. Budesheim, a Public Utilities Consultant, living in Silver Spring, Maryland. He told his account of Rice's catch, explaining that he and another 17-year-old had been in the front row of the bleachers at the point where Sam Rice hurtled into them. "I caught Sam full across the chest and arms as did my friend," Budesheim began.

"When Sam went out of the park [over the barrier] he had the ball in his glove definitely. However, upon hitting us, he definitely dropped the ball. I wish to emphasize he rolled off our laps and was flat on the ground in the tight space between our legs and feet and the barrier and I [was] frantically trying to get the ball—me to give it to him and he to get it himself naturally. ...Sam beat me to the ball. When Sam says 'at no time did I lose possession of the ball,' he is generally and literally correct in that I never got it and he had it under control so to speak but not necessarily in his glove without interruption."

Sam might have been a bit ingenuous in how he framed his claim, but his witness of the catch made nearly 50 years earlier verified Sam Rice's account and accepted the truth as deemed by the outfielder.

Game Four was a great triumph for Walter Johnson. Some observers said he was not quite as fast as he had been in the opener, but his curve and control were sharp. The Senators scored four runs in the third inning, and Johnson pitched a six-hit shutout for a 4-0 win. Johnson had led off the fourth inning with a single but had been tagged out at second base trying to stretch it to a double. He had already slowed up rounding first base when Barnhart had trouble picking up the ball hit down the left-field line. In starting up again, Johnson pulled a muscle in his leg. He finished the game without difficulty, but afterward it tightened up and ultimately proved to be a serious handicap.

The carnival atmosphere of the previous year was missing from the nation's capital. With the Senators leading three games to one, the team's supporters prepared to revel again. It would lack the surprised spontaneity of 1924, but would be an outlet for civic pride and confirm the rightness of Walter Johnson's team retaining its World Championship. All that was needed was for Stan Coveleski to chip in his certain win. Pittsburgh, however, had other ideas about that. Bill McKechnie rallied his team, and they began one of the greatest comebacks in World Series history.

Vic Aldridge, winner of Game Two, and Coveleski reached the seventh inning locked in a 2-2 tie. It was the veteran who cracked. A one-out walk followed by three successive singles brought the spitballer's exit. Two runs were in and runners were on first and third. Win Ballou, a 28-year-old rookie lefty, was Harris' strange choice to pitch to Pie Traynor, one of Pittsburgh's devastating right-handed batters. Perhaps reverse logic worked. Ballou fanned Traynor. Then, when Barnhart broke for second base, Muddy Ruel faked a throw and then whipped the ball to Bluege to trap Cuyler off third base.

After opening the home half of the seventh with a double and a run-scoring single to close the margin to one run, the Senators' rally sputtered out. Ballou, lifted for a pinch hitter, was replaced by another lefty, Tom Zachary. The wisdom of not risking lefthanders against the Bucs was reaffirmed this time. Zachary was touched up for a run in the eighth and another in the ninth before Fred Marberry came in to get the final out. The sportswriters had plenty to second-guess about, asking why Marberry or Allan Russell had not been used instead of Zachary. Now, instead of a victory parade along Pennsylvania Avenue, the World Series troupes headed for Pittsburgh. The Senators were confident. They needed only win the sixth game and the title was theirs. If worse came to worst, Walter Johnson would pitch the seventh game. When that did happen, it was worse than Johnson's fans expected.

Alex Ferguson pitched well enough to win the sixth game, taking an early 2-0 lead into the third inning, when the snakebit Roger Peckinpaugh made another error. He didn't boot or drop the ball; this time he failed to step on second base as the pivot man on a double-play ball. The Bucs tied the score and won it in the fifth when Eddie Moore hit a wrong-field homer into the temporary right-field stands. Remy Kremer held Washington scoreless, although they threatened in the eighth. Hank Severeid, catching in place of Muddy Ruel, opened with a single, and McNeely, who ran for him, promptly stole second base. He stayed there as Leibold, pinch-hitting for Ferguson, popped up, Rice grounded out, and the veteran Bobby Veach, batting for manager Bucky Harris, also failed. In the ninth, with one out, Joe Harris doubled off the screen in deep center. It would have been his fourth home run of the series in a ballpark with less daunting distances. Judge and Bluege failed to bring him home, and the outcome now rested in a seventh game, with Walter Johnson pitching his third time.

An unrelenting rain poured down on Pittsburgh the next day. Restless crowds were turned away and visitors scrambled to renew hotel accommodations. The delay gave Johnson a needed extra day to get ready. Now he would pitch the final game on three days' rest. However, as he explained after winning the fourth game, "I didn't have the stuff I had in the first game…I had plenty of rest before that game, but three days' rest is all I had since. You know, that's all right for a youngster. Ten years ago three days of rest was even too much for me. But now it's different."

Trainer Mike Martin massaged Johnson's arm and wrapped his

strained leg muscles. While the patched-up veteran would be pitching on three days' rest, he was not the tireless machine of earlier years, and he had a gimpy leg as well. Sadly, athletic idols are held to high expectations until their careers finally end. Fans remember occasions to which they can no longer rise. So it was with Walter Johnson. He had already won twice, the fans reasoned, why not a third time? This was the Big Train, the King of the Mound, the greatest pitcher in the history of baseball. Why not?

The rain, the strain, and an intimidated Judge Landis ruined Johnson's chances. Had the game not begun at all, called off because the field was already too muddy for playing the final game of the World Championship, it would have been a sensible decision. However, Landis was impatient. Important people had been inconvenienced by the extended series and two days had already been lost from busy lives. Once underway, had Landis accepted that the game was being played under conditions which would have sent picnickers scampering for cover, Walter Johnson would have been the winner of a rain-shortened game. Washington led, 6-4, after five innings. No tarpaulin hastily spread until the rains stopped would have helped restart the game. It would only have covered an already unacceptably muddy infield. When Pittsburgh splashed its way to a tie in the seventh, a judicious decision would have been to call off the game right then. The teams could have resumed a day or two later, when the ball field justified the settling of a championship.

However, the egoist in the soggy, floppy hat, seated with his chin resting on the railing of his field box, grimly peered out from beneath his shaggy eyebrows. Sitting in the rain, he remembered 1921 when, conducting his first World Series, he had been convinced by the umpires that darkness would fall before a final inning could be played in a tie game between the Yankees and Giants at the Polo Grounds. When he allowed the arbiters to stop play with the sun still shining, a mob of angry fans besieged him. After that he had reserved to himself all decisions about starting and stopping World Series games. Now in a persistent rain storm it was his decision to make. As long as some semblance of a baseball game could be maintained, both teams were equally disadvantaged, Landis thought. It would take a bolt of lightening, a game-ending sign from the heavens, directed at an immobile man in a soggy fedora to stop the game.

The last game of the 1925 World Series has been written about many times, jubilantly by Pittsburgh writers, mournfully by most observers who felt bad for Walter Johnson. Maintenance of a playing field, even for a World Series, was primitive in the 1920s. Sawdust to soak up moisture once a game was underway was the only resource. The Pittsburgh ground crew used it liberally when it would be to the home team's advantage. The pitching mound was a slippery hill. Before each inning, improved footing for the Pirate pitchers, Aldrich, Morrison, and Kremer—McKechnie threw all his starters into the fray—was provided with a wheelbarrow of sawdust. It was never available when Johnson took the mound. He carried sawdust in his baseball cap to try and gain a footing each time he went out to pitch another intolerable inning.

Bucky Harris stuck with his ace. He never wavered in his decision, he told questioning reporters afterward. "Walter Johnson is my best pitcher. In a tough spot I want the best pitcher in the game."

Ban Johnson, in a venomous postgame diatribe, berated Harris for failing to win for the American League. He had stayed away from the World Series, bitter that it was Landis' domain. However, when he learned the outcome, he wired Bucky Harris, "You sacrificed a World's Championship for the American League through your display of sentiment." Even Judge Landis, when the telegram became public, said, "That was a lousy thing for Ban Johnson to do." Washington's manager stood up to the tyrannical league president and repeated his belief that in staying with Johnson he was applying the best baseball wisdom. You always went with your best. That he was also following the dictates of his heart and of fans everywhere was obvious.

Washington even edged ahead again in the top of the ninth, but the beleaguered Johnson could not hold the one-run lead. The unrelenting rain pelted down while the Pirates rallied with two out and tied the score. Again, an inning could have ended had an awakened sense of justice stirred Landis to stop the absurdity that was being played out on the mud-covered diamond. To halt the game at that point would have reverted the score to the last completed inning, the eighth, with both teams equal in the scoring. The idea never crossed the mind of the jurist who was then baseball's czar.

Again the star-crossed Peckinpaugh had the ball hit to him, a routine ground ball which would force the runner from first and end the inning in a tie. Harris splashed over to the bag for the throw, but Peckinpaugh flipped it wildly for his eighth error of the series and all runners were safe. The game went on, and KiKi Cuyler then drove home two runners with a ground rule double that bounded into the crowd edging into right field. He had fouled off three pitches after Johnson's first pitch was called a ball. Then Johnson cut the plate with what should have been strike three, but National League umpire Barry McCormick failed to call it. Muddy Ruel forever insisted it had been a strike and that the ump had refused to acknowledge it. It was a game that triggered postmortems.

Washington was still dangerous and, in the wildly inclement weather, might have surged back. Now, the canny Scot, Bill McKechnie, played his trump card. He had Red Oldham ready to finish off the ball game. In his undistinguished career, spent mostly in the American League, Oldham had been an average pitcher against all clubs with one exception. The Washington Senators were his eternal victims. With Detroit he had never lost to them and had beaten them eight straight times. Oldham had last faced Washington in 1922, but the three batters coming up had been easy for him to get out then. The left-handed Oldham struck out Sam Rice and, after Bucky Harris lined out to second, struck out Washington's other left-handed star, Goose Goslin.

Pittsburgh went wild and erupted into a celebration no rain could dampen. In Washington, at the White House, Grace Coolidge switched off the radio and went to tell her husband the sad tidings.

Walter Johnson did not duck the reporters who came to the losing team's clubhouse looking for quotes. He said, flatly, "I tried my best; gave 'em everything I had but it wasn't good enough. I had plenty of stuff, my left leg was all right, but it was no day for pitching. It's tough but they had the better club out there and they won."

Bucky Harris railed against the adoption of the new system in which one team hosts the first two games and, if a sixth and seventh game became necessary, also the balance of the games. Nineteen twenty-five was the first season for this arrangement. In the past, the teams flipped a coin to decide which would be home team if a seventh game was necessary. Harris contended that was the fair arrangement even if it had caused difficulty with ticket distribution.

The *New York Times* followup stories about the World Series contrasted the ecstasy of 1924 in Washington with the indifferent treatment of the 1925 losers. The final game lost in the rain revealed many of the Senators' supporters to be fair-weather fans.

Walter Johnson went back to Washington to use his $3,786 loser's-share World Series check toward the purchase of a larger house. With four children, the house on Irving Street in Washington was too small. It had been all right for summers during the baseball season. There had been a farm in Kansas to winter in, with barns for livestock and fields for his dogs. This year, there would be no Walter Johnson Day game played in Coffeyville. He never lived there again and only visited rarely.

Hazel and Walter found a large house on eight and a half acres of good Maryland farmland on the Georgetown Road in the Alta Vista section of Bethesda. Mostly chickens were raised on the farm, and his foxhounds, too, had new kennels. The house is still there at 9100 Georgetown Road.

Johnson no longer planned on being a minor league owner. He was already signed to a 1926 contract and would stay with Washington until something developed. After all, he had just won 20 regular-season games and two more in the World Series. It was hardly time to call it a career. Had it been only a matter of his pitching arm, he might have gone on for years. However, his legs, which he acknowledged were critical to successful pitching, were getting beyond trainer Mike Martin's ability to keep flexible. In recent years he had wintered in Reno and hiked the trails into the mountains. Hunting with his field dogs over rough, but flat, Maryland countryside would have to take the place of the Rocky Mountain foothills.

33
Twilight Begins
to Darken

THE WASHINGTON SENATORS again prepared to defend their American League Championship in Tampa, Florida. Several things made spring training in 1926 unusual for Walter Johnson. He was spared the customary case of springtime sniffles. His progress toward opening day readiness was unimpeded by even a common cold. When the team headed north, he was also spared the ordeal of the obligatory appearances to meet the expectations of fans along the exhibition trail. While the Senators and Giants traced a 13-game path from Florida to its weekend conclusion in Washington and New York, the Big Train was allowed to run as an express directly from Tampa to Washington. After a five-inning workout against the Giants in Tampa on March 27, Johnson and catcher Hank Severeid set their own pace until the teams met at Griffith Stadium on April 10. Although he was hit hard, giving up seven hits and five runs in a brief three-inning stint, Walter Johnson was ready for Opening Day.

The team that Bucky Harris and Clark Griffith sent out to defend its league championship was unchanged except at shortstop. This proved to be the critical flaw as the season was played out. Roger Peckinpaugh was played sparingly; the explanation was that the Senators thought he would do better by waiting for warmer weather. The reality was the veteran, who had been the previous year's Most Valuable Player, had lost the edge of assurance with which he had always played after making eight errors in a losing World Series. Instead of the team captain, Washington sent a rookie, Buddy Myer, to do the job. Charles Solomon Myer was a rare Jewish ballplayer, whose ethnicity made no difference in the national capital. In New York City, John McGraw tried in vain to develop a Jewish gate attraction. Myer was everything he was expected to be, except a big league shortstop. He had only one season of minor league experience, and his

231

.336 average at New Orleans masked his .938 fielding average and an error rate of one in less than every three games. Another deceptive stat was Myer's success at stealing bases. A future big league leader in stolen bases—30 in 1928—he showed how fast he could run in a straight line. Unfortunately, he lacked comparable lateral movement in the field. In 1926 he was not only last among shortstops in fielding average but also in chances handled per game. Despite hitting .304 for the season, his influence on team play can be judged by Washington's sharp decline in double plays. In 1925 they led all teams with 166 and, with Myer at short instead of the slick Peckinpaugh, made only 129, fewer than any team except the St. Louis Browns. The Senators would lead the league in batting but almost fell out of first division because of a defense weakened at its most critical position.

On Opening Day, Johnson showed the wisdom of being allowed to follow his own preparation formula. While the schedule allowed an opportunity for President Calvin Coolidge to throw out the first ball of the season, the president's father had recently died and the family was in mourning. Vice President Charles Dawes, a ranking fan in his own right, substituted for Coolidge from a field box. The march to the flagpole in center field to raise the 1925 pennant was led by Secretary of War Dwight Davis. In sports, he is more associated with tennis as the donor of the Davis Cup for international competition.

If there were any questions whether the Big Train had been permanently derailed in the fiasco of the final game of the previous World Series, Walter Johnson answered them with the greatest opening day game anyone ever pitched. Only Bob Feller's no-hitter in 1940 competes for this claim. Feller won 1-0 in nine innings; Johnson won by the same score but dueled with Eddie Rommel of the Philadelphia Athletics for 15 innings before the Senators could score a run. Bob Feller was 21 in 1940. Walter Johnson was 37 and starting his 20th major league season when he spread six hits over 15 innings to start what appeared, at first, to be another triumphant season.

Johnson's next start, against the New York Yankees on April 20, caused alarm that not even a week's rest after his marathon stint was enough. Babe Ruth demonstrated he was back at full strength after his illnesses in 1925. He homered off Johnson his first time at bat, and although Washington's ace lasted only three innings, the Babe added two doubles and a pair of singles for a five-for-six day.

Johnson's next start came against the youngster who had taken over as strikeout king, Philadelphia's Lefty Grove. Walter Johnson registered no strikeouts in the April 23 game at Philadelphia, but outlasted the usurper to the strikeout crown. Washington won, 9-5, with Johnson getting two hits himself. Then Johnson settled into a winning stride to bring his record to 6-1 by mid-May. On May 11 he beat St. Louis, 7-4, at home, for what was then hailed as Walter Johnson's 400th victory. He had actually reached that landmark three games sooner, on April 27, with a four-hit, 9-1, win over Boston.

Suddenly, Johnson's winning ways waned. He lost 4-2, giving up but two earned runs, and 5-3 in a rough outing that Firpo Marberry could not save. He lost his next five games, *all by one run*, including a 1-0 loss in Detroit. It took a favorable one-run margin to win the game that put the brakes on his slide on June 26 when he topped the A's, 3-2. The win which halted his own losing streak also ended an eight-game drought for the Senators. They were now in last place.

Two unearned runs beat Johnson again, on July 1, in his next negative one-run decision, 3-2, against the Yankees. After he won two starts he was literally knocked out of the box, on July 11. George Burns, the hard-hitting Cleveland first baseman, smashed a line drive back at the mound and Johnson could not skip aside fast enough. The ball caromed off his ankle, and he had to be helped from the field.

Walter Johnson and the Senators struggled toward the comparative respectability of .500. Before he could raise his total of victories on the diamond, Walter and Hazel added a fifth child to the Johnson household. Barbara Joan, a seven-pound, six ounce baby girl, was born on July 18. There were now three sons and two daughters dependent on their famous father continuing to bring home paychecks.

Johnson managed to level his season at 10-10 with a peculiar win over Detroit on July 21. Coasting behind a 7-1 lead, Johnson over-relaxed and the Tigers scored six runs in the fourth inning to pull even, 7-7. Johnson then blanked Detroit in the final five innings for a 10-7 win.

Washington headed west on a road trip, where Johnson won in Chicago on July 27, 7-2, then pitched his first shutout since Opening Day against the St. Louis Browns, on July 31, winning 9-0. He almost lost the shutout with a typical kindhearted Walter Johnson gesture. Ernie Nevers, as great an All American fullback as Walter Camp ever named, was trying a pitching career. The previous year he had led Stanford into battle against the Four Horsemen of Notre Dame in the Rose Bowl, playing savagely before being ridden down by the Fighting Irish, 27-10. Nevers is honored in both the College and

Professional Football Halls of Fame and his name is on a plaque in Cooperstown. There's a list of Babe Ruth's home runs when he hit 60 in 1927. Among the pitchers who gave up the round-trippers, Nevers appears twice being responsible for Ruth's eighth and 41st homers.

In the memories of the National Football League, Nevers holds the oldest record still on the books. Playing with the Chicago Cardinals in 1929 against their crosstown rivals, the Chicago Bears, Nevers scored six touchdowns and kicked four PATs for 40 points, a one-man scoring spree no one has ever equaled.

On July 31, Nevers relieved Milt Gaston after Washington had opened an early 5-0 lead. He never forgot what happened the first time he came to bat against Walter Johnson. "It was one of my very first appearances at bat," Nevers told Dr. Stanley Grosshandler in a magazine interview many years later. "He threw two strikes past me so fast I never got the bat off my shoulder. Following the second pitch, Walter walked in to get the ball from the catcher and said, 'Be ready son, the next one will be right down the middle.' I looked at the catcher, and he said, 'If Walter said it, that's where it will be.' I started to swing as Johnson started his pitch, and I hit the ball up against the right-field wall for a double. When I got to second, I saw Johnson was as happy as I was."

Johnson's record dropped below .500 again on August 13 when Lou Gehrig hammered two home runs in the five innings it took to rout the slowing Big Train. Not since 1914, when Jake Fournier hit two inside-the-park homers off him, had any batter taken such a liberty.

On August 26, in a doubleheader win over the White Sox that was reminiscent of the previous season's one-two punch, Walter Johnson and Stan Coveleski beat Red Faber and Ted Lyons, 9-3 and 1-0, in 10 innings. All four pitchers have been elected to the Baseball Hall of Fame. The schedule sent the Senators on a road trip for the final month of the season, and Walter Johnson lost his last three games when his team could score only one run in each game. He lost the final two decisions, 2-1. This dropped him below .500, winning 15 games but losing 16. He was beaten by a ninth-inning home run by outfielder Bill Barrett of the Chicago White Sox for his final decision, on September 25, at Comiskey Park.

The Senators won 81 games and lost 69 to finish fourth, eight games behind the New York Yankees. Babe Ruth almost won a triple crown, losing the batting title to Heinie Manush, .372 to .378, while dominating in both home runs, with 47 to runner-up Al Simmons' 19, and runs batted in, with 145.

Although Walter Johnson failed to lead the league in any category, his stats were highly respectable. The veteran of 20 seasons was fourth to Grove in strikeouts, 125 to 194. He was third in complete games with 22, and fourth with 262 innings pitched. Again, he could not find a compelling reason to end his career at this point. Not while still trying to choose how he would raise and educate his growing family after the paychecks from the Senators stopped.

34
The Curtain Rings Down on Johnson's Career

WALTER JOHNSON'S SPRING TRAINING MISFORTUNES reached their peak soon after the 1927 camp opened in Tampa, Florida. He was on the mound, pitching batting practice. Today he would be throwing from behind a screen. Even the most expendable and unproven pitching prospect would be protected. The Washington Senators were not that prudent. A sizzling line drive off the bat of Johnson's roommate, Joe Judge, smashed into his ankle and knocked him off his feet. Al Schacht, always looking for a gag opportunity, rushed over and began counting 10 over the fallen pitcher. The joke was as lame as its subject would be. Trainer Mike Martin knelt beside Johnson and probed to learn the damage. All he could confirm was that it must have hurt. The stoical Johnson tried to dismiss everyone's concern, but an x-ray later found a broken bone in the left ankle. Spring training was over for Walter Johnson and, except for an attempt to play out a partial season, so was the greatest pitching career in baseball history.

When the mighty are fallen, they don't stay down to take the count, they struggle to get back to the top. Johnson's foot was put in a cast and he was sent to Washington to heal. Hazel and the children helped him pass the time at home while his leg mended. He was fitted with an iron brace and limped around Griffith Stadium waiting for the team to arrive. Someone else would have to pitch the opening game. Stan Coveleski was promoted to the role, and President Coolidge was on hand to resume his part in the ceremony.

This time, with a politician's eye for the best opportunity, he winged the ball to Tris Speaker, who had resigned as manager of Cleveland and signed with the Senators for a reported $75,000. With Ty Cobb, Detroit's manager who also had departed from his team between seasons, Speaker had been accused of rigging a ball game years earlier. Judge Landis' investigation cleared both superstars, but both elected to end their careers with other teams. Cobb joined Connie Mack's Athletics where, after the season with Washington, Speaker would join him in 1928 for a swan-song season for both.

Coveleski won the opener from the Boston Red Sox, 8-2, but hurt his back and, unable to regain his form, was released in mid-June. Roger Peckinpaugh had been traded to the White Sox during the winter, and the disappointing shortstop replacement, Buddy Myer, was soon traded to the Red Sox for Topper Rigney, hailed as a "real short-stop." He was even less capable than Myer, who the Senators retrieved from the Red Sox after a brief exile. It cost them heavily in a player trade a year later, but once Myer was played at second base, the Senators had a star for a decade.

Nineteen twenty-seven simply belongs to the New York Yankees: Babe Ruth and his fellow sluggers of Murderers' Row, Gehrig, Meusel, and Lazzeri. By the time Walter Johnson could return to action, the Yankees were clear of the pack and Washington was striving to find a place in first division. The Yankees were in full flower, and the Athletics' were getting ready to bloom next.

Walter Johnson reported he was ready to go to work at the start of May. Actually, he was ready to resume the preparation to pitch which had been aborted in Florida. Tempting fate, he began by pitching batting practice. Then he pitched an exhibition game against the Baltimore Orioles on May 24. He scattered five hits over five score-less innings and said he was ready to make his delayed 1927 debut.

When the Senators reached New York on May 27, the Sportsman's Brotherhood presented Walter Johnson with a medal. It recognized his unique achievement. In 21 major league seasons Johnson had never been put out of a game by an umpire.

Walter Johnson's 1927 debut on Memorial Day was a splendid return to glory, but it faded immediately after he beat the Red Sox, 3-0, allowing only three hits. It was the last shutout he would pitch. He lost his next three starts before Firpo Marberry saved an 8-7 win from the Red Sox on June 26.

On July 4 Johnson was used only to mop up after the carnage of a Yankee doubleheader in which they scored 33 runs, beating the Senators 12-1 and 21-1. Washington had won 10 straight games and was in second place before the Yankees crushed them. At that, only Walter Johnson had pitched well for the Senators that day. He struck out eight in the final four innings of the first game.

Johnson looked good on July 9, pitching a complete game, at Cleveland, to win 3-2 while fanning eight. In that game, Tris Speaker became the first Senator that season to reach 100 hits. Walter Johnson was backed by a Hall of Fame outfield with Goose Goslin and Sam Rice flanking the Grey Eagle, who drove in two runs to win the game.

Johnson won again in Chicago, taking the second game of a dou- ble- header from Ted Lyons, 7-4. Speaker had four hits in five times at bat. He stumbled in St. Louis, giving up seven runs in the first three innings. Johnson's record was level at 4-4. Back home in Washington he won easily, 12-2, from the White Sox. It proved to be his last vic- tory. Two subsequent decisions would go against him, but mostly he appeared in no-decision games.

The most celebrated of these was played on August 2, the 20th anniversary of Walter Johnson's major league debut. Again, the Detroit Tigers were his opponents, and Billy Evans was again an umpire. He would have been behind the plate but had injured a leg in the series opener with the Tigers. Using crutches, Evans made a token one-inning appearance at third base. Before the game Walter Johnson was honored for his long service to the American League. Ban Johnson was ill and would resign after the season. Frank Kellogg, Secretary of State, subbed for the American League president. Herbert Hoover, a prospective opening day first-ball thrower, had as the Secretary of Commerce, chaired the Anniversary Committee.

Walter Johnson was given a Distinguished Service to the American League medal, in the form of a gold Maltese Cross with 20 diamonds, one for each completed year's service. There were 19,974 fans on hand, in perfect weather. The Senators donated $15,000 in cash from the day's gate receipts. Missing from the spectrum of political celebri- ties on Walter Johnson's Day was Calvin Coolidge. He stole the head- lines the next morning when it was reported the taciturn leader had declined renomination by saying succinctly, "I do not choose to run."

After waving his cap to the cheering crowd, Walter Johnson tried to roll back the calendar, and for four innings he did. His shutout string was snapped in the fifth inning, but he took a 5-4 lead into the ninth inning. Johnson was tiring. He no longer deemed it a matter of honor to pitch a complete game. Harry Heilmann singled, but Johnny Neun forced him at second. Then Neun stole second base and Ivy Wingo came in to pinch-hit. After Johnson missed the plate with two pitches, he agreed with manager Bucky Harris that it was best to turn the job of holding the lead over to someone else. Garland Braxton had replaced Firpo Marberry as the team's stopper and led the league with 13 saves. He also led in relief losses with seven and was charged with one of them in this game. Braxton completed a walk to Marty McManus, who scored the winning run. Larry Woodall's long fly ball bounced out of the glove of Earl McNeely for a triple as he tried to make an over-the-shoulder catch. The fans told each other that Tris Speaker, watching from the bench, would have snared it and saved the game. The loss was charged to Braxton.

Johnson continued to pitch in turn, and his record had again leveled off when he had his fifth loss, to Cleveland. He had been roughed up for five runs and left in the sixth inning. A 10-day layoff ended when he turned over a 5-3 lead to Garland Braxton after pitching six innings. Washington subsequently lost the game in 12 innings.

Johnson's last decision was a 7-3 loss to Detroit on August 22. He gave up three earned runs, and three Washington errors gave the Tigers their four-run margin. During September Johnson made only two brief relief appearances. In one, on September 11, Johnson had pitched runless eighth and ninth innings. Then, trailing 5-1, the Senators rallied with four runs to send the game into extra innings. With Hod Lisenbee now pitching for Washington, they won 6-5 in 12 innings. No decision for Walter Johnson, of course.

The last pitching appearance by Walter Johnson came on September 22, at home, against the St. Louis Browns. Still hoping to even his record for the season, Johnson was knocked out of the box in the fourth inning. However, before he left the game, he homered in the bottom of the third inning. Washington eventually won the game, 10-7, but Johnson did not get the decision.

After the game, questioned by reporters whether he would end his career with the 1927 season, Walter Johnson said he might try another season, or he might not. "My arm is as good as ever, but there are other troubles. The leg I broke bothers me a lot and not where it was broken. You see when the legs get bad and you lose the old zip on the ball, you find pitching a lot harder and you find you are not effective. I figure another season at any rate will be enough. Perhaps when I settle down for the winter I will not pitch in 1928. It's worth plenty of thought."

Wait. While Walter Johnson was pondering his future, was a possible trivia contest question in the making? In homering on his last time at bat in the last game he would pitch, had Johnson preceded Ted Williams as a Hall of Famer who homered on his last time at bat?

To the disappointment of trivia buffs, Johnson made one more plate appearance. It came, as was so often the case, in a game made historic by someone else. On September 30, in a season-ending game at Yankee Stadium, George Herman Ruth commanded the day. He set a new home run record by lofting his 60th round-tripper of the season off Tom Zachary. Lost in the excitement of the game was a ninth-inning pinch-hit appearance for Zachary by Johnson. On what was to be his final time at bat, he flied out to Babe Ruth.

35

Exiled to Newark

P AUL BLOCK, a successful newspaper publisher, wanted to join the ranks of big league baseball owners. As there were no major league franchises available where his daily newspapers were published in Pittsburgh, Toledo, and Newark, he went after the International League franchise across the Hudson River from New York City. At the end of the 1927 season, Block bought the Newark Bears in a receivership auction and promised readers of his paper, the *Newark Star-Eagle*, a team which could win the pennant the next year.

His first need was a manager, and his first choice was Walter Johnson, who had resigned as a player with the Washington Senators in mid-October following the 1927 World Series. Block visited Johnson at his home outside Washington, and the two men hit it off. With the blessing of Clark Griffith, who promised to send prospects to Newark for Johnson to develop, Block signed the Big Train to a two-year contract on October 26th. It would pay him his Senators' salary of $20,000 a year and make Johnson the highest-paid man outside the major leagues. Paul Block said, "I am not only exceedingly pleased, but very proud to have a man like Walter Johnson associated with me. I don't think there has ever been a baseball player with a finer character and better standing than Walter Johnson. He will, of course, run the team and I am sure all the players of the Newark Club will be happy to have such a man at their head." Block's assumptions, unfortunately, went awry. He wanted a winner, and his way to put one on the field was to sign veteran players for Johnson to manage. Unfortunately, many of them were unmanageable, particularly by such a mild-mannered leader as Johnson.

Paul W. Eaton, who had reported Walter Johnson's entire 21-year career in the sporting weeklies, had not expected such an outcome. In his wrap-up report in *The Sporting News* on the passing of Walter

Johnson from Washington to Newark he wrote, "Some critics think that Johnson is too easy-going to be a successful manager. Barney is a good fellow and a helpful teammate, all right, but he can bear down when necessary. Most players will be glad to give him their best efforts, and if any are bad actors they will find their teammates' sympathies will be with the manager. I feel certain that Johnson will be a success as a pilot." Eaton's conclusion was optimistic.

On the good side in Johnson's future as Newark's new leader was Jack Bentley, who had dueled with Johnson through the extra innings of the final game of the 1924 World Series. A lifelong friend, Bentley was a carryover from the 1927 Bears. Another veteran with a tie to Johnson's past, Jake Fournier, was signed to play first base. In 1914, Fournier had hit two successive home runs after Johnson came into a game with the White Sox in the eighth inning to preserve a 3-2 lead. Fournier, the first batter Johnson faced, tied the game with an inside-the-park home run to center field, and when he came to bat again in the 10th, repeated the home run act. Johnson could hope Fournier's bat was still lively. It was: he hit 22 home runs, but his defensive range had narrowed to playing on the proverbial dime.

On the bad side was "Good Time Bill" Lamar. Two years after he hit .356 for the A's, they traded him to Washington when the 1927 season ended. Lamar refused to report without a raise, and Clark Griffith let Paul Block sign him for an undeserved $8,500. Lamar was a lazy, indifferent boozer who gathered a clique of dissolute dissidents around him. The other major disrupter of team harmony was Hugh McQuillan. "Handsome Hugh" was vain about his appearance, quarrelsome with teammates and management, and quick to offer unsolicited opinions on all subjects. Paul Block's good intentions had set a trap for his new manager. It took time for Walter Johnson to learn what a disruptive lot of clubhouse lawyers he had been asked to lead. And even before he could start managing the team, Walter Johnson had to experience his almost annual springtime respiratory problem. This time it was worse than any in the past.

The team had just set up spring training in St. Augustine when a heavy cold sent Johnson to the infirmary. The team was taken over by coach George McBride, the longtime star shortstop and short-time manager of the Senators. Johnson's condition worsened into pneumonia, and he was finally invalided home with nurses to care for him en route. A picture taken as he left Union Station in Washington, D.C., in a wheelchair shows a very ill man. He entered a hospital and, although optimistic bulletins were issued, there was no expectation he would return to active duty soon. Not only was Johnson battling a new problem, a kidney infection, but an infected tooth undermined his whole system. More than 30 pounds underweight, he gave up expectations of being an active player for 1928. He did not make his first appearance in a Newark uniform until May 14. By then the team was already in second division.

The Bears had opened optimistically with a gala inaugural. The debonair mayor of New York City, Jimmy Walker, was a guest of the owner, but the eyes of the fans were on Hazel Johnson and her son, the 12-year-old Walter Jr. They were there to represent the family. Walter had wired George McBride, "I am sorry I can't be with you fellows today. I am glad, however, that I will soon be able to join you, and I know you will give them a battle. My best to all the boys."

Al Mamaux, who was to opening day pitching assignments in Newark what Johnson had been in Washington, responded, using the microphone of radio station WOR which broadcast the game: "Hello, Walter. I hope you're feeling well today. I'm a better pitcher than a radio announcer, and I'll say so long, assuring you that myself and the rest of the team will be out to win every game for you. We hope you will soon be back with us."

Mamaux make good on his immediate promise, pitching a 4-0 win over Toronto. Jocko Conlan, later to become a Hall of Fame umpire, was one of the all-out players on the team. He hit a leadoff home run and had two other hits. After the season, in sizing up individual talents, Johnson praised Conlan and promised he would have a major league career if "only he would learn to lay off swinging at high pitches off the plate." Conlan's brief time in the major leagues might have lasted longer had he taken Johnson's batting tip. Then, if he had made good as a player, he would probably never have become an umpire, let alone one of the few exceptional enough to be enshrined in Cooperstown.

Hazel had rented a house for the family as it was the intention of the Johnsons to be part of the community, at least during the summers. Walter Jr. joined a boys' baseball team, the Millburn Terriers, as a pitcher and second baseman.

Paul Block organized a Walter Johnson Day to formally welcome the Big Train. Sixteen thousand cheering fans turned out on an overcast Saturday, June 23. Walter took the mound in a slight drizzle to make a token appearance. Maurice Archdeacon, a minor league speedster, led off and walked on a 3-1 count. Johnson turned the pitching over to Hal Goldsmith and retired to the bench. He watched his team beat the Bisons, 5-4. During the season Johnson also pinch-hit six times, getting one hit for a .183 average. His last appearance in organized baseball came on September 16, when he grounded out third to first.

The season Walter Johnson endured trying to cope with the Newark Bears hardly served as a fair judgment of his managerial ability. In a 1947 interview by Frank Graham in *Baseball Magazine*, Jack Bentley said about Johnson, "The way he talked to us would have brought tears to the eyes of a hobby horse. But, I regret to say some of the fellows couldn't have been listening because the things they did to him were a crime." As the season went on, Johnson became frustrated by the indifference and boneheaded play of the soured veterans he had to use.

While still expecting to serve the second year at Newark, Johnson announced changes that would be made. He put most of the team on waivers, having had a final confrontation with Lamar. "Good Time Bill" had given Johnson a bad time once too often. Coming off the field to lead off an inning at bat, Johnson heard Lamar instruct one of his buddies to bring his bat to the plate for him. That was the last straw, and Johnson yanked Lamar from the game. In the midst of one of Bill Lamar's sulking fits, Jake Fournier told him, "If you think the International League is too small for you, soon you'll be playing in the Blue Ridge League and lucky to have a job."

In a post-season news conference the embittered manager said, "I regret that we did not get rid of Lamar and McQuillan the first week of the season. I can see now that was the wise move, but we had so much money tied up in them I took the long chance that they would straighten out and play the kind of ball of which they were capable. It was not due to soft-heartedness on my part, but because I was hoping they would mend their ways." Tris Speaker affirmed Johnson's plight the following season when he took over as manager of the Newark Bears. "Never in all my baseball experience," said the Grey Eagle, "have I seen so many cliques on one ball team."

A definitive baseball biography has not yet appeared to tell us the Clark Griffith story. His influence on baseball history can only be guessed at in some instances. One of these covers the departure of Bucky Harris from the Senators and the return of Walter Johnson. "The Old Fox," had made a 28-year-old gloveman, with a more than adequate bat, his "Boy Manager" in 1924. The result had been two pennants in a row. Since then the New York Yankees had dominated the American League and the Senators had slipped out of contention. In 1928 they finished below .500. Also, the "Boy Manager" was now at the end of the road as an everyday player. He played only 96 games at second base and batted a mere .204.

Like everyone else, Griffith coveted a young second baseman with Detroit, Charlie Gehringer. Perhaps his intention to change managers began with a hope to change second basemen. As it developed, after a negotiated resignation from his job of leading the Senators and a period during which Walter Johnson was chosen to replace him, Harris no longer had to covet Gehringer or play second base himself. The Tigers hired him to replace George Moriarty, who went back to umpiring after a two-season stint as a manager. Harris went on to complete a 29-season career as a big league manager, including returning twice to the Senators for long managerial periods. He won no more pennants for Clark Griffith, but he did lead the 1947 Yankees to a World Championship.

However, although there was resentment at the departure of Harris, the return of the Big Train more than offset any displeasure the fans felt. When Johnson knew that Bucky Harris was finished in Washington, he approached Griffith during a game of the 1928 World Series in New York. The Old Fox, delighted to be asked, explained that Johnson would have to get Paul Block's consent to release him from the remaining year of his contract. First, Walter Johnson made a trip to Coffeyville to see his mother and, perhaps, ask her opinion. He might have thought managing, even the Senators, something not worth doing after the bitter season he had spent in Newark. Always among the options was a return to the life of a Kansas farmer.

Johnson's mind was made up. If he could get the manager's job with Washington, he and Hazel and the five Johnson children would settle permanently in the Washington area. Paul Block was gracious in freeing Walter Johnson to accept a three-year contract to be the new manager of the Washington Senators.

36

The Hero Returns
—But Not to Conquer

I T WAS A HOMECOMING for Walter Johnson when he took charge of
the Washington squad and prepared them for the 1929 season.
Again, Clark Griffith chose Tampa for the spring training site.
Johnson named his former roommate, Joe Judge, captain of the team
and began writing familiar names into the lineups for pre-season
games. The fourth-place finish of the previous year could not be
blamed on the carryover veterans of the 1924 and 1925 pennant winners. Sam Rice and Goose Goslin could be expected to provide aggressive bats, and a youngster, Sammy West, had showed speed and a .300
hitting style as a rookie the year before. The infield was set at its cor-
ners with Judge and Bluege. The middle of the infield would be
improved by the return of Buddy Myer. He had played well his two seasons in exile with the last-place Red Sox. He had again failed as a shortstop but, when shifted to third base, became another kind of player altogether. Johnson decided to use him to plug the vacancy at second base
left by Bucky Harris. Myer made the switch comfortably, leaving shortstop open as a question mark. However, the answer was already on
hand. There was a newcomer in camp who had played briefly with
Pittsburgh and had been viewed as promising in the half-season he
played the previous year with the Senators. A lantern-jawed Irishman
from San Francisco, Joe Cronin would solve Washington's shortstop
problems and later become Clark Griffith's second "Boy Manager."

Catching would be a problem. In 1929 Muddy Ruel could no
longer catch 100 or more games or bat over .300. Ben Tate, his backup, fell short of replacing him as the regular catcher. A non-roster
player in camp caught Johnson's attention. A teenaged Californian
was released with a comment from the new manager that he was certain to reach the majors in a few years. Instead, Willard Hershberger
ended up in the Yankees' chain, starred at Newark in the 1930s but, a

left-handed hitter, was blocked from advancing by the presence of Bill Dickey with the Yankees. Traded to Cincinnati, Hershberger next had to play behind Ernie Lombardi. The moody player ended his life and still-promising career by committing suicide in a Boston hotel during the 1940 season.

The pitching staff had been erratic the year before and would be the main reason for the team's downfall in Johnson's first year. It was hoped the veteran Sad Sam Jones would lead the staff. Instead, he led the first rebellion Johnson would have to quell. Picked up on waivers from the St. Louis Browns the year before, Jones had won 17 games and lost only seven for Washington. Clark Griffith had continued him at his $10,000 St. Louis Browns' salary. But Jones demanded $15,000 from Washington, considering them a more affluent employer. Clark Griffith offered a $1,000 boost and negotiations stuck at that point. The dispute was turned over to Walter Johnson to handle, and he convinced Jones that $11,000 with a team that could be considered a contender for World Series money was worth taking.

One familiar face missing from the Senators was Tom Zachary. He had been allowed to move to the Yankees during the previous season. In 1929 he would win 12 games and lose none pitching for New York. Johnson could have used him. Garland Braxton and Bump Hadley had joined the Senators in 1927 and were expected to form the front line of pitching. Neither ever reached the stardom Johnson expected of them. Hadley constantly disappointed and only achieved substantial success years later under the stricter discipline of Joe McCarthy and the Yankees of the late-1930s.

Fred Marberry was asked to continue alternating between relieving and starting. Johnson decided to use him to start games more often than Bucky Harris had, but Marberry would also lead the league with 11 saves. In Johnson's first year as manager, he led the staff with 19 victories, 16 as a starter and three in relief.

Walter Johnson was hailed in the Washington papers for getting his team off to a winning start in spring training. Johnson said he wanted to instill a winning attitude right off the bat. It worked fine until the real season began. After winning 20 of the 24 pre-season games, including 14 from major league teams, the Senators stumbled badly coming out of the starting gate.

With Ban Johnson no longer president of the American League, a new custom, to start the season a day ahead of everyone else with Washington at home, was now possible. President Herbert Hoover showed top form at the opener, winging the ball to George Moriarty, who was back to being "a man in blue" again. Moriarty made a jumping catch of the president's throw, and the ball was returned to Hoover as a souvenir. Johnson no longer collected opening day baseballs. His collection had been completed when he pitched that 15-inning shutout to start the 1926 season. As the 1929 season approached, the "Presidential Baseballs," starting with Taft's autographed ball from 1910, and Johnson's trophies were displayed in the window of a downtown Washington department store.

The showcase advantage of playing a day ahead of the other teams was lost when the opener had to be canceled. The next day the president wore a top coat and his wife, Lou Hoover, wore her furs when the inaugural game was played in the cold and rain. The managers shook hands for the photographers, and the captions which ran with them in the newspapers pointed out that Johnson was the youngest manager in point of service and the 67-year-old Connie Mack had managed more years than anyone. Mr. Mack was about to unveil his last dynastic team. Foxx, Cochrane, Simmons, and Grove dominated the opposition and started right in with a 13-4 drubbing of Johnson's team. The next day Washington lost, 8-2, and after a week, during which three of seven games were canceled due to rain or cold weather, Washington was in last place.

Walter Johnson's inaugural year as a manager was a struggle to avoid the cellar. Injuries played a major role in the team's inability to win even half of its games. Ossie Bluege missed almost half the team's games, but the hardest blow came when Goose Goslin's arm went lame. After several months, while Johnson had to decide whether Goslin's bat compensated for the way base runners ran on him, Goslin was sent to Atlantic City and told to sit on the boardwalk and rest his arm. The world wrestling champion, Ed "Strangler" Lewis, who was appearing there, took time from tossing opponents out of the ring to counsel Goslin. He explained he once had the same problem until his doctor diagnosed it as neuritis. The treatment was simple: avoid eating meat. Goslin abstained and soon was back in the Senators' lineup, and once again he was cutting down venturesome base runners. The downside of the arrangement was that, possibly because he was deprived of energy-giving red meat, Goslin's hitting fell off alarmingly. In 1928 he had won the batting title with a .379 average. In 1929 he dropped to a weak .288.

Walter Johnson had somehow avoided his customary spring training respiratory problem. It took until May before he succumbed. This time his condition was the result of sitting on the concrete steps of the dugout in Cleveland on a cold day after pitching batting practice and hitting fungos to his outfielders. Johnson developed a severe cold, which turned into a kidney infection. The attack came on suddenly, and Johnson was sent home for treatment. He returned to the same hospital in which he had been bedridden the year before. This time he recovered more rapidly, and when the team returned to Washington, he took up his duties again.

The Senators played winning ball from mid-season on, but were much too far behind the runaway Athletics to challenge them. The A's romped home 18 games ahead of the second-place Yankees. Washington was 34 games behind, in fifth place. In the World Series, Connie Mack surprised everyone by starting the veteran Howard Ehmke in the first game. Ehmke surprised everyone except Mr. Mack by striking out 13 Cubs and setting a new World Series record. Ed Walsh had fanned 12 in 1908 and, although Walter Johnson had also struck out a dozen batters in the opening game of the 1924 World Series, he had taken 12 innings to do it.

Herbert Hoover was another United States president with a true liking for baseball. He drove up to Philadelphia to see Game Three of the World Series, which had opened in Chicago. He was warmly received by the fans at Shibe Park. It was the twilight of his popularity. On October 29 the stock market collapsed, and Hoover became a depression-era president. The next time he went to a ball game, he would be booed more lustily than the umpires.

The Johnsons were now year-round residents of Washington. He no longer pitched in post-season exhibition games, but as manager, he attended the annual meeting of the American League with Clark Griffith. They went hoping to make trades or buy talent that would strengthen the team for the 1930 season. The newcomers who would vastly improve the team didn't join the Senators until later, after the 1930 season was underway.

As usual, the Senators got ready in Tampa and lined up a testing series of pre-season games with mostly National League opponents. Again, Johnson evaded a training period cold and brought his team north ready to play. Before the Senators reached Washington, Johnson learned that his oldest son, Walter Jr., had been seriously injured. A motorist had struck the 15-year-old, who was riding a bike, and both of the boy's legs were broken. Johnson rushed north ahead of the team and took up a bedside vigil. Both of his son's legs were in casts, and later it was learned than one leg had not healed properly. For a time it was feared the leg would have to be amputated. The distressed parents were finally relieved as Walter Jr. not only recovered but by mid-July was pitching for a local Bethesda boys' team.

As the Senators began the 1930 season, the sportswriters and fans did not expect a pennant winner or even a serious challenger. The Athletics seemed set for another romp unless the Yankees recovered from the loss of their manager, Miller Huggins. The Yankee leader had died at the end of the 1929 season, and Bob Shawkey, a veteran pitcher with the team, was to lead them in 1930. Washington was relegated to having a chance to edge into first division. Instead, the team, despite losing the advanced opening day game, started fast. The Senators and Athletics jousted for the league lead almost all season. The Senators were one strong starting pitcher short of having a pennant-winning rotation. Also, unlike the A's with Lefty Grove, they lacked a pitcher who could win crucial games.

Early in the season Clark Griffith, with Walter Johnson's concurrence, made a bold move just before the trading deadline. On June 13 Washington sent the popular Goose Goslin to the St. Louis Browns in exchange for Heinie Manush and Alvin Crowder. Goslin and Manush were practically an even swap, except that Goslin's arm problems were never quite overcome. In 1926 Goslin and Manush waged a head-to-head duel for the batting title that ran the month of September before Goslin edged home a winner, .379 to .378. Manush was a line-drive hitter, whereas Goslin lofted the ball over the fences and drove in more runs.

It was Alvin Crowder who was coveted by Griffith and Johnson. Washington had him once but let him get away in a trade to retrieve Tom Zachary, who had been inopportunely dealt to the Browns in 1927. In 1928 Crowder rose to stardom with the Browns. He led the American League in winning percentage with an .808 mark and a 21-5 record. In 1929 he slipped to 17-15 and, when the trade was made, was struggling at 3-7. With the Senators he returned to top form, winning 15 games during the rest of the season. Had he anchored the Washington pitching staff the full season, they might have overtaken the Athletics. As it was, except for a short stay at the top of the standings in mid-July, the Senators leveled off in second place, and neither rose nor dropped back, maintaining an even pace behind the Athletics until the season ended. Although Walter

Johnson's team won 94 games, a gain of 23 wins over the previous season, the Athletics piled up 102.

A less beneficial acquisition followed a week after the Goslin for Manush and Crowder trade. The Chicago White Sox had a problem child on their team named Art Shires. A Texan with a flamboyant knack for self-promotion, Shires had already tested the patience of Judge Landis. Among Shires' delusions was that he could hit opponents in the ring as effectively as he could belt baseballs around a ballpark. He had not reckoned that baseballs don't hit back. An off-season heavyweight bout between Shires of the White Sox and George Trafton, one of the first Monsters of the Midway to play for the Chicago Bears, was arranged. It was a fiasco between two gladiators who each viewed the other more apprehensively than was warranted. After three rounds of mutual respect, the contestants called it off.

Nonetheless, Shires was a genuine big league hitter. He played first base where the Senators were still well represented by veteran Joe Judge. To shorten Shires' prospects even more, in July Washington bought a truly sensational first baseman from Kansas City. Joe Kuhel would succeed Joe Judge and be the Senators' first baseman for as long as Judge had. However, his arrival, with press notices that demanded he be played to verify them, tested Walter Johnson's loyalties. Judge was his best friend among the players. Judge was not visibly slowing down. However, Clark Griffith had invested substantially in the future development of Kuhel. Johnson benched his buddy and played the new kid on the team. The fans protested and Johnson put Judge back on first base. Either way, the manager had a good bat in the lineup and a sure glove in the field. The next year, however, youth would have its way and Joe Judge went to the bench.

The Senators played evenly during the last half of the season. However, while the fortunes of the Senators did not vary, the misfortunes which haunted Walter Johnson brought him the most tragic event of his life.

37
Hazel's Tragic Death

T HE LONG HOSPITALIZATION of her oldest son and his recovery at home had been stressful for Hazel Johnson. The four younger children, particularly her daughters, Carolyn, 7, and Barbara, 4, demanded her attention. With young Walter now able to get about and care for himself again, the Johnsons planned a vacation for Hazel and the younger children.

As the Senators would leave on a long western trip right after the July 4 holiday, Hazel decided to take her restless brood to visit their grandmother and aunts, uncles and cousins in Kansas. It was a long way to travel, but Hazel had driven it several times. She was a safe driver and a resourceful traveler. The trip west was uneventful, and the stay of several weeks a pleasant family get-together.

Some who have reconstructed what went awry with the planned return trip believe the intention was for Johnson's family to visit him in St. Louis when the team reached there, then store the car and take a train back to Washington. From St. Louis, where the Senators played July 20-23, a four-day stop at Chicago followed before turning for home.

At some point a decision was made for Hazel and the children to drive back to Washington and not wait to take a train. It was a bad decision and a fatal one. The nation had entered a widely pervasive hot spell, the sort which often blankets the Midwest in agonizing heat. Nineteen thirty was a time when roads, while not primitive, were far from being the superhighways of today. Air conditioning was unknown. The most luxurious automobiles lacked any method of cooling the occupants other than opening the windows and air vents. When the temperature outside was over 100 degrees, the movement of air through the car brought little comfort.

While Walter Johnson and the Senators went to Chicago, Hazel and the four children pushed east, hoping to find cooler weather once they emerged from the Midwest. Unfortunately, the East Coast, too, was baking under a relentless sun. The children were fretful, diarrhea became a problem, and when the family stopped for a night, Hazel had little chance to sleep.

Finally, on July 29, the worn and weary family reached Washington, but Johnson himself was not yet there to welcome them. By the time the ball club returned, Hazel had been admitted to Georgetown University Hospital. She suffered from dehydration and exhaustion; hospitalization was expected to restore her. Johnson felt reassured enough to lead his team in their games against the Philadelphia Athletics on July 29 and 30, but was called at the ballpark on the 31st by the doctors at Georgetown University Hospital, who warned that Mrs. Johnson was in a dangerous condition. He raced to the hospital and tiptoed into her room. He sent Walter Jr., who had kept a vigil throughout the day, home and sat quietly with his wife for the final hours of her life. She passed away at 4:30 A.M. on August 1. Walter Johnson's grief was starkly evident, but unspoken. He never discussed his distress over the decision for Hazel to drive back to Washington, D.C. It would haunt him forever.

The public responded to Johnson's tragedy in the ways by which we acknowledge death. The spiritual solace of the Christian faith by which the Johnsons lived and raised their family was invoked in the prayers of friends and strangers. The family in Coffeyville left immediately, with Mrs. Frank Johnson, to whom Hazel had been like a daughter, accompanied by Walter's brothers, Earl, Leslie, and Chester. Mayor Edwin E. Roberts, Hazel's father, rushed east from Reno, Nevada.

A steady stream of floral tributes arrived at the Johnson home, where Walter Johnson kept an unwavering vigil beside Hazel. For four days he steadfastly refused to leave, neither sleeping nor eating, while the time ticked away until, the weekend passed, it was time to bury his wife of 16 years.

Although the ball club, with Joe Judge as acting manager, had continued to play during the days following Hazel's death, the Monday, August 4, game in New York with the Yankees was postponed. Johnson's players were present for the burial service, with Clark Griffith, Joe Engel, and Mike Martin serving among the pallbearers.

Hazel Johnson was buried with a simple Episcopal service at the Rockville Union Cemetery with funeral services conducted by the

Rev. Joseph E. Williams of the Bethesda Episcopal Church. Dry-eyed but visibly broken by the loss of his wife, Walter Johnson leaned heavily on the arm of his mother throughout the service.

Clark Griffith paid tribute to Hazel Johnson and the special devotion of the couple. "Why, Walter was just one of the kids in the Johnson family. Mrs. Johnson bought his clothes for him, babied him when he was not feeling well and took all the burdens of his household from his shoulders. She often called Walter one of her children, mothered him exactly as she mothered the three boys and two girls."

Griffith told his manager he could return to the club whenever he wished or remain in seclusion. He told the press it would probably do Walter Johnson more good to get back to leading the team in the pennant fight, no matter how poignantly he felt the loss of his wife.

Close friends and neighbors of Walter and Hazel, Tom and Therese Flaherty, tried to console Walter and contain five active children. Even with help from Hazel's dear friend, Addie Hugenin, a secretary who had worked for Representative Roberts, it was too much. Minnie Johnson rented out her house in Kansas and moved to the Maryland farm to complete Hazel's role of home maker. With her came the widowed son-in-law John Burke and his sons, Jack and Jim. They all settled onto the Johnson farm. Johnson would never marry again or cease to mourn the loss of his wife. His life without her would last as long as their life together had, 16 years. Meanwhile, two weeks after Hazel was buried, Walter Johnson returned to work.

In assessments of the performance of the Washington Senators in 1930, writers of the time never factored in the impact of Hazel Johnson's death on Walter or how his personal loss might have affected the play of the team. When he had been named manager of the Senators, popular opinion was that he would set such a sterling example of dedication that the players would make him their model. Just by his presence, it was believed, Johnson would free the team of cliques, self-interested players, and indifferent ones. It did not happen. Johnson's belief in the goodness in others was read by some of the players as a chance to perform at less than maximum effort. Not all, not even many of those who played for him in Washington took advantage of his easy ways. There were no "Good Time Bill" Lamars or Hugh McQuillans on the Senators roster, but a pitcher with a hangover can lose a critical game he would have won had he gone to bed early the night before.

The 1930 Senators were a team which, judged against the strength of the pennant-winning Philadelphia Athletics, was by any measure the second best. The teams which followed under Johnson's management had much the same characteristics. In fact, Johnson's final three years produced season records that were remarkable for their winning consistency. In some seasons the total victories by the Senators would have been enough to finish first. Pennant winners who topped 100 games won, particularly for a 154-game schedule, are less frequent than those who ended up below that mark. It was Johnson's fate that the Athletics won 102 in 1930, 107 in 1931, and, in 1932, the resurgent Yankees also won 107. Johnson's teams won 94, 94, and 93 games in each of those years. They lost 60, 62, and 61, a most remarkable stretch of consistency at a pace that would have won pennants in other years. It really had little to do with the job Johnson did as manager; he probably got as much from his material as any other manager would have gotten. The trouble was that he was the Walter Johnson of legend. He was expected to win with the same certainty when leading others as he had when he was the King of the Mound.

The frustration of near misses, of season-long pennant chases which fell short, changed Walter Johnson. He managed more, left less to the judgment of the players, began to call pitches from the bench, and displayed a coldness toward the failures of others, which replaced the forgiving shrug that had characterized his playing years. The most telling incident happened close to the end of what was to be his final season as manager of the Senators. Johnson never explained his motivation for inserting the team's most effective pinch hitter, Dave Harris, in a game which was helplessly lost. Detroit's Tom Bridges was within one out of a perfect game and leading 13-0 when Johnson sent Harris to bat. Bridges had struck out seven, mainly with his sharp-breaking curve ball, and only five balls had even been hit to Detroit's outfielders. Harris hit the first pitch into left field for a single. After Sam Rice grounded out to end the game, shocked Washington fans let Johnson know they would rather have seen a rare perfect game than a meaningless base hit. The public was confused by Johnson's decision to pinch-hit with two out in the ninth and trailing by 13 runs. This wasn't a game managed by John McGraw or some hard-bitten scrapper. It wasn't that Dave Harris had been determined to improve his batting average regardless of the game's situation. Harris was only at bat because Walter Johnson had decided to put him there.

Walter Johnson's three-year contract had been extended to cover

1932. When renewal was at hand, Clark Griffith had a long talk with his friend and explained he wished to make a change. Perhaps a different managerial approach would move the Senators to the top of the league again. The last time they won the pennant the team had been led by Bucky Harris, a playing manager. Griffith believed he could once again work the wonder of another Boy Manager with his incumbent shortstop, Joe Cronin.

Walter Johnson accepted his dismissal gracefully, saying all the expected things. He apologized for a winning record that was not quite adequate to produce a championship. He made no excuses, thanked the management for his opportunity, and slipped quietly into the anonymity of life outside of baseball.

38

The Cleveland Disaster

W ALTER JOHNSON experienced the same ambivalence other men do when they retire from a lifelong profession. Being free of the routines of past years was a new experience, although he would have to enjoy it alone. Hazel would not be there to share the pleasure of spending the spring and summer with their children. After a quarter of a century of getting ready for a baseball season and the excitement of Opening Day, now he could just read about baseball in the papers. The 1933 season began without Walter Johnson. He was not even there to watch someone else pitch the opener or lead the Senators onto the field.

Life was busy enough for Johnson, at least as the season rolled along. He followed the fortunes of the Senators with interest, envious to some degree of the young manager, Joe Cronin, and curious whether he could improve them. Johnson had his pack of foxhounds and, for closer protection and companionship for his children, a large police dog. He built up his poultry stock, literally an "egg money" crop for his mother. There were visits from friends, particularly those who no longer could be suspected of celebrity cultivation. His closest friends were men who shared his conservative views and sense of neighborliness. It was an easy life, but one easy to abandon when he was contacted by his longtime friend and admirer Billy Evans, who was then the general manager of the Cleveland Indians. Johnson's former teammate and good friend Roger Peckinpaugh was about to be deposed as manager after failing to raise the Indians above their customary fourt-place status in the league standings. A local boy who had made good but not quite good enough as manager of his hometown team, Peck had come from the sandlots of Cleveland to be a great shortstop but a bland field leader. Why Evans chose Johnson to inspire a dispirited squad of players when he was known to be the same type of manager as Peckinpaugh can only be attributed to misdirected loyalty. Evans needed a manager, Johnson needed a job, and the mismatching to accommodate those needs was overlooked.

Walter Johnson was a legendary name whose arrival to lead the Indians was hailed with optimism and expectation by Cleveland's civic leaders. Mayor Ray T. Miller, heading a large welcoming committee of businessmen, proclaimed Sunday, June 10, when Johnson would take charge of the team, "Walter Johnson Day." The *Cleveland Press* ran an editorial urging the fans to show their support by attending Johnson's managerial debut game. They saw what was hoped to be the transformation of a team of uncertain performance into one where decisive dugout decisions would make a difference.

The opponents for the debut game were the St. Louis Browns, and the tides of change had floated Bump Hadley—a disappointment to Johnson in Washington—to the mound for the Browns. Johnson countered with the rising star of the Indians, Mel Harder. The two dueled for nine scoreless innings. Then, in the top of the 10th, Harder weakened. The Browns loaded the bases with one out, and Walter Johnson walked from the dugout and signaled for a relief pitcher. One of the unproven prospects on the Indians staff was Oral Hildebrand. Johnson had commented favorably about him in his first press conference, remembering a game the previous season against Washington when Hildebrand, scarcely past rookie status, had challenged Heinie Manush after a spiking incident. It had impressed Johnson, and, needing a pitcher in a tough spot, he turned to Hildebrand. In storybook fashion, the lean righthander got pinch hitter Carl Reynolds to pop up and Jim Levey to hit into a force play. In even greater storybook tradition, Hildebrand was allowed by Johnson to bat with two out in the bottom of the 10th and the winning run on third. He drove a single to right-center to score Joe Vosmik and win Johnson's first game as the new manager.

Johnson's crowd-pleasing performance had impressed 12,000 fans, and the next day he continued his inaugural magic. This time fate placed Tommy Bridges of Detroit on the mound. Although he did not flirt with a no-hitter this time, Bridges was hooked up in another scoreless duel. Johnson had come right back with Hildebrand, who was pitching one of the six shutouts he hurled during the season. Before Hildebrand could come to bat with Joe Vosmik again perched on third as the winning run in the bottom of the ninth, Frank Pytlak, a rookie catcher, singled to drive the runner home.

Despite the predictions of the press before Johnson's tenure began, the initial successes raised expectations. Cleveland, however, was a much better team at home, and when the schedule took them on the road, Johnson's hunches or judgments went astray.

Stuart Bell, the sports columnist of the *Cleveland Press*, had set the journalistic tone for the advent of Walter Johnson as manager: "Johnson comes to the Indians without any outstanding performances as a leader, but he didn't have the softest spot in Washington, where a pilot does not have free rein and the Nats apparently were not good enough to finish any higher than the third-place notch in which they finished the last two seasons under The Big Train." Bell pointed out, "Johnson and Peck are of the same type, quiet, phlegmatic and without outward show of fire." Bell then assessed the team Johnson was taking over: "The players are in harmony among themselves, and if there has been any laxity in obeying training rules, the owners are as much to blame as anybody, for they have coddled and pampered some of the players, entertained them, and generally tried to run the team on the 'one big happy family' idea, which they will find won't work in baseball. The Indians are in a crisis of despondency now from which it will take some inspiring force to lift them. Everybody hopes Walter Johnson is the man who can turn the trick, and we wish him all the luck in the world."

Luck was something which abandoned Walter Johnson after the 12th inning of the final game of the 1924 World Series. Fate, which had placed pebbles in the path of ground balls which became base hits by hopping over Lindstrom's head, had perversely strewn boulders in his path ever since.

Johnson's initial success did not last long, and the Senators contributed to the dimming of fan optimism. They arrived in Cleveland for a five-game set and, on June 25, won an opening doubleheader, 9-0 and 10-1. They then took two of the three remaining games.

Walter Johnson had a chance to reverse this showing early in July when he returned to Washington for the first time in an enemy uniform. Matters did not break as Johnson would have hoped. Instead, the Indians lost another doubleheader, 6-2 and 5-4, on July 8, then a single game on Sunday, July 9, and finally won a 12-inning struggle, 3-2, before leaving town. The Senators, meanwhile, were in hot contention for the pennant, with the team Johnson had left behind.

Although Cleveland played well in August, taking three of five when the Senators came to town, and briefly moved into third place ahead of the Athletics, September was a disaster. The Indians managed only seven victories in 19 games, lost on October 1, and disbanded after yet another fourth-place finish. Johnson did not seem to have made a difference either way, but off-season assessments suggested an improvement might be gained the next year.

Cleveland trained in New Orleans, and Walter Johnson made fitness a priority. He believed that a player's legs, particularly a pitcher's, had to be strengthened before other playing skills were worked on. It had been his way of getting ready, and he ran his players ceaselessly. He was quoted by the *Cleveland Press* as favoring married players, provided they were wed to a good woman. "A bad wife can ruin a good ball player faster than anything else," he cautioned. He also made his standard pronouncement against cigarette smokers, citing the obvious nicotine culprits panting as they circled the field under Johnson's baleful eye.

The pre-season assessment consigned Cleveland to the fourth-place finish they had occupied the past four seasons. To Johnson's credit, he had moved them up a notch. The fans and press were dissatisfied; he should have done better. The novelty of having the legendary Big Train as manager had worn off, and the customary carping by the press had begun. Although the team started fast, sweeping opening series with the Yankees and A's, both ranked with Washington as pre-season favorites, the schedule made success illusionary. As usual, Cleveland played much better at home than on the road. The 1934 schedule penalized them by providing only three home games in the whole month of June. Reporters traveling with the team sent back critical accounts of games in which they hinted Johnson had stayed with a pitcher too long or removed one too soon. The fans, drawing their information from writers whose biases against any incumbent manager were Cleveland tradition, echoed a chorus of criticism.

The Cleveland management, whose team was not floundering, only playing at an expected level, silenced the critics briefly by signing Walter Johnson for 1935. Perhaps they were compounding an original mistake, but Alva Bradley, the president, headed a group of businessmen who, in any dispute, sided with management. Johnson had put a $100,000 profit on the books by reviving interest in the previous year's team, and the bottom line was also helped by his payroll pruning. He weeded out veteran hangers-on and even dispensed with a coaching staff.

Soon after his contract was renewed, he entered Lakeside Hospital, felled again by pleurisy with a threat of pneumonia also hovering over him. The illness also showed how alone and isolated Johnson was. He had lived alone in a hotel since joining Cleveland. He had signed Sam Rice, cut loose by the Senators, and Moe Berg, an oddly intellectual companion, had been hired after he, too, was dropped by the Senators. However, Johnson could not fraternize too obviously with active players. Usually, a manager adds a crony to the coaching staff, but Bibb Falk and Earl Wolgamot, who had been Peckinpaugh's coaches, were not retained after 1933 and not replaced. Steve O'Neill, who would replace Johnson before the next season was over, had coached the pitchers for three weeks in spring training but left to manage Toledo during the 1934 season. He did not rejoin Cleveland until 1935. With Johnson in the hospital, the team was turned over to the veteran third baseman, Willie Kamm, to manage. This would prove to be a bad choice for Johnson, giving the ambitious Kamm the apparent cachet of the ailing manager. Johnson had covered the need for base coaches by using reserve players while coaching first base himself. Even this was dubiously regarded. Most managers who coached the bases put themselves in the third base coaches' box. That's where decisions to send or hold up runners are made. Johnson's critics said he should not merely be pointing the way to second base as runners rounded first. It would be best if he sat in the dugout and plotted strategy, they argued.

More and more Johnson became an ill-regarded managerial incumbent. If Willie Kamm did not overtly covet Johnson's job, he was a logical successor. He fit the catalog description for big league managers far better than Johnson. Except for Clark Griffith, no Hall of Fame pitcher became a successful manager. Like Miller Huggins, Joe McCarthy, Bill McKechnie, Bucky Harris, and the latest, Hall of Fame manager Leo Durocher, Kamm was a standout defensive infielder and was considered a smart player.

A third-place finish did not placate those critical of Johnson's managerial style. They pointed to the team's apparent comparable strength, position by position, to the pennant-winning 1934 Detroit Tigers and the narrowly beaten New York Yankees. Many contended the difference was in leadership, contrasting Johnson with Cochrane's fiery style and Joe McCarthy's "push button" efficiency.

39
Johnson Retires to His Farm

B EFORE THE 1935 SEASON BEGAN, despite no significant personnel changes by the Indians, a poll of American League managers rated Cleveland as the team most likely to win the pennant. Perhaps the passing of Babe Ruth from the Yankees following a season that signaled the certain end to the Babe's greatness and the humiliation of Mickey Cochrane and the Detroit Tigers by the Dean brothers and the St. Louis Cardinals' "Gas House Gang" in the 1934 World Series, moved Cleveland unreasonably ahead in the forecast. When Johnson himself revealed he had voted with the majority and considered his team capable of winning the pennant, a wave of unwarranted optimism swept Cleveland's press and fans. It was a fragile hope, and the eggshell-thin premise cracked when the team slipped slightly in the early season. Even so, looking back at the setting, with the Indians bunched with two other teams a mere three games behind the leading Yankees, it is hard to understand why the panic button was jabbed so vigorously. The season had not even reached Memorial Day and already doomsayers had launched a vicious attack on Johnson.

The trigger was the sudden news from Philadelphia on May 27 that Willie Kamm, veteran third baseman, had been told to return to Cleveland and that catcher Glenn Myatt had been released. Johnson accused the two of being "disturbers" of team harmony and closed the clubhouse doors against a press he viewed as hostile. All gloves came off and the claws most baseball writers had sheathed scratched away for an explanation that would justify Johnson's purge. Even the previously supportive *Cleveland Press* set the scene on its editorial page. In space usually reserved for political and social commentary, the newspaper editorialized about the action against Kamm and Myatt:

Presumably, these steps were taken in the interest of "harmony." "For the good of the team," is Johnson's explanation.

We do not think harmony will result and we do not think it is good for the team. It will probably create a great deal of bad feeling in the team and among the fans as well.

Johnson had not been popular with the players. Whatever else may be responsible, Johnson's own personality has been an important factor in producing this situation.

Reserved, silent, undemonstrative, he also appears to be jealous and suspicious of men who would be his friends if they met a warmer approach and who are loyal workers anyhow.

Alva Bradley, the club owner, says: "In any business we run we only have one manager." That is a principle sound enough. But this sudden disruptive order will raise the question that was in so many minds last summer whether in the baseball business Bradley had the services of even one.

The editorial was accompanied by a page-one story by Stuart Bell, the *Press* sports editor, headlined: "Players Back Kamm and Myatt In Team Purge." Bell, after detailing the events, added: "Johnson hasn't had the whole-hearted backing of his team from the beginning because he hasn't even taken the trouble to be cordial.

"Your correspondent at all times has endeavored to remain aloof from the disagreements between players and managers on the theory that he could better report what actually happened and today he could not supply this story if Johnson hadn't flagrantly violated all the rules of fair play."

Other writers for other Cleveland papers took up the cause against Johnson. Gordon Cobbledick of the *Cleveland Plain Dealer* claimed the feeling against Johnson was not limited to the players he had cited, Kamm and Myatt. "Johnson is not liked by most of the Indians, and neither has he gained their respect and admiration. If the owners of the team believe he can be a successful manager under these conditions they cannot be blamed for insisting on the right to keep him. But if they feel it is only necessary to rid the team of a few malcontents to set Johnson right, then they are making the mistake of their brief baseball careers. To stamp out the anti-Johnson faction among the Indians would be to stamp out the present baseball club."

The next day Stuart Bell, in his column in the *Press*, questioned the original decision to import Washington's idol and further analyzed Johnson's primary personality problem. "They engaged Walter Johnson to manage the Indians despite the fact he had been a failure at Newark and Washington. His mistakes in both cities were plain to all and many of them are the same he has made here. Johnson has been no more popular here than he was in either of the other cities. Even if he were a good manager, he would not be popular. Johnson hasn't the personality to which sports audiences respond. He is cold, undemonstrative and lacking in the boldness and fire that fans expect from their leaders. Johnson is not a fighter on the field or in the clubhouse. His nature is strictly a defensive one. It is a defeatist nature, unable to see the good in Bill Kamm, but inventing out of Kamm's honest desire and efforts to be helpful, a Judas after his job."

It is difficult to match the beloved Walter Johnson, warmly admired by United States presidents, subject of uplifting articles in national magazines, and revered for his wholesome qualities, to how he was perceived in Cleveland. Yet, the assessments of the baseball writers cannot be dismissed as only the customary managerial character assassination as practiced in Cleveland. Something had changed Johnson, at least during his years in Ohio. Obviously, the missing element in his life was his wife. Hazel had been the balance wheel and he now seemingly spun out of emotional control. His problems in Newark were not the result of his approach to his team. The dissonance in Washington did not begin until after Hazel's death midway through 1930. Only when he lost her counsel did he begin to slide from contemporary public favor.

The Indians management tried to pass the buck to the commissioner, but Landis, after listening to both the players and Johnson, passed the buck back. He said both sides were honorable and honest in their views, but concluded, "However, it falls upon the manager as a practical proposition to act in cases wherever there are honest differences. This is so because the responsibility is his and with the responsibility must go the authority."

Johnson claimed victory, and Cleveland owner Alva Bradley chose to stonewall against the public and the press. He soothed Kamm's feelings by continuing him at full salary while appointing him to be a special scout. Myatt was quickly signed by the New York Giants. The Indians ran paid advertisements on the sports pages which contained a statement of support for Johnson signed by all the players. Some of the players told sportswriters they had been coerced into signing, although the team leader, Earl Averill, and Oral Hildebrand, whose relationship with Johnson had been a troubled one, made statements explicitly assuring Johnson that he had their backing.

Management inserted into the ballpark programs a reprinted article from the *Detroit News* written by J. G. Salsinger, the sports editor. Salsinger was also president of the Baseball Writers Association and a leading national authority. He put the blame on the Cleveland writers, saying, "No manager in years has been the object of an attack either as vicious or insistent as the one launched against Johnson."

Salsinger called it "a bad rap" that was enhancing Johnson's reputation outside of Cleveland where he was viewed as the martyr of provincial prosecutors.

The Cleveland papers responded by digging up a three-year-old column by Salsinger about Johnson's use of a pinch hitter to deprive Detroit's Tommy Bridges of a perfect no-hit game.

The immediate consequence of the conflict was that the Indians continued to be managed by Johnson. Attendance suffered, but so did the box offices throughout the league. The country was deep into the Great Depression. The team continued at a level third-place pace, and with Mickey Cochrane again providing inspired leadership, the Tigers firmly held first place with the Yankees in close contention.

Then, on August 5, 1935, Walter Johnson offered his resignation. It was accepted with public regret and private relief by Cleveland's management. Steve O'Neill, who had been the third base coach, was given the job of leading the Indians. He maintained them in third place and in 1936 finished fifth with the team Johnson's critics had expected to win a pennant. After a fourth-place finish in 1937, O'Neill, too, was deposed. Ossie Vitt, once a victim of a rare Johnson beanball, took over the perilous manager's perch and, in a scene reminiscent of the Johnson turmoil, departed after several years when management surrendered to the team that the rest of baseball labeled "the Cry Babies." Some of Johnson's players were still on the team, and still finding managerial faults.

Walter Johnson said his only immediate plans were to "go back to the farm," his newly bought 500-acre place near Germantown, Maryland. Asked if he expected to spend much time in Cleveland for the remainder of the season as part of his new job as a consultant, he said: "I hardly think so. I'm going to leave for home as soon as possible."

The last major league game Walter Johnson was associated with was on August 4 when he managed for the last time. It was two days past the anniversary date of Johnson's debut game in 1907, and again, Detroit was the opponent. This time, 28 years later, Detroit's pitcher was Tommy Bridges, the victim of Johnson's pinch-hit decision when the Tiger was one out away from a perfect game. Bridges provided the *coup de grâce* to Johnson's career with a three-hit shutout.

Walter Johnson had purchased the farm in Germantown intending to settle down to a life of farming with his five children. The oldest, Walter Jr., was now 19 and attended George Washington University. Known as "the Little Train," he had been a pitching prospect and Connie Mack intended to start him in the minor leagues the next season. Before that happened his arm was badly wrenched by a rearing horse he was training and the promise of a big league career was lost.

Walter Jr. never lived at the farm in Germantown and, according to the next-oldest son, Edwin, seldom visited. Eddie provided writer Susan Soderberg an insightful reminiscence for her book, *History of Germantown, Maryland*, published in 1989.

"...When we first got up there the only thing there was sheep. So Dad built a dairy barn not long after we got up there. As time went by we enlarged the barn. I think we were milking maybe 50 head at one time.

"We had some hogs too, for a time, but that was a low time in farming. Prices were bad. Hogs only brought four and a half cents a pound and went down to one and a half cents a pound for old sows. We always had chickens on the farm. Dad had some that he liked to take to show."

Eddie recalled, "When we first went up to the farm we had work horses. Tractors were just coming in. We had a Percheron stallion from France which we used for stud. Grandmother was living with us since my mother died. Walter Jr. seldom came to the farm in Germantown, he was out on his own when we moved there."

A news clipping in the Johnson file at Cooperstown reported that on September 28, 1935, Walter Johnson, Jr., suffered severe cuts when an automobile he was driving crashed into a telephone pole in Bethesda, Maryland. He had fallen asleep while driving home after working all night and was not seriously injured, the article reported.

"Grandmother had a son-in-law who also lost his wife, Aunt Blanche [Walter's youngest sister]. That was John Burke and his sons were Jack and Jim. They lived with us too. There were other houses on the farm and we sometimes had relatives living there."

"Dad liked to go hunting at night," remembered Eddie, "He and his friends would gather on a hilltop and light a fire. They always did this in cold weather. They liked to listen to those dogs as they hunted. Dad's dogs would end up maybe eight or ten miles away. He sometimes had to pay a neighbor to get them back."

Eddie, who developed his own farm nearby in Comus, Maryland, has provided a family snapshot of Walter Johnson in retirement. The former baseball star established himself as a gentleman farmer, but one who was unwilling to hire out all the labor for others to do. All his life he enjoyed the regime of a farm with its ability to reward hard work with abundant crops and prize-winning cattle. Johnson's transition from major league baseball to retirement had been planned for many years. The managerial experience in Cleveland, and even in Washington, had been far less than he had wished for. Still, those years bridged a time in his life, particularly following Hazel's death, when he was making the transition from a public life, for which he was not completely suited, to a private one, for which he was ideally prepared.

40
Inducted into
Baseball's Hall of Fame

EFORE WALTER JOHNSON could settle into the refuge of retirement on his new dairy farm, he was back in the limelight again. Along with Ty Cobb, Babe Ruth, Honus Wagner, and Christy Mathewson, Johnson was elected to the new Baseball Hall of Fame. On February 2 word came that the 200-member Baseball Writers of America had voted in the first five "immortals" they considered worthy of the honor. As is still the standard, a player needed a minimum of 75 percent of the total vote. That feat is hard enough today; imagine the competition in the first election! The initial election would not be followed by formal induction for three years. In 1936 the concept was mostly an abstraction, but there were hard driving forces at work to create a permanent home for the Hall of Fame even if it was based on the myth that baseball had sprung to life in Phinney's Meadow, in Cooperstown, N.Y., in 1839. Getting most of its energy from the new National League president, Ford Frick, the baseball establishment fell in line to establish a tangible shrine to the national pastime. In Cooperstown, Stephen Clark, who was a historian, an enthusiastic collector of early Americana, and a local resident with the advantage of being wealthy and a philanthropist, pushed the concept. He had begun by purchasing an ancient ball with a torn cover that had turned up in a nearby barn for $5. Put on display at the Cooperstown library, it triggered a search for more artifacts that might support the claim made by the Mills Commission in 1908 that Abner Doubleday had "invented" baseball. The local gymnasium was taken over to house the growing collection, and the building of a museum began. The Federal Works Project built a ballpark, to be named Doubleday Field, where tradition said Farmer Phinney had let the local lads play games with sticks and balls a century before.

Commissioner Landis appointed a commission to increase the

number of players and pioneers to be included, and subsequently, the BWA added more stars of the past to join Walter Johnson and the others of the First Five. When the Baseball Hall of Fame was formally dedicated, 25 members had been selected. The impending visit to Cooperstown became one of the events Walter Johnson looked forward to as he adjusted to life outside of baseball.

A few weeks after being elected to the Baseball Hall of Fame, Walter Johnson again made the national news, on February 22, 1936, George Washington's birthday. This was when our first president was permitted a separate celebration on whatever day of the week February 22 happened to fall. In 1936, Washington's 204th birthday fell on a Saturday, which partly explains why 10,000 people showed up at an event designated to celebrate the day.

In 1800 the inventive Rev. Mason L. Weems created durable myths about the boyhood of George Washington. His chopping down the cherry tree and throwing a silver dollar across the Rappahannock River became myths imbedded in national memory. The city of Fredericksburg, Virginia, where Washington's family lived during his boyhood, planted 200 cherry trees and asked Walter Johnson to repeat the feat of throwing a silver dollar across the river.

Johnson was willing to try. He did not mind throwing away other people's money provided no one made him don a colonial costume. The crowd of 10,000 lined both sides of the Rappahannock. Most wanted to be close to the celebrities involved, but many gathered where they might catch the dollar. The Chamber of Commerce boasted about Johnson's chances, whereas Congressman Sol Bloom of New York City, director of the commission to celebrate Washington's bicentennial, set the odds against Johnson at 20 to 1. Johnson was 48 years old and the last throwing he had done was to pitch batting practice to the recalcitrant Indians the previous summer. Little George Washington had only been 10 years old when Parson Weems claimed he had astonished his elders with a child prodigy's heave. No one seemed certain how wide the river had been in Washington's time, but legend had fixed the spot from where the throw had been made at a point where the Rappahannock measured 272 feet from bank to bank.

They gave Walter Johnson three brightly minted United States silver dollars. The third one he threw would be the official toss, the first two would be as much warm-up the budget for the event allowed. Walter Johnson removed his suit coat and, despite the cold day with ice in the river and snow on the river's banks, rolled up his sleeves.

The ground was as muddy as the pitcher's mound had been during the rainy final game in Pittsburgh in the 1925 World Series. Johnson, who never used a windup, just stepped and slung with his familiar sweeping sidearm motion. The dollar went sailing across the waters but splashed down a few feet from the opposite bank. The second try plunked into the mud at the foot of the bank across the way and was never recovered. Time now for the official toss. Walter Johnson put all his strength into the throw and it cleared everything, landing amid scurrying spectators where it was captured by Pietro Yon, who was neither a baseball fan nor a student of American history. Yon was an Italian stonemason who broke off working on a nearby Civil War battlefield memorial to see what had drawn the crowd. Nonetheless, with the silver dollar grasped in his artisan's fist he shook off a banker's offer of $200 for the souvenir. With characteristic modesty, Johnson told the press he was sure the river had narrowed considerably since Washington's time, and he slipped back to his farm and his retirement.

Walter Johnson now followed major league baseball in the newspapers. As he left the baseball scene, the next strikeout king entered. Had Johnson lasted one more season in Cleveland, he would have managed his successor when the 16-year-old Bob Feller reached the major leagues. Comparisons were made between the two. Both had been raised on farms, Feller growing up amid the corn crops of Iowa. They came from families who raised them to value the ethics of hard work, perseverance, responsibility to others, and the good sense to avoid self-destructive habits. Feller comes closest to Johnson in sharing similarities in both career and personal conduct. Substitute Johnson's having pitched for years for a second-division team with the almost four full prime career seasons Feller lost to wartime service in WWII, and the total career statistics of both pitchers would be even far greater than the impressive totals they did leave behind. Yet Johnson survives with all his admirable qualities still cited whereas Bob Feller is just another immortal selling his autograph at card shows. No matter how prodigious his pitching feats and exemplary his life off the diamond, Bob Feller never touched the emotions of the fans in the way the Big Train had. Maybe we have become less sentimental and more cynical about what we read in the newspapers...particularly those published in Cleveland.

Among the stories which cling to the Johnson legends is one told by Shirley Povich as often as he has found a way to work it into his copy. Johnson went to very few games after he retired and had not seen Feller pitch. He accepted Povich's offer to watch the wunderkind from Cleveland work against the Senators. After the game, Povich asked Johnson if Feller threw the ball as fast as he had.

Walter Johnson wrestled with the question, allowing that Feller was surely very fast. Pressed to compare Feller to himself in his prime, truthfulness won out over modesty. According to Povich, Johnson finally mumbled that, no, the youngster was not as fast as he had been, and then changed the subject. Actually, Johnson had seen Feller pitch earlier that season. He had filled in as a broadcaster of White Sox games for a Chicago radio station. His quoted interview with Povich took place when the writer, covering the Senators, came through the Windy City with the team. Johnson's response to the question is true enough, but Povich's posturing about enticing The Big Train out to Griffith Stadium is self-serving.

Walter Johnson was urged by his neighbors to run for county commissioner in 1938 and was elected after a campaign expenditure of 50¢ for postage. A Republican amid a constituency of New Deal Democrats, he was elected chairman by the Democratic majority and served his term impartially. He was drawn into a larger political fray in 1940 when he was persuaded to stand for election to the U.S. House of Representatives for the Sixth Maryland District, covering Montgomery County, Maryland.

The big national issue was whether Franklin D. Roosevelt should be elected to an unprecedented third term. The Republican Party nominated an unknown Midwestern lawyer named Wendell Willkie, who launched his presidential campaign in Coffeyville, Kansas. Willkie had taught history at the high school during years when Coffeyville was Walter Johnson's hometown and the two men had been friends. Willkie asked Johnson to return and introduce him at the dinner where he would formally declare his candidacy.

Other than an occasional short visit to see his brothers and sister still living there, Johnson had not been back since Hazel's death in 1930. By then, they had sold their property in Coffeyville and, with his mother now heading his household in Maryland, circumstances had not provided "hometown hero" returns to Kansas. Willkie's candidacy was almost overshadowed, locally at least, by the presence of Coffeyville's true favorite son. Willkie, a corporate lawyer, was in need of an image to offset one coined by FDR's writers who dubbed Willkie "the Barefoot Boy of Wall Street." Coffeyville provided ample photo opportunities for the candidate to be posed beside farm tractors or admiring a silo. However, the ones with the most impact were those taken while shaking hands with Walter Johnson. Willkie shook hands with Johnson in front of grain stores, hardware stores, in school yards, on church steps, and wherever the background rubbed some of the city-slicker shine off his image. In November, both candidates lost, although Walter Johnson, in a year of a Roosevelt landslide, had come close to being elected; he lost narrowly. If he had run in Montgomery County, Kansas, and not Montgomery County, Maryland, he would have been the landslide winner. In 1942 he was returned to the county commission and remained its chairman until his death.

Before heeding the urgings of politicians to come out of the seclusion of his dairy farm, the formal induction to the Baseball Hall of Fame had given Walter Johnson the greatest satisfaction he enjoyed after his active baseball life had ended. There were 11 living inductees including Walter Johnson, and all had been his contemporaries. The oldest, Connie Mack, had managed the Philadelphia Athletics in every game they played against Washington over Johnson's 21-year career. Cy Young, whose career straddled the 19th and 20th centuries had pitched against the young Johnson. Cobb, Ruth, Speaker, Sisler, Collins, and Lajoie had batted against him. Grover Cleveland Alexander had been as dominant in the National League as Johnson had been in the American League. Honus Wagner, too, was a National League figure who had never faced Johnson. However, all the men were bonded by a special status. They were the superstars for whom a Baseball Hall of Fame had been envisioned. The founders of the on-going national shrine could hardly have anticipated the desperate search for "immortals" that would join them in the future. Players have since been installed whose achievements are insignificant when compared to those who were introduced with Walter Johnson on June 12, 1939.

Missing from the platform during the inaugural ceremony was Ty Cobb, who was late to arrive, perhaps to avoid sharing the stage with Kenesaw Mountain Landis. Speaker and Cobb never forgave the commissioner for the shoddy treatment he had given them by granting credibility to a known malcontent who had accused them of betting on a game. The inaugural was the only time Landis visited Cooperstown. Although he presided with proper ceremony, the idea of a Baseball Hall of Fame had not been his, and never had his personal approval.

The several days the great stars spent together in Cooperstown were fully enjoyed by Johnson. These were the kind of men whose company he preferred. Among them they held about every baseball record worth recording. Ruth for homers, Cobb and Wagner for batting and base stealing, Speaker, Sisler, Collins, and Lajoie for superb fielding as well as outstanding hitting. Young and Alexander, the absent Christy Mathewson, and Johnson held the records for victories. Johnson, of course, held all the strikeout marks. Matty, the only former player missing from the First Five, had a ceremonial jump on the others. A bronze bust of the great pitcher of the Giants had been given to the museum by Matty's widow and was unveiled two weeks earlier. The presentation was part of ceremonies which included a ball game between Mathewson's alma mater, Bucknell, and St. Lawrence University. The 100th Anniversary of Baseball, as acknowledged at the time, was celebrated by events all summer in 1939, starting with those honoring Christy Mathewson. Except for their encounter in Tulsa, Oklahoma, when Walter Johnson pitched for the world-touring Chicago White Sox against Matty and the New York Giants, the two great pitchers had not met on a ball field. Nor could Johnson compare memories of games played against Honus Wagner; but both were outdoorsmen who hiked into the woods with their shotguns and hound dogs. Johnson would not match Ol' Pete Alexander drink for drink in the taproom of the Otsego Hotel, but they could compare a boyhood in Kansas with one growing up in Nebraska.

It was the right occasion for the great players of the past to divulge their assessments of their peers. There is no reason to assume the Johnson's views had changed from those given in his autobiographical series in the *Washington Times* in 1925. Then, he had answered the rhetorical question about Cobb and Ruth: "Who would you sooner have on your ball club?" Johnson had written that Babe Ruth would be the more valuable. Johnson was weighing in Ruth's years as a top pitcher and his winning record against the Big Train. Johnson also admired Ruth's defensive ability over Cobb's, particularly his throwing arm.

Johnson recognized the importance of Cobb's base running and aggressive play along with his unprecedented string of batting championships. Johnson believed in the fellowship of sports. He had never carried a grudge off the field and wanted everyone else to be friends when not opponents in a game. Johnson cited the off-field friendship between Cobb and Ruth, commenting that they had ridden to the ballpark for the 1924 World Series in the same taxi and sat side by side during the games. Johnson would not have known it at the time but, during World War II, Cobb and Ruth would be paired in golf matches to sell war bonds. As for Cobb and Johnson, theirs was a mutual admiration society. Frank Graham, columnist for the *New York Journal-American,* wrote of riding back from the

Cooperstown event with Cobb and Johnson. They shared a table in the dining car of the special train returning them to New York, and Cobb urged Johnson to tell of his three shutouts in four days against the New York Highlanders.

The day of the induction ceremonies was a full one and included a baseball game between active players from the American and National Leagues. Babe Ruth got into the game as a pinch hitter, wearing a Brooklyn Dodger uniform. He had coached them in 1938. If he had asked for the use of his old Yankee pinstripes with the numeral three, he would have been told that George Selkirk had first call now. Lou Gehrig, whose number four would be the first to be retired a few weeks later on July 4, was missing. On June 12 he was making a final appearance as a Yankee in Kansas City, Missouri, in an exhibition game against the Yankee farm team, the Blues. From there he went to the Mayo Brothers Clinic in Rochester, Minnesota, to learn his illness was fatal.

On Dedication Day the upstate New York country town was swarming with 10,000 visitors, forerunners of the millions of baseball pilgrims who come annually to renew their faith that baseball is truly the National Game. Other sports have mimicked baseball and established Halls of Fame. They have extended their playing seasons to ridiculous lengths and encroached on a calendar which was once neatly divided by weather-appropriate sports. Baseball belonged to the warm-weather months, to sunshine and grass. Now baseball, too, is extended to preposterous lengths, played indoors, on synthetic turf, conducted almost clandestinely after dark, and denies youngsters the chance to watch the World Series even on weekend afternoons. Hypocritically, organized baseball postures as the heritage of American youth while shutting them off from participation in anything other than merchandised trash. If baseball truly cared about its roots there would be knothole-gang days, the All-Star game would take place when kids could play hooky to watch, and the World Series weekend games would be played when youngsters could see them.

In 1939, the transition to present-day baseball was underway. Night baseball had taken a toehold. None of the players inducted then had ever played a major league game after dark. Another transition was also underway. None of the original members of the Hall of Fame were black. If any of them felt guilty about this, they did not mention it; nor did the Lords of Baseball who made the speeches. Blacks were an invisible part of baseball's "first hundred years."

41

The Big Train
Is Stopped

IN 1939 WALTER JOHNSON returned to baseball as a broadcaster. He became "the Wheaties Man," describing and commenting on the games of the Washington Senators. Arch McDonald, who had pioneered baseball broadcasts on WJSV (now WTOP), moved to New York City. The Yankees and Giants, after years of stonewalling the fans who wanted to listen to games, had been forced out of their boycott. Larry MacPhail, the Brooklyn Dodger general manager, imported Red Barber to broadcast the team's home games, and the move was a success.

A young broadcaster from the South had hoped to take McDonald's place in Washington, but Walter Johnson's celebrity won out over Mel Allen's exuberance and far better voice. Surprisingly, it is possible to compare Johnson broadcasting in 1939 with Allen's style and presentation.

In one of those happy coincidences which result from baseball research of another subject, a transcription of a game broadcast by Johnson and his partner, Harry McTigh, was located. It is available from a firm which sells sports tapes. The earliest baseball broadcast in the catalog of Sports Direct, Inc. (P.O. Box 342, Dept. C2, South Windsor, CT 06074) is the September 21, 1939 game with Cleveland playing Washington at Griffith Stadium. SABR researcher Bob Boynton was curious about the brief career of pitcher Dick Bass. Again, Walter Johnson is connected to an unusual event. Bass pitched only one major league game. Others have also been limited to a single appearance as a starter, but Bass held his own the longest and was the oldest to have such a truncated career. At 33, he had been brought up after pitching the Chattanooga Lookouts to the Southern Association pennant. He blanked the Indians for seven innings before being hit hard in the eighth and losing the game.

The radio station chose the date of September 21 to make a permanent audio record of its broadcast hours. A series of recordings (tape had not yet been perfected) began with a redheaded deejay plunking a ukulele and cheerfully urging Washingtonians to get out of bed. The career of Arthur Godfrey was underway. Although the game at Griffith Stadium began at 3:00 P.M., the station did not start coverage until 4:00 P.M., when the game had reached the fourth inning.

McTigh picked up the cue from the studio and set the stage, gave the lineups, and turned the broadcast over to Walter Johnson for a play-by-play account. The broadcasters switched roles for the rest of the game, with Johnson most frequently limiting himself to observations. He focused on Dick Bass, the new pitcher, and, speaking more loudly than his partner McTigh, said, "All right, good afternoon ladies and gentlemen…and Bass, the [pause] boy [pause] just up from [very long pause as Johnson probably had to check] Chattanooga walks out on the mound, starts tossing a few to Rick Ferrell—Bass mixes 'em up pretty well down there, has a fairly good fastball. He's supposed to have a good knuckler; it looks like he has a pretty fair curve. He's just been a little bit wild. Apparently he has something on that ball; he's had three and two on most of the batters, and usually when they get a pitch where he's got to come down in there to them they get ahold of that ball, but they're hitting a little bit late, those righthanders hitting the ball off to right field."

Johnson, whose voice was flat and delivered in a matter-of-fact style, also doubled as the public-address announcer. He is heard in the background informing the fans that Dick Bass was making way for a pinch hitter, Al Evans, in the eighth inning. The games were sponsored by General Mills and Johnson was identified as the Wheaties announcer. There were no commercials between innings and few product plugs during the games. Bob Boynton's curiosity as a researcher led him to time how long it took to make routine moves during a game in 1939. Teams changed sides each inning in a minute and 30 seconds average. Today it takes a minute longer, mostly to accommodate the extended commercial span promoted by Peter Uberroth when he was baseball commissioner. A marketing and merchandising whiz, Uberroth's contribution to baseball in the late 1980s consisted of finding ways to squeeze more revenue from the game.

During the resurrected broadcast we learn that Walter Johnson will appear at Miller's Market at 2134 4th Street N.E. between 7:30 and

9:00 that evening. Johnson said he'd sign anything from Wheaties boxes to ball gloves. No one was expected to pay to have Walter Johnson sign. Johnson's local appearances were probably part of his contract obligations, and he was also happy to have an excuse to spend an evening in town. In another auxiliary role, Walter Johnson picked the most valuable player in each game. A technique was used which would have gratified those who make baseball judgments by quantifying the factors on which they are based. Johnson was an early SABRmetrician. Each player's performance was assigned points according to the importance to the outcome and lost points for failures. Not just errors, but lackadaisical base running and failure to hustle after base hits, were weighed into the final total for each player. Johnson took this seriously, and it might reflect the way he measured his players when he managed. The *Washington Post* printed Johnson's daily judgments as part of its "Man of the Month" feature. At the end of each month, the Senators player with the most points received a trophy from the newspaper, presented by Walter Johnson.

By 1939 his children were growing up and edging out of the nest. Only Barbara, the youngest daughter, still lived at home year-round. The others were away at school and caught up in their own activities when at home. The family remained closely knit, but Johnson looked to old friends for company during his later years of retirement.

Joe Williams filed one of his daily *New York World-Telegram* columns describing a visit to the retired Big Train in 1937. Even then the tasks of a working farmer were not able to compensate for a widower's lonely life. Walter Johnson never concealed his mourning for Hazel. He questioned little that his middle-road Protestantism required of him but could never understand why God had taken Hazel when she was so young.

Williams described Walter Johnson as unchanged since he had left baseball except for the way he dressed as a farmer. "He wore heavy, mud-caked boots, blue denim overalls that had been patched more than once, a leather windbreaker and a battered felt hat," wrote Williams.

Johnson told the writer, "I guess this is where I belong," pointing toward the rolling fields. "It sort of comes natural to me, anyhow. You know I was born on a farm."

Walter Johnson commented about the Cleveland Indians he had left behind. Despite the furor of Feller's coming, in 1936 they had landed in second division. "They will never win a pennant until something is done to correct certain internal conditions that exist. The players don't pull together. There are several cliques on the team, each more interested in individual performances than team play. ...Just thinking about my experience out there makes me happy I'm out of baseball and on my farm."

When Joe Williams asked about the baseball prospects of Johnson's sons, the pitcher spoke frankly, more as a judge of baseball talent than a parent. "To tell the truth," he said about his namesake, "I don't think Walter's ever going to make much of a pitcher. He's too impatient, expects success overnight. Walter's a funny kid. I can't get him to live out here with us. Thinks I'm crazy, and says it's like living in a graveyard."

Johnson then pointed to his next-oldest son and said, "Eddie there, he likes the farm. Comes down from college every chance he gets and stays right here. I think he's going to be a real good baseball player, too. He's an infielder, plays with the University of Maryland, hits well and can throw."

Before Joe Williams ended his visit, Walter Johnson returned to assessing his oldest son. "He thought he wanted to be a G-man this fall, so I got him a job in the department, but because they didn't send him out to capture five or six murderers right off, he quit. Said it wasn't exciting enough. That's what's wrong with him, all right; wants to get on top too quickly."

Other than his restrained campaign for Congress in 1940 when his public-speaking appearances drew more questions about baseball than lend lease and the approaching war, Walter Johnson's life was that of a farmer. After the United States entered World War II, Johnson's life on the farm pinned him down. Walter Jr. was a bombardier cadet with the Air Force. The men with whom Johnson had run his dogs and hunted were mostly younger and were entering military service. It was difficult to hire farm labor and he did more and more of the work himself. Still, when an invitation came to go to New York for a War Bond Drive appearance at Yankee Stadium, he jumped at the chance.

In 1942, Major League Baseball voted to donate the money from a home game by each team to the Army and Navy Relief Fund. The Yankees, with the biggest ballpark and the biggest potential, picked a Sunday doubleheader with the Washington Senators. The game, which raised $80,000, was played on August 23 and 69,000 people turned out. Most of them came to see Babe Ruth try to hit a home run once again, and Walter Johnson was invited to pitch to him.

The old adversaries dressed in the Yankee clubhouse while the first game was being played. The Babe had been issued a Yankee uniform again after eight years, and the number three was on the back of the pinstriped shirt. Walter Johnson brought a 1942 Washington uniform with a shield patch. Many more reporters swarmed around Ruth's side of the locker room. Joe Cummiskey, reporting for *PM*, a short-lived New York City tabloid, wrote: "The Babe arrived at the Yankee Stadium gates at 2:30. I caught up with him at 2:40. He was eating a thick ham and cheese sandwich and washing it down with Ruppert's beer. In the dressing room down the corridor he ripped off his shirt and wiped the steam from his wide face and plumped on his chair in front of his old locker—the first one to the left as you go through the Yankee portals."

Cummiskey reported that the lean and lanky Walter Johnson walked in. "Hiya, Babe," said Walter, sticking out his long right arm. "Hiya, Walter," said Babe, grabbing his fist. They both told the other how good the other one looked. Then they got ready to go out on the field.

The players came out early to see the Babe and the Big Train try to re-create enough of their ability to satisfy the fans. Walter Johnson later told Bugs Baer for his column in the *New York American* that he had not thrown a baseball in six or seven years and that he did not practice for this appearance because he felt he could only make the effort once. He said he expected he could get the ball over the plate about a dozen times and did not want to waste his energy practicing. He did throw a half dozen warm-up pitches to Benny Bengough, a coach for the Senators who had been a Yankee catcher in the years they featured their "Murderers' Row" lineup. Behind the plate was Johnson's great admirer Billy Evans, wearing an inflated chest protector.

Tom Meany, also writing for *PM*, described the action: "Ruth nailed Johnson's fifth pitch for a line drive homer into the right field seats, just inside the foul line at the 296 mark. Walter continued pitching and Ruth, after a string of fouls, belted one high into the top tier in right field, foul by a few feet. It was a tremendous, soaring drive and Babe, with his inherent sense of the dramatic, made it his exit cue, mincing his way around the bases as though it were a bona fide homer. The crowd roared its appreciation at the sight. It was the twentieth pitch served up by The Big Train."

Later, Johnson told reporters he had been there simply to serve up straight balls for the Babe to hit. "No one came here today to see me try to strike out Ruth," he told them.

The two veterans left the field together, arms over each other's shoulders. They waved a farewell and disappeared into the shadows of the dugout, went down the corridor to dress and go back to their after-baseball lives. Sadly, it was their last time together. Johnson would die in four years and Ruth in six. Walter Johnson made several other Old-Timer Day appearances to help wartime causes, and Ruth had his own farewell to Yankee Stadium shortly before his death in 1948.

Walter Johnson's last appearance at Griffith Stadium was Opening Day 1945. President Franklin D. Roosevelt had died a few days earlier on April 12. The new president, Harry S. Truman, was too occupied picking up the reins of the office to attend. The European invasion was pending, and an epochal decision regarding the developing atomic bomb was to be made. Sam Rayburn, the Speaker of the House and next in succession for the presidency, made the ceremonial toss. Walter Johnson was part of the presidential party and is seen in a photo of Rayburn's throw. Rayburn stands with the managers, Joe McCarthy of the visiting Yankees and Ossie Bluege, the Senators field leader, on one side and his fellow Texan and congressional protégé Lyndon Johnson on the other. Walter Johnson, looking older than he had when he made his appearance with Babe Ruth, stands behind Sam Rayburn smiling.

Early in 1946, Walter Johnson complained about pain in his left arm and gradually lost the use of it. His physician, Dr. Thomas F. Keliher, directed him for diagnosis at the Georgetown University Hospital and Johnson never left. An inoperable tumor was found. It blocked an artery to the right side of the brain and produced a paralytic attack on his left side. Johnson's mind was clear during most of the eight-month ordeal which followed, and he received visits from former teammates and, particularly, Clark Griffith. The 77-year-old Washington Senators president was an almost daily visitor. Griff and the others spent hours reminiscing with Johnson about the past. When he could no longer speak, Griff held his hand and the dying ex-pitcher responded to questions by squeezing back his "yes" and "no" replies.

Johnson retained his interest in baseball during much of the time he was in the hospital. A woman who attended him reported, "Every morning, Mr. Johnson holds out his hand for the newspapers. I fold them back to the sports pages and he reads them carefully. But what he thinks about baseball today, I couldn't tell you. He never talks about it afterward."

Johnson's plight was monitored by the press as life and the 1946 baseball season went on. On September 21, 1946, thinking the end was close, Clark Griffith dedicated a game to Walter Johnson. Twenty-four thousand people stood in silent prayer for the Big Train, who had lapsed into a coma. Still, Johnson staved off defeat by death as determinedly as he had battled baseball foes. Then, on December 10, his final hours began. His five children, his brother Earl, and Clark Griffith waited at Walter Johnson's bedside. At 11:40 P.M., in the same hospital where his beloved Hazel had died 16 years earlier, Walter left this world to rejoin her in the next.

42
The Legend Lives On

THE FUNERAL OF WALTER JOHNSON began in the splendor of the Washington Cathedral and ended in a windswept hillside rural cemetery. The Very Reverend John W. Suter, Dean of the cathedral, presided at both places. There had been no eulogy at the solemn church services where a thousand mourners had prayed for baseball's departed idol. However, in one prayer, Dean Suter expressed appreciation of those who had gathered to share the loss with Johnson's family. The Dean offered a prayer of thanksgiving "for all the goodness and courage which have passed from the life of this, Thy servant, into the life of others, leaving the world richer for his presence…For a life's task faithfully and honorably discharged, for gracious affection and kindly generosity, for sadness without surrender, and weakness endured without defeat."

The cathedral's main altar was banked with floral tributes, including those sent by President Harry S. Truman and flowers from "the children of Washington's playgrounds." Two hymns were sung by the cathedral choir, "Abide With Me" and "Oh, God, Our Help In Ages Past." In the front pews were Walter Johnson's five children, Walter Jr., Edwin, Robert, Carolyn, and Barbara, and his mother, Minnie. His brothers, Earl and Leslie, also fronted the casket. Clark Griffith sat with the family, and behind them came those from the baseball world. The active pallbearers were: Ossie Bluege, Tom Zachary, Roger Peckinpaugh, Muddy Ruel, Sam Rice, Joe Judge, Nick Altrock, and Mike Martin. Also present were Clyde Milan, Bucky Harris, George Weiss, and Jack Bentley. Each had special memories of Walter Johnson.

The cortege carrying Walter Johnson to the Rockville Union Cemetery was a long procession of limousines and passenger cars. Along the route, people stopped to stand respectfully as the Big

Train passed from the city, where he had been triumphant, to the countryside, where he had quietly lived out his years as a dairy farmer. The simplicity of the graveside service marked the modesty of the man who was being buried. Walter Johnson was laid to rest beside the grave of his wife, Hazel, who had been buried in the family plot 16 years earlier.

The nation's newspapers carried accounts of Walter Johnson's life in baseball, retelling the accomplishments and settling for the statistics which the writers of the time believed were beyond surpassing. Many were and still remain credited to Walter Johnson, although some proved vulnerable to the changes in the way baseball is played. It was announced that Walter Johnson would be memorialized with a bas-relief plaque at Griffith Stadium. When it was suggested that the fans be asked to contribute to the cost, Clark Griffith claimed the right belonged to Johnson's team, and he commissioned Edward J. Landow to create and cast the plaque.

When it was unveiled on June 21, 1947, by President Harry S. Truman, it became a fixed attraction inside the entrance to Griffith Stadium. Fans who remembered the Big Train and those who came along too late to have seen him pitch, could view a full-length portrait in bronze of Walter Johnson as he completed a sweeping sidearm pitch. The legend beneath his portrait read: "A Champion On And Off The Field—His Greatness An Enduring Contribution To Baseball." His major records were listed below. President Truman said, "I am honored and privileged to be called upon to unveil this plaque to a man who in my opinion was the greatest ballplayer who ever lived. He was a great ballplayer, great American and great citizen of the United States."

The Walter Johnson memorial was removed when the original Senators left for Minnesota. It was relocated to the Walter Johnson High School in Bethesda, where it was displayed inside the main entrance, illuminated by a spotlight. The memorial has been subsequently promoted to a position of greater prominence and is the centerpiece of a landscaped entrance to the high school.

Meanwhile, Coffeyville, Kansas, which considered itself Walter Johnson's true hometown, pined to memorialize its former native son and local hero. The baseball field, Forest Park, was renamed Walter Johnson Field. The diamond where the annual Walter Johnson Homecoming Day games had been played is still in use. High schools, the American Legion, and Babe Ruth League teams play their games where once Walter Johnson took on a series of local challengers after completing a major league schedule.

A duplicate of the Walter Johnson Memorial that had been installed at Griffith Stadium was ordered from the artist, Edward J. Landow. On June 25, 1954, Mrs. R.M. Tongier, who was Walter Johnson's sister Effie and a Coffeyville resident, unveiled the duplicate memorial in front of the baseball stadium at the park. Edward B. Eynon, longtime secretary of the Washington Senators and a close personal friend of Walter Johnson, represented Clark Griffith at the unveiling. Eynon, who had suggested the design of the memorial, helped the Coffeyville Chamber of Commerce secure a cast of the original work.

The Coffeyville Public Library is "the keeper of the flame" and has an impressive selection of materials about Johnson. Not just reports from the local newspapers but copies of many national articles about the man who, during his prime years, was billed as "the Coffeyville Express," are cared for there.

Minnie Johnson survived most of her children, living to be 100 years old in a nursing home in Sandy Spring, Maryland. She was visited by Sam Rice on her centennial anniversary and a photo of her sharing a single-candled cake with the 77-year-old Hall of Fame outfielder appeared in the *Washington Daily News*. Her birthday was observed a week earlier than its actual March 14 date. She had a pleasant day with her family, which by then had extended beyond her three living children, Effie in Coffeyville, Leslie in Faulkner, Maryland, and Chester, the youngest, of Austin, Texas, to include 20 grandchildren, 58 great-grandchildren, and 18 great-great-grandchildren, the youngest of which was less than a year old. When Minnie passed away several months later her body was sent to Coffeyville, Kansas, for burial in the Johnson family plot. Her husband, Frank, and the granddaughter Elinor who had died in early childhood had been buried there many years before.

The dark shadows that dimmed much of the luster of Walter Johnson's later years partly fell upon his children. His youngest son, Robert, died in 1954 at 32 years of age when a car in which he was a passenger was involved in an accident. Walter Jr. died of Hodgkin's disease in 1961. Edwin, who inherited his father's love of the land, lived on his farm in Comus, Maryland. Carolyn married Henry W. Thomas and lives in Washington. Her son, Henry Thomas, a SABR member, has spent many years researching his grandfather's life with the expectation of publishing a biography. To that goal, he withheld access to the family's history from this work. The youngest daughter, Barbara, became Mrs. Robert Pogue of Chappaqua, New York.

In 1985 Bob O'Donnell, a staff writer of the *Washington Times* provided readers who lacked a contemporary team to follow, with a seven-month series that recounted the 1924 season in the writing style of the period and detailed the season's sentimental course. Current baseball fans could find relief from salary squabbles, drug and sex charges, the sulking, overpaid athletes, disabled lists that seem longer than rosters were in Johnson's day, and the tedious detail of present-day reporting of items more suited to the business pages. They could read about a World Series, something no one could do in 1994.

On November 6, 1987, the Walter Johnson High School in Bethesda, Maryland, rounded off the first 100 years following the birth of the Big Train by holding a birthday party in his honor at the school. Governor William Donald Schaefer of Maryland proclaimed the centennial date as Walter Johnson Day.

The family of Walter Johnson retains many of his souvenirs. The scrapbooks, kept during Johnson's career by Hazel, are guarded by the Thomas family. The most historically interesting item, the collection of Presidential Autographed Baseballs, was donated to the Baseball Hall of Fame in 1968 by his son Eddie. When a younger member of the family visited Cooperstown several years later he asked to see the exhibit. Lamely, the museum staff displayed the mahogany box in which they had been kept. A neatly printed card explained what the box had contained, especially the ball autographed by President William Howard Taft in 1910 that had began the custom of presidents throwing out the first ball on Opening Day. The actual baseballs had disappeared. At best, it can be hoped they are secreted away by a private collector who gloatingly relishes the clandestine possession of this unique set. They might yet emerge from the estate of the thief who either stole them or bought them from whoever did.

Walter Johnson left an imprint on baseball, and his astonishing statistics still deserve the wonder of those who consider them. They do not, of course, fully measure the impact Johnson had on his time in baseball. They were compiled over the 21 years in which he was backed by a winning team in less than half the seasons. In ranking the pitchers of the past, *Total Baseball* places Walter Johnson at the top. This encyclopedic work weighs into judgment all of a pitcher's values, including fielding and batting. This last is a plus only in one league now, ironically not Johnson's American League. However, fielding deficiencies have cost some pitchers higher places on the grading scale. Nolan Ryan, whose fastball prowess has drawn comparison with Walter Johnson, is rated 69th on the list.

Rather than play the numbers game, which so easily becomes a substitute for rational thought, we will pass over claims for those who came after Johnson's time which are based on statistics alone. The only pitchers who are ranked close to Johnson by *Total Baseball* are those who were his contemporaries or, like Cy Young or Lefty Grove, overlapped a part of Johnson's career. Tom Seaver fares best among moderns, ranked seventh.

In reviewing the life, the attitudes, and the *unrealized* potential of Walter Johnson, one must wonder what totals he would have left behind had he an agent to negotiate performance clauses into his contracts. Johnson was ever alert to opportunities to pick up extra money so he could build up his farm property. He pitched exhibition games at every chance and endorsed products as unlikely as pipe tobacco. What would have been his attitude when, cruising along behind a safe lead, he saw a weak-hitting batter come to the plate? We know he was benign by nature, often grooving a pitch to make an opponent look good when it did not threaten the outcome of the game. However, suppose his earnings would have been increased by bonuses paid for the number of batters he struck out. By the shutouts he pitched. By rewards for pitching no-hitters. Would he have borne down on the easiest batters to fan? We think he would. Would Ty Cobb have safely crowded the plate? We think not. And, suppose Walter Johnson had pitched when antibiotics were available. How many games he missed because of colds, flu, grippe, pneumonia, mumps, malaria, and other preventable or quickly cured health problems, would have been pitched and how many more winning feats been accomplished?

In a tribute to Walter Johnson following his death, Bob Considine, then at the top of his popularity as a columnist and writer, concluded the only man of the past to whom Walter Johnson could be compared was Abraham Lincoln. We agree.

WALTER JOHNSON • 1907-1927

Year	Won	Lost	G	GS	CG	ShO	Relief W - L	Svs	AB	H	R	ER	ERA	BB	SO	Opponents InP	B.A.	Relief G.	Relief Finish
1907	5	9	14	12	11	2	0 - 2	0	408	100	35	23	1.88	20	70	110.1	.245	2	2
1908	14	14	36	30	23	6	0 - 1	1	921	194	75	47	1.65	53	160	256.1	.211	6	6
1909	13	25	40	36	27	4	1 - 2	1	1120	247	112	73	2.22	84	164	296.1	.221	4	3
1910	25	17	45	42	38	8	1 - 1	1	1278	262	92	56	1.36	76	313	370.0	.205	3	3
1911	25	13	40	37	36	6	1 - 1	1	1228	292	119	68	1.90	70	207	322.1	.238	3	3
1912	33	12	50	37	34	7	6 - 2	2	1321	259	89	57	1.39	76	303	369.0	.196	13	13
1913	36	7	48	36	29	11	7 - 0	2	1239	232	56	44	1.14	38	243	346.0	.187	12	11
1914	28	18	51	40	33	9	4 - 3	1	1321	287	88	71	1.72	74	225	371.2	.217	11	9
1915	27	13	47	39	35	7	2 - 0	4	1205	258	83	58	1.55	56	203	336.2	.214	8	8
1916	25	20	48	38	36	3	4 - 3	1	1319	290	105	78	1.90	82	228	369.2	.220	10	10
1917	23	16	47	34	30	8	5 - 1	3	1173	248	105	80	2.21	68	188	326.0	.211	13	12
1918	23	13	39	29	29	8	3 - 4	3	1149	241	71	46	1.27	70	162	326.0	.210	10	10
1919	20	14	39	29	27	7	2 - 4	2	1073	235	73	48	1.49	51	147	290.1	.219	10	10
1920	8	10	21	15	12	4	1 - 2	3	549	135	68	50	3.13	27	78	143.2	.246	6	6
1921	17	14	35	32	25	1	1 - 1	1	1007	265	122	103	3.51	92	143	264.0	.263	3	2
1922	15	16	41	31	23	4	1 - 1	4	1060	283	115	93	2.99	99	105	280.0	.267	10	9
1923	17	12	42	34	18	3	1 - 2	4	977	263	112	101	3.48	73	130	261.0	.269	8	8
1924	23	7	38	38	20	6	0 - 0	0	1041	233	97	84	2.72	77	158	277.2	.224	0	0
1925	20	7	30	29	16	3	1 - 0	0	867	217	95	78	3.07	78	108	229.0	.250	1	1
1926	15	16	33	33	22	2	0 - 0	0	986	259	120	105	3.63	73	125	260.2	.263	0	0
1927	5	6	18	15	7	1	0 - 0	0	407	113	70	61	5.10	26	48	107.2	.278	3	2
	417	279	802	666	531	110	41 - 30	34	21649	4913	1902	1424	2.17	1363	3508	5914.1	.227	136	128

Compiled by Frank J. Williams from Official Score Sheets at the Baseball Hall of Fame Library.
Scoring rules which were in effect when games were played have been applied.

Index

288

About the Author

When Casey Stengel reached 75, the New York Mets retired him. He did not want to go, but observed: "Most people my age are already dead. You could look it up." When Jack Kavanagh retired, he started a new career. He had always wanted to be an author, but a steady paycheck was more important than bylines and book credits. By the time he reached 75, a new career would be well underway.

In one form or another, the written word has always been a part of his work. In high school he was sports editor for the school paper. An obnoxious teenager named Howie Cohen had previously held the position; he later changed his name to Howard Cosell, but remained as obnoxious as he had been at Alexander Hamilton High School in Brooklyn, New York.

Born in Brooklyn in 1920—when the Robins lost a World Series to the Cleveland Indians, partly due to running blindly into an unassisted triple play by Bill Wambsganss—Kavanagh grew up with only Prospect Park between his home neighborhood and Ebbets Field. He hung around the ballpark learning as an impressionable boy that baseball players are cheap. Greed is not a singular contemporary trait. When the 1933 season ended, he begged one of the Dodger players for his cap. He got the cap. The player sold it to him for $5.

Baseball was the topic which linked him to his father, a bat boy in 1903-04 at Washington Park, the pre–Ebbets Field home of the Brooklyn Dodgers. For the son, three years as an usher at Ebbets Field, culminating with the Dodgers' next pennant in 1941, was following in his father's footsteps. Baseball has also provided Kavanagh an unfailing topic with his own son, Brian.

Brian's handicaps, paraplegia and mental retardation, decided Kavanagh's career. After a successful career as an administrator with New York City, national advertising agencies, and in the emerging television industry, he resigned from Capital Cities Broadcasting to become an administrator of services for the handicapped. He was serving as the Director of the Washington County (RI) Association for the Mentally Handicapped when Brian's transfer to a group home made retirement and a switch to writing possible.

His daughter, Beth, has added five grandchildren to the family. The three grandsons are ballplayers and fans, and the two granddaughters accept this in good spirit. All of the family live in Rhode Island. The only sad note is that Sally, after 50 years of marriage and tolerating a husband's fascination with baseball, died shortly before the book about Walter Johnson was completed.

Kavanagh's post-retirement writing career got its toehold in SABR publications, which led to a series of juvenile biographies for ages 10-14. Inevitably, his sights were set higher, and a full-length biography of Walter Johnson, one of the players included in the "juvvies" series, is the result.

He sees no point in slowing down. Casey Stengel never got another managing job, but Jack Kavanagh has a new assignment to write a full-length biography of Grover Cleveland Alexander. This is a fine way, he believes, to have the cup runneth over after having already enjoyed a full life. Kavanagh says he will keep coming back for seconds as long as God grants him the health and energy to do so. Baseball will provide the material.